Business Systems Engineering

Business Systems Engineering

MANAGING BREAKTHROUGH CHANGES FOR PRODUCTIVITY AND PROFIT

Gregory H. Watson

John Wiley & Sons, Inc.

New York ♦ Chichester ♦ Brisbane ♦ Toronto ♦ Singapore

This publication is designed to provide accurate and authoritative
information in regard to the subject matter covered. It is sold
with the understanding that the publisher is not engaged in
rendering legal, accounting, or other professional services. If
legal advice or other expert assistance is required, the services
of a competent professional person should be sought.

Library of Congress Cataloging-in-Publication Data:

Watson, Gregory H.
    Business systems engineering : managing breakthrough changes for
productivity and profit / Greg H. Watson.
        p.   cm.
    Includes bibliographical references and index.
    ISBN 0-471-01884-8
    1. Organizational change—Management. 2. Industrial management.
I. Title.
HD58.8.W39   1994
658.4′063—dc20   94-32752
                                                                     CIP

Printed in the United States of America

10   9   8   7   6   5   4   3   2   1

*To Jeff and Ginger Watson, my twin brother and his wife of over
25 years, in appreciation for their shared values, mutual commitment,
and long-standing, supportive, loving relationship that has produced
a great outcome: three wonderful young men—
Ted, Steven, and Brian.*

Acknowledgments

To hold on to the Way of the present—
To manage the things of the present,
And to know the ancient beginning,
This is called the beginning of the thread of the Way.

Lao Tzu, *Te-Tao Ching*

Each of us is the product of his or her history, environment, and relationships. We develop our own working style through role modeling things that we observe and like in others. This means that no book is the individual product of a single author, but is the result of many interactions with a variety of mentors and colleagues. In particular, this book is the product of many experiences that began during my service in the United States Navy, developed into a business focus at Hewlett-Packard, blossomed into a managerial perspective at Compaq, and matured into a broader executive viewpoint at Xerox. I have been blessed with many wonderful experiences in each of these organizations and am grateful for the opportunities that I have had to participate, observe, and learn from others.

Dr. C. Jackson Grayson deserves a special acknowledgment for his continuing encouragement and support. Jack has been an inspiration to me both personally and professionally. His driving dedication to the improvement of the United States economy through the application of quality principles has been a major influence on my own thought processes. In particular, he has helped me to understand the business impact of quality in terms of productivity. Thanks, Jack.

Many others also deserve a word of thanks—especially some colleagues from Xerox. Dick Leo, my boss at Xerox, provided a wonderfully stimulating environment for rethinking quality and business relationship issues within the context of Paul Allaire's architectural changes of Xerox. Over the past two years, I have had some wonderful conversations with members of the Xerox quality community: Dick Palermo, John Swaim, Art Coles, John Cooney, Mark Shimelonis, Dottie Elias, Masataka Yoshizawa, Dave Terry, John Thomas, Tom Lynch, Denny Gerbassi, Kevin Lewis, Sam Malone, Mike Haravich, Tim Gilbert, Rich Menefee, and John Hansen. They have helped to hone my understanding of management and change initiatives that are facilitated through the combination of strategic benchmarking, quality assessment, and policy deployment. In addition to these direct colleagues, discussions with some of the individuals who have implemented the systems approach to business process engineering have been helpful including: Ennala (Ram) Ramcharandas, Constantine Kazatas, Claudette Ettenberg, Mary Colecera, Cindy Gordon, Bill Joiner, and Ted Richman. Many of these discussions and considerations have spilled over to influence my way of thinking about the management of business change. Norm Rickard deserves a special expression of appreciation in his role as president of Xerox Business Services for the quality way in which he has developed an empowered environment for individuals to grow and contribute to the future success of Xerox through productivity enhancements.

This book was developed through the encouragement of Mike Hamilton, senior editor at John Wiley & Sons, who saw the need for a more detailed description of the "hot topic" called Business Process Reengineering. This work has profited from the efforts and insights of those whose earlier books have preceded it. In particular, this book supports and further refines the concepts found in Michael Hammer's popular book, *Reengineering the Corporation,* that brought broad exposure for the practice of Business Process Reengineering. As Mike Hammer has been the evangelist preaching the need for radical redefinition of business processes, it is my hope that this book will extend the "religion" into a business practice that is capable of being grasped by all organizations.

I would like to provide a brief explanation of the reason I selected the writings of Lao Tzu to introduce each chapter. Lao Tzu is an anonymous "old master" who wrote the *Te-Tao Ching* or "the book of the way and its power" around 300 B.C. He addressed this book of poems as a guide to the thinking of those who would take leadership positions in Chinese society. The underlying current is about the responsibility of leadership for making change happen on a grand scale. I selected some of the excerpts from this religious text to introduce common themes that appear in business today. Many of the challenges facing the leaders of early China are the same challenges that face senior management as we approach the twenty-first century. I appreciate what the "old master" recorded in his poetic musings on the nature of change and wanted to share them with the readers of this book.

Preparing real case studies is one way to ground the ideas of a subject in the basis of reality. I owe much gratitude to the following individuals who provided insights and assistance in the development of the case studies: Paul Schattenberg, Phil Grossman, Bill Flynn, George McCall, Ken Graham, Linda Bond, and Rebecca P. Cartall—all of USAA; and Bob Beach, Nemo Azmanian, and Nora Hahn of Compaq.

In addition to those who have stimulated my thoughts, a whole cast of characters has provided support from the pragmatic perspective of producing a book. In particular, I would not have been able to produce this book without the dedicated case study writing support from Gary Taylor, a freelance writer in Kerrville, Texas, and a friend from shared days at Compaq Computer Corporation. I also appreciate the efforts of Joy Holland of the American Productivity & Quality Center, who provided able assistance in background research. The management of the administrative details of publishing a book go well beyond my abilities to research or keyboard on a word processor. Special appreciation goes to Impressions for their support in guiding this book to its final form.

Finally, I reserve my greatest expression of gratitude: "Thank you, Joelyn," my loving wife, who has worked with me in developing and editing all aspects of this book. She has always been an encouragement to me in everything.

Gregory H. Watson
Victor, New York

Preface

As soon as we start to establish a system, we have names.
And as soon as there are set names,
Then you must also know that it's time to stop.
By knowing to stop—in this way you'll come to no harm.
Lao Tzu, *Te-Tao Ching*

It seems that every magazine or journal I pick up today has a leading story on the subject of Business Process Reengineering. Ever since Michael Hammer's 1990 article in *Harvard Business Review* ("Reengineering Work: Don't Automate, Obliterate," July/August 1990) announced the topic and promoted the phrase—Business Process Reengineering (BPR)—it has grown in both popularity and application. Because he came from an information technology background, Hammer focused on information technology—computer systems and software—as the driver of Business Process Reengineering. Since this initial statement of the subject, interest has grown to include other professions: Industrial engineers, quality managers, and human resource managers all have jumped on the "reengineering" bandwagon. Each community has taken a parochial perspective to the subject, seeking to carve out a niche in the overall reengineering effort. But, no matter what perspective has been taken initially, the final result appears to have a similar emphasis; it takes a cross-disciplinary and cross-functional approach toward reengineering to enable it to address the needs of the entire organization. This includes aligning customer needs with business processes to eliminate waste and cost, and to reduce cycle time, thereby driving the improvement of productivity that provides an opportunity to achieve the business goals of both profitable revenue growth and market share expansion. And, of course, the end result is one that everyone agrees is good for almost any organization.

That's why Business Process Reengineering is a hot topic in today's business discussions. Everyone has questions, opinions, stories, or myths about the subject. So why add another book to those already released? Because I found the previous books to be missing some basic linkages to organizational principles—and some of those have proven themselves over the years. In short, I believe that we should firmly ground our "advances" in their historical context, before we rush to embrace a "new" approach to organizational development.

This book is different from the previous writings on the subject of reengineering primarily because I regard the term "reengineering" a misnomer. I believe that the term *business systems engineering* is a more accurate description of the work activity that is needed in most organizations. Moreover, I prefer a systemic or holistic organizational view by merging the contributions of all business change support disciplines into a single, unified approach for delivering breakthrough business systems change. And finally, I build upon the language and methods of the Total Quality Management (TQM) worldwide movement as the context for change that most major business organizations have adopted and deployed throughout their ranks. By building upon the language and methods already placed within many working team structures, this approach finds many natural allies who can readily accept the methods and are therefore more willing to focus on delivering the desired changes.

This book is divided into five parts. In the first part, the roots of business systems engineering are described: learning, change management, innovation, productivity, competitiveness, and quality. This part demonstrates that business processes can be represented as open systems that are capable of improvement and adaptation. In the second part, the foundations of business systems engineering are described: its needs, structure, and elements. This part demonstrates how to represent business processes as systems in order to identify needs and select initiatives for strategic change. In the third part, tools of business systems engineering are presented: process analysis methods for work redesign, benchmarking for external learning, information technology advances that have changed the workplace, and policy deployment that is used to coordinate, implement, and review breakthrough change efforts. This part demonstrates how to make the change happen through the coordinated use of analytic tools. The fourth part of this book provides a potpourri of case studies that grounds this theory of business systems engineering in reality and describes how various organizations have applied aspects of this methodology. A survey of the automotive industry illustrates how change within one company can influence the actions of competitors. A second case study illustrates how Motorola used the principles of systems engineering to increase the competitiveness of its pocket pager line in the mid-1980s. A third case study illustrates the need for rapid action when faced with rapidly changing market conditions, as Compaq Computer Corporation needed to redo its entire business within less than a year. A final case study illustrates how United Services Automobile Association (USAA) has learned from its past "reengineering" efforts to build its strategic change upon the foundation of its quality methodologies. These case studies illustrate how companies have made system-level changes happen using some of the tools that are described in the prior section. The final part describes lessons learned from these case studies, presents an implementation methodology, and then pinpoints the most pressing management challenges for strategic business change in today's economic environment. This part provides an economic basis for a new perspective on productivity that is based on a systems approach and recognizes the contribution of the knowledge worker.

Contents

PART I

Introduction

1

Learning: The Root of Change

Disaster is that on which good fortune depends,
Good fortune is that in which disaster's concealed.
Who knows where it will end?
For there is no fixed "correct."
The "correct" turns into "deviant";
And "good" turns into "evil."
People's state of confusion
Has certainly existed for a long time.

Lao Tzu, *Te-Tao Ching*

REENGINEERING OR ENGINEERING?

What is "reengineering" and how can we "reengineer" a business process if we have never engineered it in the first place? I faced this interesting dilemma when I was attempting to develop a training course on the subject of Business Process Reengineering (BPR) for use at Xerox Corporation. I discovered that Xerox was using seven different approaches to reengineering—one for each consultant who had captured its business! In order to provide clarity of language for all of the Xerox employees who had long-standing experience using the tools of Leadership Through Quality, I devised a simplified approach building upon this methodology. This resulted in a simplified, work-process centric model for engineering the business as a holistic system. It is built upon the tools and processes of both industrial and quality engineering that were deployed to support the efforts of Xerox teams

3

in the continuous improvement of their business processes. As if to confirm the approach that I defined at Xerox, Robert C. Stempel, former chairman and chief executive officer of General Motors, made the following observation: "As companies we have to do more than reengineer the work process, we must create a whole new attitude about how we learn. . . . For example the word 'reengineering' is nothing more than a wholesale acknowledgment that we did not do it right the first time. More importantly, it gives us permission or official sanction to do it again. Of course, speaking as an engineer, it also assumes that we engineered it in the first place."[1]

While discussing this systems engineering approach to business with senior management from other companies two trends became clear: first, that an information-technology centric approach to Business Process Reengineering was dissatisfying and, second, that a systems engineering approach was more congruent with Total Quality Management (TQM) language and methods. This observation raises two very interesting questions. First, should it be important to build change methods upon an organization's history of lessons learned? While others may argue that it is time to move beyond TQM—some say by eliminating TQM practices—I believe that the benefits to organizational restructuring should be grounded in what has come before. The second question is also provocative: How is a holistic, business-process centric approach distinguished from the more popular information-technology centric approaches that are commonly discussed today? The answer to the first question is embedded within the concepts of adult learning theory, while the answer to the second question is found by contrasting the systems engineering methodology against the mainstream, information-technology centric thinking about process reengineering. Let's begin our discussion on the methodology of business systems engineering by looking at the concepts behind learning organizations and reviewing some of the literature on Business Process Reengineering.

Adult learning theory holds that the experience of discovery is the best teacher for adult learners and that grounding new learning in past experience is a solid approach to getting people to learn how to change. Learning involves change—in particular, it is a continuing process of change within individuals by constantly restructuring experience to create an environment in which people recognize the lessons that they need to learn and apply them within the context of their own need. Learning has become recognized as a process of active, rather than passive, inquiry by the participants. Over the years, the emphasis on learning has shifted from the model where the role of the teacher is "subject authority" to a model where the teacher is the "facilitator of learning."[2]

Thus, adult learning theory helps us to answer the first question: By anchoring the process of "reengineering" in the historical lessons learned by individuals who have been practicing TQM, we are providing an experiential context to which the vast majority of employees can relate as opposed to the more technical focus of the information-technology centric approach, which tends to generate technophobia among a great majority. In simpler terms, the systems engineering approach provides a natural transition from TQM applications of continuous improvement at the process level to the systems level of breakthrough change. There is continuity in the methodologies of TQM and systems engineering even though its application may be slightly different.

This leads naturally to the second question: What is the difference between these two approaches—process reengineering and systems engineering?

Michael Hammer, the leading proponent of Business Process Reengineering, defines it as "the fundamental rethinking and radical redesign of business processes to achieve dramatic improvements in critical, contemporary measures of performance, such as quality, cost, service and speed."[3] At the heart of his definition is the idea of *discontinuous thinking*—"identifying and abandoning the outdated rules and fundamental assumptions that underlie current business operations."[4] Hammer seeks ambitious solutions that provide breakthrough levels of improvement, encourages reengineers to start with a clean sheet of paper rather than the old process and structure (which wasn't working anyway), and recognizes that information technology is the key enabler that allows organizations to do work in radically different ways. The fact that a process wasn't engineered in the first place, however, does not mean that it is ineligible for treatment by "reengineering."

The first major distinction between the ideas of Business Process Reengineering and the systems engineering approach was hinted at in the preface to this book. Hammer and Davenport[5] both provide methods of reengineering that are developed from the perspective of the chief information officer. They present information technology as the solution to as yet undefined problems—they put the technology in the driver's seat and seek solutions where it can apply. The approach you will discover in this book subordinates information technology to the process of identifying alternative process solutions and considering all potential methods for their resolution, whether they be related to the design of the process, training or capability of the people, structure or design of the data and information, or the enabling systems technology. The systems engineering approach does not lead with the system; it leads with the thorough analysis of the business process and uses technology assessment as the vehicle to introduce potential information systems contributions.

The second difference involves the perceived value of benchmarking. My own business experiences have convinced me that benchmarking is another business practice that leads "reengineers" toward implementing strategic change initiatives in key business processes. However, Hammer takes a divergent view. From Hammer's perspective, benchmarking restricts the framework of the reengineering team by limiting it to its own industry. Clearly, Hammer's narrow perspective of benchmarking as limited to competitive studies would not permit the use of what Xerox calls "creative imitation." This results from conducting generic benchmarking studies across industries where targeted benchmarking partners are selected based on analogous business functions and processes.[6] Indeed, the highest value outcomes of benchmarking studies come from thinking "out of the box." This observation is even borne out in Hammer's own description of Ford Motor Company—it did not gain the insight into the problems with its own accounts payable process until it observed how much better the process operated at Mazda Motors. This benchmarking provided Ford with two valuable insights: realization that its process performance was not in a leadership position and, second, that Mazda had taken a totally different design perspective for its process.[7] This is clearly an example where benchmarking enabled the basic discovery that permitted the reengineering project to succeed. By recognizing a larger role for benchmarking and more clearly linking it with the strategic business change process, we see our second major distinction between the two methodologies.

The third difference lies in the way quality technologies are used. In addition to Hammer and Champy's book, Davenport, Johansson et al.,[8] Morris and Brandon,[9] Hunt,[10] Shores,[11] Roberts,[12] Lowenthal,[13] and Osborne[14] have all recently released books that describe their approaches to Business Process Reengineering (a complete annotated bibliography on reengineering is included as an appendix). Each has taken a slightly different approach to the subject relative to the quality and industrial engineering methodologies that help to facilitate the reengineer's basic understanding of the fundamental work processes. Davenport's book is also driven from a framework of information technology, but he recognizes the need for a more holistic approach, including the contribution of benchmarking to process innovation, the use of industrial engineering tools for better process definition, the need for a change context within the overall management planning and implementation system, as well as the human or interpersonal aspects of change management. Johansson's book builds specifically upon both TQM and Just-in-Time manufacturing or cycle time reduction for their toolbox of Business Process Reengineering. Hunt's book has a singular focus on applying reengineering to develop an integrated product development process, as does Shores's book, which describes a tool kit of methods to apply to the reengineering of manufacturing. The best-selling book by Osborne and Gaebler seeks to apply business process innovation to the bureaucratic structure of government and encourages a more entrepreneurial approach to the way that governments at all levels operate. Rather than provide a tool-driven methodology for change, it provides a compelling argument for the framework of change based on analogies built from mission-oriented, results-driven entrepreneurial businesses.[15]

The basis for the third distinction is in the omission of a key methodology from the basic principles of Business Process Reengineering. It is interesting to note that both Hammer and Johansson miss the linkage of reengineering to policy deployment—an advanced quality planning methodology for deploying strategic cross-functional change initiatives that are targeted to make breakthrough performance happen. (Policy deployment also goes by its Japanese name, *hoshin kanri*. It was introduced into the United States by Hewlett-Packard in late 1983 and by consultants from the Japanese Union of Scientists and Engineers in 1984.) While Davenport does cite policy deployment as influential in change management, he has not clearly specified how to drive the structural change using this quality management methodology. This provides a third distinction between Business Process Reengineering and my model for business systems engineering. The deployment method of organizational change is not a "one-off" special project, but an integrated part of the entire organization's change management system—integrating both breakthrough change and continuous improvement.

These three distinctive differences provide historical linkages to other management practices and indicate that reengineering is not, as Hammer and Champy claim, "a new endeavor,"[16] but that it is based on a holistic approach that incorporates the integrated use of such business practices as Total Quality Management, benchmarking, business process improvement, policy deployment, industrial engineering, teamwork, problem solving, as well as information technology. I call this integrated approach to change *business systems engineering.*

It is interesting to note that in Hammer's own experience roughly 50 to 70 percent of all reengineering efforts fail to deliver the promised dramatic improvements in business process performance.[17] But, we demand a better payoff potential! How can we ensure that we get a successful payoff from such visible change initiatives? How can we make the desired change happen? Perhaps, by more clearly linking the reengineering approach to its related methodologies, a synergy will be created that will vastly improve the ability of organizations to produce significant results from their strategic change initiatives. Before we define the specific methods of business systems engineering, a historical perspective as to its intellectual evolution will be helpful.

THE EVOLUTION OF BUSINESS SYSTEMS ENGINEERING

The concepts behind business systems engineering are not new ones.[18] Related concepts have been maturing within innovative businesses, and its intellectual roots may be traced back into the nineteenth century. Charles Darwin, the nineteenth-century biologist, introduced the idea of natural selection—only the strongest species will survive in the competition for scarce resources. Even earlier, Thomas R. Malthus in his 1798 *Essay on the Principle of Population* had built upon the observation of Benjamin Franklin that population in the American colonies tended to double every 25 years. Malthus postulated that population size would double every generation—up to a point of diminishing returns, which was the limit of the land's ability to produce food. Change Masters (an older and more apt term for reengineers coined by Rosabeth Moss Kanter)[19] make the point that current systems have grown like Topsy over the years and that they have reached a point of diminishing returns—ineffectiveness and inefficiency— which needs to be addressed through a radical transformation where only the strongest processes can survive to the new age. These are key observations for Change Masters to make if they are both to anticipate and lead the organization in the deployment of productive, strategic changes.

Another foundation for business systems engineering is the linkage of innovation (so necessary to produce breakthrough thinking and initiatives) with the idea of drastic restructuring of an organization. The linkage is found in economic theory. Joseph A. Schumpeter (1883–1950), the Austro-American economist, believed that capitalism would be destroyed by bureaucracy. He believed that the entrepreneur's role was to introduce innovations that would break down bureaucracy. Schumpeter defined innovation as "creative destruction"[20] and believed that firms must organize for the systematic abandonment of the established, customary, familiar, comfortable way of doing things. In this environment, productivity is the result of breaking down the current system and innovating through the development of new combinations of productive factors. The resulting productivity increase among the Baby Bells following the divestiture of the Bell system is perhaps the most interesting modern example that lends credence to Schumpeter's thesis. Certainly, the need to "radically restructure" by starting with a clean sheet of paper to begin the redesign is a recurring theme among reengineers. At Xerox this approach is called "breaking glass" (Davenport refers to this same idea as "breaking the china"). Perhaps an even better description of Schumpeter's "creative destruction" is provided by Peter Drucker when he links innovation with the idea of planned obsolescence: "Indeed, organizations increasingly will have to plan abandonment rather than try to prolong the life of successful product, policy, or practice—something that so far only a few large Japanese companies have faced up to."[21] Drucker sees the answer for developing plans to abandonment throughout the systemic process of continuous improvement (or as the Japanese call it, *kaizen*, the daily improvement activities within their *hoshin kanri* system) as being exploitation of organizational learning and knowledge, and applying innovation as an organized, systematic process.[22]

Another contributor to the idea of "clean sheet" designs is found in Peter A. Phyrr's book *Zero Based Budgeting*.[23] This book served as a guidebook to drive the United States government under the Carter administration to reconsider how the federal budget was allocated by considering each budget element as if it were independent from its sunk costs and prior history. Zero based budgeting, like Business Process Reengineering, required starting the budgeting process from scratch and shifted the burden to justifying doing anything at all, rather than merely continuing past practices and only providing an incremental analysis of the budget submission.

Change Masters must also be able to see the organization as a whole enterprise where business processes are woven into a system that produces outputs. Jay W. Forrester, professor emeritus of systems theory at MIT, set a goal of "enterprise design" to create more successful management policies and organizational structures. He applied computer simulation techniques to large-scale business models to evaluate the dynamic effects of change. *Industrial Dynamics*[24] is the study of the behavior of these large-scale systems to determine the interactive effects of business policies, structure, decisions, and delays on its growth and stability. Many of the reengineers use large-scale enterprise models as the starting point to evaluate which cross-functional business processes are the most critical to the corporation and deserve the reengineer's attention.

As described earlier, benchmarking is a key enabling process for engineering business systems. Why has benchmarking caught on so strongly in many organizations? Perhaps it is the linkage to some early principles of good management. *In Search of Excellence*,[25] by Tom Peters and Robert Waterman, made popular the idea of examining how other organizations perform in order to generate better concepts for changing your own organization. Xerox built upon this learning approach with its development of the practice of benchmarking—studying other businesses to identify leading examples of performance excellence and learning how to transfer that performance to its own business. The application of Management by Wandering Around (or MBWA as Peters and Waterman have abbreviated it) to other companies provides a rich source of learning experiences that stimulate the Change Master's environment.

The introduction of information technology to the mainstream of organizational dynamics owes much to John Naisbitt and Patricia Aburdene. In *Re-inventing the Corporation*,[26] they described how the labor market at the end of the twentieth century will become increasingly more restricted and that labor shortages will demand that we reinvent work to take advantage of the new capabilities offered within the information society. Soshana Zuboff built upon this vision and recognized the ability of information technology to "empower" ordinary people with systems knowledge, which makes them capable of making more demanding decisions where "jobs are comprehensive, tasks are abstractions that depend on insight and synthesis, and power is a roving force that comes to rest as dictated by function and need."[27] Zuboff developed the vision of the emerging workplace as an *informated* workplace, where fully integrated information technology (both hardware and software) systems work in harmony with their human counterparts to produce business outcomes. This vision gives rise to the development of the knowledge workers in a business where information management has become a key economic ingredient.

Peter Senge recognized the significance of Forrester's work and linked it with the theories of John Dewey, the American pragmatist and educator, to describe the future workplace of the knowledge worker as the "learning organization." By the learning organization, Senge means ". . . an organization that is continually expanding its capacity to create its future."[28] Senge bases his description of the learning organization on the theory of adult learning. He observes that "organizations learn only through individuals who learn. Individual learning does not guarantee organizational learning. But without it no organizational learning occurs."[29] Thus, organizational learning requires an organization's commitment to individual learning. But, this can be threatening because it builds the organization's core competency into particular knowledge workers who are mobile and, as Peter Drucker observes: "The more an organization becomes an organization of knowledge workers, the easier it is to leave it and move elsewhere." As a result, every organization "is always in competition for its most essential resource: qualified, knowledgeable people."[30] This creates a learning imperative. According to Peter Drucker, the only way to attract and retain the best people is to provide them with an environment that allows both learning and innovation to flourish. As another outgrowth of the emphasis on the learning organization and its knowledge workers, Drucker cites the change in hierarchical structure. "Because the modern organization consists of knowledge specialists, it has to be an organization of equals, of colleagues and associates. No knowledge ranks higher than another; each is judged by its contribution to the common task rather than by any inherent superiority or inferiority. Therefore, the modern organization cannot be an organization of boss and subordinate. It must be organized as a team."[31]

The concept of the learning organization supports the adult learning theory of Malcolm Knowles. According to Knowles, there are two styles of learning that teachers can use for educating others: pedagogy and andragogy. The pedagogical style gives the teacher full responsibility for the learning process: what will be learned, how it will be learned, when it will be learned, and the determination if it has been learned. This style assumes that learners only need to know what the teacher provides and, therefore, requires that the learner (child figure) become dependent upon the teacher (parental or authority figure). The learners' life experiences are of no value as a resource for the learning process; learners must become aligned with the teacher's point of view if they want to succeed. Pedagogy organizes learning by subject matter, and implies that learners are sufficiently motivated by the grading system and its related social pressures. Indeed, the word pedagogy means the art and science of teaching children. Knowles proposes an alternative to this pedagogical educational style that he calls andragogy. The andragogical style is based on the adult learner's need to know why it is important to learn something before beginning to study the topic. In this style, the instructor's job is to help learners become aware of their need to know. Since the learners are adults, they have strong self-concepts and feel capable of making their own decisions. As a result, they are self-directed in their outlook and are more excited by an empowered environment, where they participate actively in the governance of the process, than when submitted to a more dependent environment where they are merely the mechanistic recipients of the outcome of decisions. In addition, they have rich life experiences to draw from as a basis of learning, and they readily learn those things that are natural extensions from life experiences. This is what provides the personal interpretation or perspective of "truth" or "reality." The focus of adult learning is not on the subject matter, but rather on something they perceive as helping them to perform tasks or effectively deal with the problems they face in their real life situations.[32]

Margaret Wheatley, author of *Leadership and the New Science*, describes this dynamic structure of the new genre of these new learning organizations—how "dissipative structures demonstrate that *disorder* can be a source of *order*, and that growth can be found in disequilibrium, not in balance."[33] Her concepts build upon the systems perspective of Forrester, support the worldviews of Schumpeter and Senge, and reflect the chaos and upheaval that is felt during major systemic changes. But despite the chaos, Wheatley observes that, "Changes do not occur randomly, in any direction. They are always consistent with what has gone on before, with the history and identity of the system."[34]

Contributions to business systems engineering also come from the manufacturing and industrial engineering community. In particular, the focus on waste elimination and cycle time reduction taught by Japanese industrial engineers has been especially influential. Taichi Ohno, the business systems architect of the Toyota Production System, taught his people that the goal was a tenfold increase in productivity and that *kanban* —the Toyota approach to Just-in-Time manufacturing and cycle time reduction—is the primary approach to achieve this end.[35] In support of Ohno's streamlined production system, Ryuji Fukuda, in his book *Managerial Engineering*,[36] described the development of reliable work methods at Sumitomo Electric Industries—methods that inevitably lead to success when they are followed on a rigorous step-by-step basis. The functional basis for these reliable methods comes from the integration of quality control methods with those of industrial engineering and operations research and their application within the context of the total quality system.

Let us complete the historical sketch by considering the quality contribution. Drs. W. Edwards Deming, Joseph M. Juran,[37] and Armand V. Feigenbaum created an underlying culture for continuous improvement focused on achieving business objectives through their contributions to statistical process control and TQM. Contributions by the quality movement include the concepts of policy deployment (or *hoshin kanri*), quality assessment, and strategic benchmarking, which focus on identifying specific initiatives where making breakthrough improvement is possible. These ideas build upon *kaizen*, the incremental change process used by teams to keep work standards and processes improving by continuously increasing their effectiveness and efficiency. A robust TQM system should embody both the *hoshin* and *kaizen* objectives in a single set of related change initiatives. This degree of maturity is found only in the most disciplined quality systems: AT&T, Florida Power & Light, Hewlett-Packard, Intel, Procter & Gamble, Southern Pacific, and Xerox to name a few companies in the United States. Included among the Japanese companies who practice this integrated version of TQM are: Bridgestone Tire, Honda, Kansai Electric, Komatsu, Sumitomo, Toppan Printing, and Toyota. Indeed, this mature version of TQM is a model for the deployment of the major change initiatives of business systems engineering.[38]

All of these elements, taken together, have created the environment to look at business in a fundamentally different way. And yet, we must be cautious not to throw the baby away with the bath water. As Rosabeth Moss Kanter in one of my favorite writings on the process of business change has advised: "The architecture of change thus requires *an awareness of foundations.*"[39] Kanter's perspective of change is close to Schumpeter's idea of innovation: "Change involves the crystallization of new action possibilities (new policies, new behaviors, new patterns, new methodologies, new products, or new market ideas) based on reconceptualized patterns in the organization. The architecture of change involves the design and construction of new patterns, or the reconceptualization of old ones, to make new, and hopefully more productive, actions possible."[40] Thus, Kanter's contribution serves as a twofold reminder. First, plans for change should be possibilities for action that are subsequently driven into existence and become new organizational patterns based on the past. Second, Kanter reiterates the necessity of historical linkages that we first discussed as part of the fundamental need for learning and are reinforced by our brief encounter with Wheatley's ideas around organizational chaos, which is grounded in the historical identity of the system. Essentially, learning is the root of business systems change.

FACTORS THAT ENABLE CHANGE

Leading organization-wide change is the greatest challenge facing the executive teams within today's threatened corporations. The ability to integrate change elements within the context of the organization's business culture, operating history, and philosophy of management is an essential ingredient for the successful implementation of strategic change. For change to take hold and become long-lasting, positively influencing the organization in the desired manner, it must be congruent with the organization's internal pressures. It must be accepted by the people and embraced as their own. It must be reinforced by management communication, which signifies its importance and their interest. It must be supported by information to allow midcourse corrections and improvements during the change implementation. And, it must result in repeatable, reliable process performance. The key enablers of change are: people, process, and information. These three elements of change are woven like threads into the warp and woof of the organization's fabric of change, and their proper engagement provides the basis for exercising the implementation process in a way that ensures success.

ENGAGING THE LEVERS OF CHANGE

Archimedes once said that "with a lever long enough . . . single-handed I can move the world." What are the levers that can move the organization? Finding appropriate change levers is a key enabler of systemic change. Briggs and Peat state that "The ability of a system to amplify a small change is a change lever."[41]

In most organizations people, process, and information are the primary factors that can create significant organizational leverage when they are moved together to make business change happen. Interestingly enough, these three change levers are the focus of three cross-functional organizations: quality, management information systems, and human resources. Often, these three groups stumble over each other as they seek to conduct very similar business. While each of these groups has a unique functional or technical perspective, they all share a similar approach to the same set of customers—the process owners who are charged with the management of the business and work processes, and thus with their continual improvement.

Edgar Shein[42] describes the common activity of these three organizations as process consulting—individuals who attempt to change the processes of others without the direct authority to influence the behavior change. These three organizations must attempt to influence situations without any formal power to make change happen. In addition to this "process skill," these individuals bring their technical skills to bear: information technology, organizational development, quality and statistical tools, and project management. Coordinating the activities of these three staff functions can lead to a major breakthrough in the effectiveness of an organization in planning and implementing strategic change initiatives. By effectively using these three ingredients, change initiatives may be more successfully implemented.

RECOGNIZING THE NEED FOR INNOVATION:
THE NEXT STEP

What does all this historical perspective and intellectual gobbledygook mean for the pragmatic manager who is faced with an organization that has declining productivity, plummeting market share, and decreasing customer satisfaction? The next step is to generate the innovation that leads to more productive processes. How does that happen? Well, as long-time radio commentator Paul Harvey regularly says to his audience across the United States as he breaks for an advertisement: "That's the rest of the story."

2

Innovation Seeks Productivity

People delight greatly in tortuous paths.
Lao Tzu, *Te-Tao Ching*

PRODUCTIVITY: THE CORNERSTONE OF COMPETITIVENESS

Several years ago, I discovered a central truth of management: *Productivity—the key to business profitability—is the result of how we manage the processes for producing goods and services and is driven by implementing innovations in both products and their customer delivery processes.* Innovative products alone are insufficient to generate long-term productivity growth. The United States automobile industry proved this point in the 1970s as it unsuccessfully competed against Japanese manufacturers for market share using a strategy that relied only on new product development. It took a major loss of market share for U.S. manufacturers to recognize the need for change—but their lack of process-focus prevented them from seeing the appropriate way to make the required capital investments to correctly engineer their business and work processes. Despite their massive multibillion dollar capital investments in computer-integrated manufacturing, they realized little improvement in their relative competitive position. This was a natural outcome of their process myopia—because they had not improved the productivity of the processes that they had automated, there were no significant gains to be realized. Innovation in business processes is a necessary condition to increased business competitive-

17

ness. From this lesson, I have constructed my approach to business systems engineering: *Innovation should be introduced into business organizations through managed strategic change initiatives that drive productivity in key business processes through the combined introduction of product and process innovations.*[1]

When I first studied the theory of quality management, I read the obligatory "guru" tome of the late Dr. W. Edwards Deming, *Out of the Crisis.* I discovered many gems in this material. One of these gems was the linkage of quality and productivity. Quality is a popular topic that can engage enthusiastic discussions with the working level without creating personal anxiety, while productivity is a more "academic" topic that not only bores people but also generates personal fears of having one's job made redundant and becoming a candidate for "the pink slip." Deming described the *chain of quality,* which starts with the improvement of product quality, which drives process productivity, which then provides an opportunity for cost reduction, which, in turn, can increase market share. Deming believed that product and process innovation can only exist in an environment where senior management is concerned with the continuous improvement of both quality and productivity, thereby ensuring the long-term viability of the business system.[2]

What is productivity? Productivity measures the return from an investment (at the highest level of the firm, return on assets is a measure of productivity), and on a national scale it is typically expressed as output divided by input (for example, gross domestic product per employee). International competitiveness is composed of two aspects: maintaining a growing standard of living and staying ahead of other nations in that standard of living. At the level of the firm, productivity is the amount of revenue normalized by size of the labor or asset base (for example, revenue per employee), and the surrogate for competitiveness is market share (relative to competitors). Productivity measures both efficiency and effectiveness and can result from downsizing (eliminating jobs), upsizing (adding workers, shifts, or capacity), doing different things (new products or services), or doing things differently (new or changed business or work processes). Over the long haul, the nation with the highest productivity will lead the world economically.[3]

Jack Grayson's latest book, *American Business: A Two-Minute Warning,* is a call to arms for American industry—if an increase in productivity does not come, then Japan may succeed the United States to become the world's productivity leader, followed by world's economic leaders. In particular, Grayson and Carla O'Dell, his learned coauthor, warn both industry and government that they must adopt an agenda for change if they expect the American economy to maintain its current leadership position. Their agenda presents two interesting perspectives: first, the need for leadership and, second, the need for redesigning business organizations to become integrated operating systems.

Why is leadership an issue worthy of concern in a discussion about work productivity? It is because leadership, in an economic race, whether between nations or firms, can generate complacency from its comfortable position of affluence. Some inadequate responses of leaders to the threat of competition may be: disregard for potential competitors, belief in the invincibility of their own position, or reaction to a new challenge with a predictable formula or historical response. Leaders tend to overlook the relative imbalance of their productivity position compared with their competitors—it is considered to be too insignificant to care about. *But,* remembering the lessons of history, in the eighteenth century England displaced the Netherlands as the world leader in productivity by closing their growth gap at only a half a percent annually. No difference is too insignificant to ignore if its effect is compounded over time! As Grayson and O'Dell conclude: "The world is not a safe place for leaders."[4]

As an interesting aside, Grayson and O'Dell note that copying other nations is a long-standing trend. They also note that those who are gaining on the leaders tend to be those who are the copiers. They observe that "all nations copy from one another, directly and indirectly."[5] They illustrate this trend by citing several historical cases: Ferdinand Braudel observed that England's first factory in the industrial revolution was copied from an Italian silk mill; Angus Maddison observed that many of the elements of the British infrastructure (banking, shipping, canal building, and agriculture) were replications of the Dutch model; E. E. Williams noted in his 1890 book *Made in Germany* that the Prussians imitated the English as best they could in the establishment of their industries. Even the United States may be accused of copying from others—Alexis de Tocqueville, from a French perspective, deplored the United States as "a land of copiers," and F. A. McKenzie believed the Americans to be economic "invaders" by usurping the natural position of British goods in the marketplace. And today, we refer to the Japanese as the greatest imitators of all. It seems that it is natural for humans to label those who are closing in on becoming the world's economic leader as "copiers"!

The second point of interest is the need to redesign the operating systems of firms to help them compete better in the global market. Grayson and O'Dell observe that the most competitive firms have the following ten characteristics, which others should consider for themselves:

1. Small operating units with fewer, more highly skilled people per unit.
2. Few management levels.
3. Team structures.
4. Customer-driven schedules and procedures.
5. Flexible product mix potential.
6. Minimal inventories.
7. Faster startups.
8. Flexible equipment, some designed in-house.
9. Higher productivity and lower unit costs.
10. Higher quality and a focus on customer-supplier relations.[6]

As Grayson and O'Dell read the economic tea leaves, it appears that American industry will need to focus on redesigning, rediscovering, reinventing, restructuring, reengineering, renewing, rejuvenating—practically speaking, redoing everything in an effort to return itself to a more competitive position relative to its Japanese opponents. With this desperate a change manifesto, one must ask: What is the role of product and process innovation in the apparent American decline and the Japanese ascendancy? Let's consider the distinctions between the American and Japanese approaches to innovation.

THE JAPANESE WAY TO INNOVATION

A historical perspective of Japan is a necessary starting point to understand its current emphasis on innovation. In 1853, during the Meiji Restoration period, Commodore Perry attempted to force the Japanese to open their trade doors. Ever since that time, Japan has been invaded by foreign ideas. However, this invasion has never conquered the culture of Japan. The Japanese have adapted those perceived strengths from other cultures and made them their own—for example, they adapted their language and a strong religious influence from China (Japan emerged from the shadow of the Chinese culture in the Heian period—A.D. 710–794—and created its own unique culture). In response to the appearance of Perry's black fleet, Japan has been trying to catch up to the level of economic performance of Western governments. Indeed, they coined the phrase *wakon yosai*—"Japanese spirit and Western knowledge"—to describe their assimilation of Western concepts. Even the primary goal following the World War II would support this continued thrust: Economic growth was to be Japan's primary national goal.[7] The emphasis on modernizing the industrial base of Japan has its roots in the Meiji Restoration period with reinforcement through the Yoshida Doctrine following World War II. This trend continues today as a national policy. It is interesting that in the Japanese government Science and Technology Agency's 1981 White Paper on International Competitiveness the Agency's Minister, Mr. I. Nakagawa, referred to 1980 as "the first year of the era of Japan's technological independence."[8] This signals that Japan has moved from a local manufacturing-based society to a global research and knowledge-based society. This reference was made because in 1980 the rate of growth for investment in technology surpassed that of both the United States and Germany. These investments, largely made by the *kaisha,* large Japanese corporations, will lead to the conclusion that the *kaisha* will be the major source of innovative technology for the world as they continue the trend to expand their business emphasis from operational excellence in production toward technological excellence in design.[9] By 1989, the Ministry of International Trade and Industry (MITI) had concluded that Japan was on an equal competitive footing with the United States in a variety of high technology areas: copiers, laser printers, microprocessors, integrated circuit memories, superconductive materials, optomagnetic disks, midrange computers, computer-aided design and manufacturing (CAD/CAM), and communications satellites.[10] How did this transition happen from a nation that has been branded copycat and imitator?

T. W. Kang, a Japanese businessman, provides a clear statement of the postwar criticism that has been leveled against the Japanese in his book *Gaishi: The Foreign Company in Japan*: "It is clear to me that there are two very different types of know-how: one that encourages revolutionary creativity and the other that encourages [for example, evolutionary—author's note] operational improvement. They both involve a variety of factors, including culture, motivation, the relative power of each function, and turnover. Just as many U.S. firms do not understand how their Japanese competitors can manufacture so efficiently, so the Japanese do not understand how Americans can do so many innovative things. The Japanese, who strive for orderliness and discipline, are baffled when Americans produce energetic ideas through a seemingly disorderly clash of polar thoughts. One of the most valuable things I gained from working in an American company was the understanding that managed chaos can lead to revolutionary breakthroughs. The excessive emphasis the Japanese place on industriousness hinders creativity."[11] But, we must ask ourselves, are we making our comparisons between the two nations from a level playing field?

Shintaro Ishihara, the outspoken, controversial coauthor (with Sony's Akio Morita) of *The Japan That Can Say No,* is a staunch defender of the innovative methods of the Japanese culture. He believes that many aspects of the nature of Japanese creativity are not understood by Westerners. He has stated: "Americans assert that Japanese are 'just imitators.' We should not be daunted by American charges that Japanese are just copiers. Creativity in Japan is not limited to a scientific or cultural elite. You see it everywhere, among people from all walks of life. Our supremacy in high technology stems from an alert, innovative labor force. Everyone in a company contributes from top to bottom."[12]

Yes, Americans have criticized the Japanese for being mimickers, copycats, good at improvement on the inventions of others and yet unable to deliver the breakthrough Nobel laureate level of scientific knowledge. However, we must look at the facts clearly. For instance, the Japanese have created 74 totally new types of business since the end of World War II.[13] This is a truly remarkable feat for a nation that is not innovative! Another aspect of this discussion that must be questioned is the presumption that the awarding of a Nobel Prize, as esteemed a worldwide recognition as it is, is the appropriate measure for business-based technological innovation. A better metric may be the number of patents awarded, which indicates the progress of pure technology toward pragmatic applications. While the number of Nobel Prizes may indicate a national priority for pure research, the number of patent applications provides a measure of a nation's priority for applied research. In this area, Japan is clearly outstripping American industry on its own turf. In 1978, the top five companies who led in patents issued did not include any Japanese organizations; however, by 1990, four of the five were Japanese.[14] To reinforce this perspective, consider the observations of John Young, former president and CEO of Hewlett-Packard Company and president of the Council on Competitiveness. Young believes that the copycat characterization of Japanese industry is a myth and that citing the number of Nobel Prizes is misleading in two ways. First, it is not clear whether the technology represented by the Nobel Prize "breakthrough" will lead to increased competitiveness and, second, although there may be a significant number of current Nobel Prizes awarded to American researchers, the funding trend in research is down in the United States. This indicates that we are becoming complacent in our pursuit of new technology and may not continue our performance trend using this measure.[15] More support to this idea may be added from James C. Abegglen and George Stalk, Jr. In their study of Japanese business, Abegglen and Stalk observed that, "Leading *kaisha* (Japanese corporations) are now spending more of their incomes on research and development than their Western competitors."[16] To fall behind one's competitors means that profits will not materialize and that cash flows will not be available to fund future growth and product development research. To minimize the risk of losing ground to the competition, Japanese competitors keep close tabs on all business activities of their competitors. In 1989, more than 50,000 Japanese scientists and engineers went overseas to study, while only 3,633 researchers from the United States went to Japan.[17] We must truly question whether or not we are investing appropriately in our ability to maintain viable economic growth through the stimulus of both product and process innovation. The Japanese appear to be seeking innovation everywhere in the world, while we seem to be sitting at home—contemplating our navels—waiting for the muse to strike us with a bolt of lightning. The clean sheet stays clean unless it is stimulated by some external thoughts.

There is a distinct difference in perspective—Japanese automakers have been delivering a myriad of innovative features in their products (electronically controlled suspensions, turbochargers with inter coolers, synthetic voice warnings, nonmetallic body panels, and ceramic engine components) and have thereby gained the leadership role in this industry.[18] None of these innovations may be worthy of the Nobel Prize—that is not their objective—however, they are worthy of the investment by customers and the resultant growth in market share. Perhaps we are using the wrong standard by which to judge innovation.

Perhaps the warning voiced by Akio Morita, founder and chairman of the Sony Corporation, in his book *Made in Japan* is the right one to heed as we consider the roots of Japanese culture: "If you go through life convinced that your way is always best, all the new ideas in the world will pass you by. Americans tend to think that the American system is the way things should work all around the world, but they should not be blind and deaf to how things are done in other countries."[19] So, how should one look at creativity and innovation from the perspective of the Japanese culture, and what learning is available for consideration and adaptation by the foreigner or *gaijin*?

In his delightfully informative book, *Created in Japan*, Sheridan Tatsuno describes the evolution of creative Japanese ideas as a pathway of knowledge from the basic level to development of proficiency, to mastery, to a state of intellectual enlightenment, to the ultimate Zen-like state of spiritual enlightenment. During this journey, he observes that different types of creativity are achieved, and he contrasts them against their Western counterparts.[20]

Tatsuno describes a juxtaposition between the different Western and Japanese approaches to creativity. He is careful not to make a judgment regarding which approach is better. The Western approach to creativity features breakthroughs (the big product idea), spontaneity, individual freedom to develop, linear or Cartesian logic, and a focused functional application. The Japanese approach to creativity is more adaptive, cultivated and deliberate, group-oriented, nonlinear, circular or fuzzy in logical structure, and multifunctional in application.[21] Just as the yin and yang are merged into a whole in Chinese religion, so both of these concepts must be blended to achieve a holistic approach to creativity. In the final analysis, balance between these approaches should lead to the best, most innovative results.

In reality, the Japanese have a more rigorous process for innovation than exists anyplace else in the world. Their focus on developing the ideas of the group ultimately leads to breakthroughs as well as incremental improvements, and the Japanese have excelled in using benchmarking to generate new ideas. Akio Morita observed that "there are three creativities: creativity in technology, in product planning, and in marketing. To have any one of these without the others is self-defeating in business."[22] While Morita's model stresses creativities in specific business processes, it is particularly interesting to note that he has selected three of the principal business processes that must be integrated in order to deliver competitive products to the marketplace. Behind Morita's statement is the very subtle meaning that both product and process innovation must be integrated to deliver increased business competitiveness.

But how, specifically, are creativity and innovation fostered in Japanese organizations around the process and resulting outcome of product development? Creativity in the development of products and planning for their production by Japanese businesses is based on ideas of minimization—reducing waste—which comes from a long tradition of managing scarcity in economic resources. Many of the historical Japanese cultural arts exhibit the essence of the cultural developments and trends in design thought patterns of modern business: Cultivating *bonsai* trees has led to miniaturization; folding *origami* figures out of paper has led to manipulation of complex three-dimensional computer forms; using the *sorobon* or Japanese abacus has laid a foundation for personal productivity products, for example, calculators and tape recorders; and even the folding fan (*sensu*) of the geisha has provided a model for the efficient use of space in collapsible products such as laptop computers.[23] Many product innovations come from the development of analogies to the events and culture of the society's daily life.

The same is true in process improvement. Incremental improvement may, in itself, be a more rigorous way to drive breakthrough performance in the long run. As an example, David Lu provides an operational definition of incremental improvement that is based more strongly on long-term, goal-directed behavior than is presumed in many Western explanations of *kaizen*, which make it appear that change is only planned in small increments that take an exceptionally long time to accumulate.

> If you get to the one-half mark,
> Cut the remainder in half, and
> Cut the remainder in half again, and
> Then cut the last remainder in half.[24]

This progression of incremental improvements at the rate of 2^4 power over the prior level of performance results in the final process performing at either 16 times or $1/16$ of the original level (depending upon whether a reduction or an increase in performance is desired).

In other words, a breakthrough level goal (greater than 10X) was attained through the rigorous application of four cycles of incremental process improvement. The only possible criticism that could be voiced over this type of approach to process improvement (*kaizen*) is the time that it may take to achieve these four iterations of change. But, for most managers, I suspect that the net result would make the time element more or less a moot point.

Incremental improvement can occur in both products and processes. Consider the Lexus product development. The Lexus LS400 is produced at the Tahara plant in Japan where workers actively "strive for the relentless pursuit of perfection" by relentlessly seeking continuous improvement to their daily work. One example cited is the reduction in dies for a particular assembly from ten components and fifteen dies to two components and eight dies—with the engineering team believing that they need to work on further reducing the number of dies.[25] These engineers prove that the slogan is not just an advertising tag line, but a philosophy for the daily management of the business. Simpler, cheaper ways of making things are constantly sought. These small, incremental changes result from the daily experience of the factory workers who contribute their creativity to the product design and the production process. The Lexus example reinforces the idea that Ishihara pointed out: In Japan everyone participates in the design process—not just the engineering team. In addition, the Japanese do not just focus single-purposefully on product innovation, but they combine it with an even stronger emphasis on process innovation—*kaizen* or continuous improvement through employee involvement and team participation—which results in making significant operational improvements.[26]

Peter Drucker has written that many of the Japanese companies he has observed actually follow a three-pronged approach to developing creativity: (1) continuous improvement of the current product in production, (2) coupled with the simultaneous development of a variant product in a rapid turnaround (10 to 15 months) where the product characteristics are just different enough to have a perceivably different product, and (3) also pursuing a breakthrough technology that would result in an innovative clean sheet design. As an example, in the copier business, Fuji Xerox continuously improved the copiers that were on the production line while product teams designed variant products using its current light lens copier technology and developing digital technology copiers in the R&D laboratory. Drucker wrote: "Increasingly, the leading Japanese companies organize themselves so that all three tracks are pursued simultaneously and under the direction of the same cross-functional (design) team."[27] How many American design teams want to handle their new product development simultaneously with making service engineering improvements on fielded products and developing variant versions with incremental features? No, the glory of the design engineer is in hitting the home run, not in keeping score or making the base hit.

James C. Morgan, chairman of Applied Materials Inc., a company that designs and develops semiconductor manufacturing equipment and is deeply embedded in the high technology culture of both Japan and the United States, has stated: "In the quest for continuous improvements, the American passion for only the 'breakthrough' solution is deleterious."[28] Perhaps our way of thinking about systematic improvement needs to be broadened.

But, we must remember that the Japanese are not the ten-foot giants that we painted the Russians during our cold war years. They have their own valid set of concerns about their position relative to the potential emergence of Yankee ingenuity and the ability to hit a home run during a stress situation. Consider my experience as a member of the Corporate Quality staff at Hewlett-Packard. I had the opportunity to interview the senior quality officers as part of a project to determine what critical personal and business skills lead to success in that position. One of the individuals who I interviewed was Katsu Yoshimoto, the quality manager for Yokagawa Hewlett-Packard (YHP). YHP had won the Deming Prize in 1982 while its quality system was under the oversight of Yoshimoto-san, and he was one of the most respected quality professionals within the entire company. I asked Yoshimoto the following question: What do you need most to learn to improve your business performance? Without hesitation, he responded that he wanted to learn more about how to generate innovation. When I probed to discover what he had in mind, he said: "How to develop innovative ways to respond to sudden changes in the business environment that arise from political, economic, or technology changes. I think innovation must spring from learnings of past experience in order to get to new levels of innovation that results in a truly creative solution." Remarkably, Yoshimoto had described Joseph A. Schumpeter's concept of creative destruction—systematically abandoning the old way of doing business to create a new way that will ensure success in the future—as the means for innovation.

So, what should Western industry do to halt its productivity decline relative to Japan? How should it use innovation to stimulate productivity? We have a pressing question—what is the answer? Perhaps the answer is the still small voice of moderation: We should issue a call for balance in the Western approach to innovation in which industry must do it all—both product and process innovations as well as both breakthrough and continuous improvement. You may agree, but you also must surely be asking yourself: "Okay, but HOW?"

INNOVATION: CATALYST FOR BUSINESS SYSTEMS ENGINEERING

Innovation for business systems means to break out of the old mold and create a new way of doing things. But, as we saw in the previous section, a balanced approach does not just include a clean sheet redesign of the system—it incorporates all aspects of change, as appropriate, to make the overall system more effective. If there are 10,000 projects of an incremental change nature occurring at the work process level of an organization, then there is a good chance that they have the opportunity to deliver more significant change than the three to five strategic change initiatives an organization can absorb at a single time. Both of these approaches must become complementary—and the opportunity for their coexistence is great because they tend to be products of different levels of the business organization.

The past 50 years have seen the reemergence of Japan from the ashes of defeat. It has had the opportunity to "create a clean sheet design" for its businesses, which has led to a significant accomplishment in growth and productivity. Maybe the Western world should look at copying the copiers! By adopting a similar, balanced innovation strategy and building upon the strong basis for innovative product and process development, Western businesses have the opportunity to make significant strides in productivity growth and revenue enhancement.

The clear call of innovation begins with the need to *stop doing business badly*—eliminate or replace those practices that are not providing benefits commensurate with their costs. This is a *kaizen* focus on continual improvement—not standing by to let the laws of economic entropy take effect and observe the business system degrade around us!

To keep in the leading competitive position requires nothing less than not falling backwards! However, to extend the economic position of our business system requires that innovation also be applied to those areas that can provide breakthrough leaps in productivity through the introduction of technologically advanced products that target customer needs and are produced with highly efficient and effective means of manufacturing. So, how do we put such a change effort together? The appetizer course is now complete, and we should move on to the main course and both innovate and implement these innovations through business systems engineering.

PART II

Foundation of Business Systems Engineering

3

Definition of Business Systems Engineering

If you wish to shrink it,
You must certainly stretch it.
If you wish to weaken it,
You must certainly strengthen it.
If you wish to desert it,
You must certainly work closely with it.
If you wish to snatch something from it,
You must certainly give something to it.

Lao Tzu, *Te-Tao Ching*

THE MEANING OF BUSINESS SYSTEMS ENGINEERING

What do we really mean by the phrase *business systems engineering*, and how does it differ from business process reengineering?[1] Perhaps it would be helpful to start by examining each of the terms used in this phrase: business, systems, and engineering.

What is the true nature of business? *Business* is the set of activities of an entity involved in commerce, manufacturing, or service that results in the production of an economic output with the intention of producing a profitable gain. It will help to understand what Alfred P. Sloan, Jr., chief executive officer of General Motors from 1923 to 1946 and member or chairman of the board for 45 years, had to say about business. Sloan has been recognized over the years as one of this century's most insightful businessmen. He was the architect of the decentralized organization structure for General Motors and led the organization through rocky decades of economic uncertainty in a developing industry. While discussing the purpose of business Sloan said: "The strategic aim of business is to earn a return on capital, and if in any particular case the return in the long run is not satisfactory, the deficiency should be corrected or the activity abandoned for a more favorable one."[2] In short, business is about making money on money in some chosen fashion. In a competitive environment, where there is an economic scarcity of customers who purchase products, a company must seek a definite advantage in order to succeed.[3]

Customer! Customer? Who Is the Customer?

We make money in a business because customers want to purchase our services. The customer is the basic unit of a competitive market. Collections of customers having common characteristics are called market segments. Market segments are targeted for the sale of products and services. The preceding pedantic sequence of thoughts indicates what most of us have known all along—customers are the most important aspect of our business![4] Being customer focused means that you are delivering value to your customer in a way that helps your customer succeed. Thus, becoming customer focused only makes good business sense. Your customers will reward you with their loyalty through repeat business. Both Business Process Reengineering (BPR) and Total Quality Management (TQM) are customer focused. However, I want to distinguish clearly what I mean by customer focused. Much harm has been done by proponents of TQM who encourage those workers who do not have a direct "line-of-sight" vision or access to the *external,* paying customer to think of the "next person in the process" as their *internal* customer. Some TQM advocates take this position because they want to have a more customer-focused organization—but it doesn't always achieve that result. Interestingly enough, this practice seems to come from Japanese TQM companies who consider the next person in the process as their customer. However, in Japan, this is not interpreted the same way as it is in the United States. In Japan the use of internal customers is interpreted within the context of a concept called *wa* or group harmony. This means that the entire group effectively works toward a singular aim. In Western culture, with its emphasis more on individuals, the idea that "the next person in your process is your internal customer" is, fundamentally, not a sound proposition. When we consider someone a customer, their requirements become important to us and fulfilling their requirements becomes our personal objective. This means that we could become unwitting coconspirators to undermine the real requirements of the end customer. Thus, the concept of internal customer introduces a potential failure point into our system. As John Guaspari noted: "The extent that the internal customer model causes people to define the fundamental process at hand too narrowly, it [referring to the concept of the internal customer] in itself becomes the source of a serious problem."[5] For instance, what happens if the next person in the process does not share the same opinion as the final customer or has misinterpreted the external customer's expectation and we see it more clearly? The internal customer concept fails because it defocuses our attention on the paying customer—the one who is funding the entire venture that we are a part of. We should treat our coworkers as associates, cohorts, colleagues, teammates, cosuppliers, or whatever else we wish to call them, who are on the same team working together to deliver the result that satisfies our external customer. However, this is a model of teamwork or groupwork, and we should not call our coworkers "customers." The term "customer" should be reverently reserved for those people who provide the capital that makes our capitalism a profitable venture. We should value our customer as a major capital asset, particularly those who follow the philosophy of Doris Bigio, a European management consultant, who says: "As a customer, it is my duty to be difficult." Such a customer is a gem—not a pain. Only from such "difficult" customers can we learn and grow our business.

Within the context of a business enterprise, what is the meaning of a *system*? A good definition of system was offered by Jay W. Forrester: "System means a grouping of parts that operate together for a common purpose."[6] Recently, Peter Senge has focused management's attention on systems thinking. He considers how businesses are bound together "by invisible fabrics of interrelated actions, which often take years to fully play out their effects on each other. Since we are part of that lacework ourselves, it's doubly hard to see the whole pattern of change. Instead, we tend to focus on snapshots of isolated parts of the system, and wonder why our deepest problems never get solved. Systems thinking is a conceptual framework, a body of knowledge and tools that has been developed over the past fifty years, to make the full patterns clearer, and to help us see how to change them effectively."[7] Webster's dictionary defines system as "a combination of things or parts forming a complex or unitary whole; a complex scheme or plan of procedure; due method, or orderly manner of arrangement or procedure. . . ."[8] The basic idea of a system is a holistic unit—a complex structure that has some form that is recognized as a set of related subelements that have some identified, structured relationship.

In a business enterprise, the business system may be considered to be the related set of business processes that produce the output of the entire enterprise. Business processes are the horizontal processes that link together the various functional activities that deliver the output of the enterprise. They consist of functional work processes that either produce and deliver the specific elements of the product or provide support services for those work processes that do. Work processes are the sets of procedures or activities, tasks, and steps where the real work of the organization is accomplished to produce the economic output that generates the profitable return on the capital employed. If you will excuse another analogy, work processes represent the "atomic" level of the business.

What is *engineering*? Engineering is the art of developing and executing a practical application of scientific knowledge to the design of a product or process. It differs from the pure science in that it seeks an implementation of knowledge, not knowledge purely for its own sake. (Thus, the measure of engineering productivity is the number of patents issued rather than achieving a Nobel Prize.) Engineers design and manage intricate enterprises and operations using the tools of information technology to help them apply scientific principles more clearly to the tasks of the business. In particular, industrial engineers apply the tools of statistics, simulation and modeling, and scientific method to the simplification of work processes with the objective of increasing the productivity of labor and work processes. Frederick Taylor introduced the ideas of time and motion studies as a basis for work simplification and thereby created the field of industrial engineering.[9]

Putting these three terms back together we get: business systems engineering.[10] Business systems engineering is a method for identifying, defining, and implementing change. It takes a perspective that employs the whole organization as a vehicle for driving strategic change. By achieving an appropriate linkage between strategic and operational concerns of an organization, management may be able to increase the probability that the organization, as a whole, will achieve its strategic intent. Business systems engineering takes a holistic approach to managing major strategic changes for a set of interwoven business processes—it can help organizations successfully introduce large-scale, complex change initiatives. Let's understand a little more about the meaning of *strategy* and *change* before we finalize our operational definition of business systems engineering.

WHAT IS STRATEGY?

Strategy is the persistence of a vision. It is the art of seeing differently, and then planning to act differently. It is the combined ability of a group to see where it wants to go, to see where it is, to identify what must be done to close this gap, and then to execute those changes that are necessary to get and stay on a track that will close this gap. For a vision to persist, it must be carried out over time. Persistent visions are therefore aligned with the long-term business objectives that state what must be done to close the gap.[11]

While we tend to talk about fixed processes for strategic planning, we also recognize that strategy formulation is not mechanistic or a linear process. It is based on strategic learning about the business environment and contains elements of surprise that are the result of technological breakthroughs, shifts in consumer preferences, the composition of a company's senior management team, and other serendipitous events. Therefore, it is an imperative that strategic plans be flowing—each iteration adaptively learning from a trial and error process where we reshape or reformulate our organization and its products according to these recognized externalities.[12]

Core competencies and process capabilities[13] are the key levers of change that may be moved to achieve the desired states of the organization. Core competence represents the collected learning of an organization—the sum of the individual competencies of its members. Process capability represents the interrelationship among business processes from a strategic perspective. The concept of core competence is humanistic in its emphasis; the concept of process capability is process centric in its emphasis. Both of these perspectives are necessary to optimize the competitiveness of a business. The identification of an organization's core competencies and process capabilities, as well as its technology portfolio and strategic alliances, are all parts of the direction-setting process that helps to define its strategic intent—a statement of a company's long-term (10–20 years) commitment to change, in a particular and focused direction, which will result in a global leadership position beyond competitors. Although this sounds easy in theory, it is difficult in practice. The organization must join hands to both develop and deploy this strategic perspective, or as the prophet says in Proverbs: "Where there is no vision, the people perish."[14] Considering that, in the legal sense, a corporation is treated as a person, there is a lot of truth to this prophecy from a business perspective!

What prevents an organization from achieving its long-term strategic intent? Have you ever wondered why your business strategy changes every year? Has your senior management team changed its business measures so often that it is impossible to reconstruct a five-year change improvement history for your company? Have you wondered why change initiatives average less than three years, being replaced by a new version before the culmination of the past initiative? Have your business goals been vague exhortations using slogans such as "Do it right the first time," "Achieve zero defects," or "Make the customer number one"? These inspirational slogans are not operationally defined so that the working level of the organization knows how such a goal should influence its daily behaviors. These types of goals result in business change initiatives that don't stick—they fade away in time as the sponsoring manager leaves for another position or the business is faced with an impending fiscal crisis. These goals also risk being displaced by a new change initiative, resulting in the sense that management uses a "Baskin-Robbins 31 flavors" approach to identifying change—they select a different flavor of change initiative as it suits their whims. These symptoms are external signs of an unfocused management effort that will not achieve the benefits desired from long-term change. However, change is not an option. The questions remain: Where will change take us—or where will we take change? Can we make change our friend—or will change become our enemy?

CHANGE AS AN ORGANIZATIONAL IMPERATIVE

Standing still—no new products, markets, or processes—means that you are actually retreating. This observation is based on the law of entropy: All things decay over time, and the only way to prevent that decay is to reverse the process over time and change the "natural decay" into "unnatural growth." Planned strategic change using the techniques under the organizational umbrella of business systems engineering provides a structured approach to change management. If a business is not growing, then it is on the cusp of decay and must determine how it can best stimulate growth. To paraphrase Jack Welch, chairman of General Electric: A business must either grow or die! There is no choice!

Change is necessary to improve productivity. If a business stands still, that means, in relative terms, that it is actually moving backward. This decline will ultimately result in insolvency. Thus, the natural laws of physics also apply to business. Consider the law of entropy that addresses the energy budget of the universe. The law of entropy says that all processes, over time and left to themselves, naturally decay. This law comes from the science of thermodynamics. Consider the analogy of a rock that has been heated by the sun. Over the night, it naturally cools as the source of the heat is removed and its stored heat dissipates as it warms the cooler night air. That's entropy, that's decay, and the same thing can happen to a business! Growth is an essential to overcoming the natural business law of entropy! But, how do you stimulate business growth? A fundamental secret is that you must learn to live with change and embrace it as the way to learn how to grow more productive. But not all change is of equal value—and not all change is positive. So, how can we select the good and avoid the bad?

Don't Institutionalize Rigidity

In short, what do we know about change that will allow us to use it for the strategic advantage of our business? There are five ways in which a business can change. First, it can stay the same or maintain its status quo—but only for a period of time. The second and third ways are opposing trends: It can either grow or decay at an incremental rate. The fourth and fifth ways are also opposing trends: The business can have instantaneous success and achieve a phenomenal growth rate, or it can have a disastrous effect that forces it out of business immediately. If we ignore the two decay conditions, this means that there are three conditions of positive change: maintenance of standards, continuous improvement, and breakthrough improvement. What do these three conditions mean for a business?

Maintaining standards of performance is important for a business. It means that the customer can expect a reliably consistent product or service and that repeat purchases will result in similar purchasing experiences. For instance, in the purchase of gasoline, we can observe that our automobiles perform differently using different products because of the combination of additives and octane levels. We expect that a brand of gasoline will maintain a control process to consistently deliver the same formula of product that performs well for the design of our automobile's engine. This type of standard maintenance builds the loyalty of customers, which is an essential ingredient to growth. Standards maintenance is a minimum condition of excellence for a business; however, it is also a potential trap. If we do not include strategies for the other two change options, then our business can become locked in a rigid formula for success, which is all too easy for our competitors to observe and devise an effective counterstrategy. So, we must effectively combine the maintenance strategy with an improvement strategy.

Continuous process improvement is a fundamental principle of Total Quality Management. It builds upon the abilities of the entire organization to contribute to the improvement of business practices, work processes, product features, service capability, and support consistency—all to deliver increased customer satisfaction and, therefore, increased sales. As discussed in Chapter 2, this is the principle of *kaizen*—continuous improvement through the active participation of all employees to make things better throughout the entire business. Some examples of continuous improvement are an organization's ability to: rapidly correct product problems and prevent their recurrence; consistently develop methods to build higher quality levels into products; doggedly pursue the elimination of non-value-added process steps, which add unproductive delay time to the manufacturing process; and relentlessly pursue the reduction of the cost of waste throughout the product delivery process. These small, incremental improvements in all areas of the business keep it from becoming rigid or inflexible and, at the same time, make it more difficult for competitors to emulate its ever-improving business practices. Over time, small improvements can accumulate into outstanding results. As significant as continuous improvement can be to a company, some of the most visible, and therefore important, gains come from making breakthrough improvements.

Breakthrough improvements come from an organization's ability to see its business in a different way—a perspective that no competitor has considered. This leads to new products that are truly different, service processes that meet needs that customers feel but cannot fully express as requirements, and performance capability that delights customers and gives them a feeling of respect for being associated with your business. Examples of this type of improvement include the development of the Lexus by Toyota, the treatment of people as "customers for life" by Carl Sewell in his Dallas, Texas, Cadillac dealership, and the IBM service response to computer problems where the company "mobilizes an army of engineers" to make it better. These types of breakthrough performance, tied to both continuous improvement and standards maintenance, can build long-term customer loyalty— repeat buyers who want to maintain a business relationship. As we engineer our business, we must consider how to use this full system of change mechanisms to build a flexible organization, one that will not rigidly hold onto the past at all costs, including its own self-destruction.

Breakthrough change can be motivated either by internal desires to engineer the business in a way that positions it ahead of the competition or by an external imperative thrust upon the organization. Schumpeterian-like examples of change are available from recent U.S. business history. For instance, in the late 1970s, Xerox was forced to share its patents and disclose its trade secrets, thereby opening the copier market to both domestic and foreign competitors and forcing it to become more competitive in its manufacturing practices. In the early 1980s, AT&T was forced into divestiture by the federal government, resulting in its need to increase efficiency throughout its operations. Likewise, in the late 1980s, Digital Equipment Corporation and IBM learned that the market can force change also, and both suffered through painful downsizing as they became "lean manufacturers." The point is that, in the recent past, "creative destruction" has been forced on American companies. Managing forthcoming breakthrough change has not been part of corporate strategic plans. Xerox, AT&T, IBM, and DEC are all now learning how to compete more effectively in the global market. Perhaps these earlier experiences provide them with a better perspective on how to manage massive organizational transformations.

The leader of another company that has weathered this type of change, John F. Welch, Jr.—also known as "Neutron Jack"—the well-respected CEO of General Electric, has said: "Changing the culture starts with an attitude. I hope you won't think I'm being melodramatic if I say that the institution ought to stretch itself, ought to reach to the point where it almost comes unglued."[15] Hewlett-Packard forced such a change process when it faced John Young's 10X goal for improvement of product reliability during the 1980s. George Fisher, as CEO of Motorola, Inc., challenged employees to achieve a six sigma level of performance for product quality in five years (1987–1992). Such a stretching of an organization leads it to breakthrough change. How do these industry role models deploy change? The answer is through considering the entire business as a system that needs to be optimized as a whole—not suboptimized in its parts. This leads us to our operational definition of business systems engineering:

> *Business systems engineering is an approach to designing business processes in a structured way that maximizes both customer value and enterprise performance.*

This type of change is needed to increase competitiveness—the question to focus upon now is how we should identify and deploy these change initiatives.

THE NEED FOR BUSINESS SYSTEMS ENGINEERING

Sometimes I believe we feel that we must always "get it right the first time" as we design systems or develop business methods. One of the lessons learned from the project sponsored by the American Society for Quality Control, called the *Stuff Americans Are Made Of*[SM], was that Americans learn by their mistakes. They tend to jump into new opportunities and work things out. According to the *Stuff* statistics, 64 percent of Americans say that they are better off having made mistakes.[16] I guess we don't like to "do it right the first time"! We do tend to learn from our past—both our own successes and failures as well as the performance results we observe from others. As Norm Rickard, president of Xerox Business Services and former vice president of Quality at Xerox, once said to me: "I reserve the right to be smarter today than I was yesterday." The question should not be whether or not change is good or right—the question really is, how should we identify what must change and how can we successfully manage it?

Hierarchical organizational change—or the move toward work group thinking and working—is a move up to the group or team level from the individual contributor, and down to the team level from the functional organization. In this level of change, there is the potential for two fatal errors, which senior management must be alert not to make:

1. Not paying attention to their own level of the organization—its values, vision, mission, core competence, strategic intent and fundamental technical advantages, the reasons for which senior management exists.
2. Micromanaging things that they have done before—not letting go of business process or work process activities.

There is an interesting corollary to the second error: A fatal error of individual contributors occurs when their reach exceeds their bounds, for example, when production workers try to change the culture of the organization (exceeding the limits or boundary of their empowerment).

As if to emphasize this point, Brian Joiner, a leading disciple of Dr. W. Edwards Deming, has said: "We need to work together to optimize the system as a whole, not seek to optimize separate pieces. Optimizing separate pieces destroys the effectiveness of the whole."[17] Joiner is absolutely right! His statement cuts to the root cause of the problem with Business Process Reengineering. It cannot treat individual business processes piecemeal and expect to make consistently effective change a reality. Problems do not present themselves one at a time; they present themselves as a system of problems that must be resolved systemically. So, the business must be engineered as a system, not put together as an off-the-rack set of casual clothes that can be mixed and matched to form an acceptable outfit to wear! Okay then, now that we have covered all of these preliminary considerations, let's ask the main question: What is so different about business systems engineering and how can it be used to drive the transformation of an organization?

BUSINESS SYSTEMS ENGINEERING AS AN ORGANIZATIONAL TRANSFORMATION METHOD

The approach to business transformation through systems engineering is illustrated in Figure 3–1. The "drivers" in the model are two methods for determining the priority for engineering processes within the business system. The enterprise model is the result of a business mod-

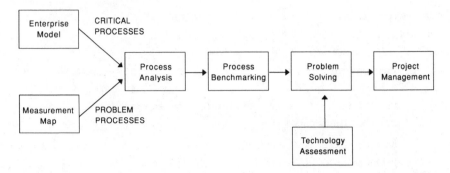

Figure 3-1.   Business Systems Engineering Model

eling methodology that identifies critical business processes that need to be changed. The measurement map is the output of an analysis of the measurement requirements for the daily operations of the business. It identifies problem work processes where controls are beyond the resource capability of their owners. (Both the enterprise model and the measurement map will be described further in Chapter 4.) During the process analysis phase, the customer requirements and business outcomes of the process are determined, and the process is documented for both sequence of events and measurement control points that may be used next for benchmarking. The process benchmarking studies should include comparisons with both internal and external partners; however, the process is halted at the end of the analysis phase when the team has identified both the measurable gaps and a set of potential enablers to improve the performance of the process. These are inputs to the next phase of the systems engineering effort, which uses a problem-solving model. The problem-solving model is used to structure the process-improvement project. The inputs from the enterprise model and measurement map, together with the results of the process analysis and benchmarking studies, are used to define the problem statement. A technology assessment provides new concepts about the application of alternative technologies (for example, bar coding, computer and software applications, networking, and automation) that may be used to generate the set of potential solutions. The outcome of the problem-solving process is the definition of a high-priority project that is managed to completion using such project methods as critical path determination and management milestone reviews. This model of business systems engineering illustrates a relatively linear picture of the methodology and does not provide a clear picture of how each of the pieces relates to a holistic, or businesswide, application. To illustrate how this occurs, let's look at how business organizations are structured and how this process can be used to support both cross-business and cross-functional improvement initiatives.

THE NATURE OF BUSINESS ORGANIZATIONS

McKinsey & Company, Inc., business consultants have made many contributions to business analysis. One of their key contributions is the idea of a business enterprise model.[18] An enterprise model is one way to depict the interactions among the customer value system and the key processes of the business that comprise that delivery system. Figure 3–2 illustrates a generic enterprise model. It shows the value delivery system at the top level as the sequence of four systems that generate the value that is delivered as the organization's output to the

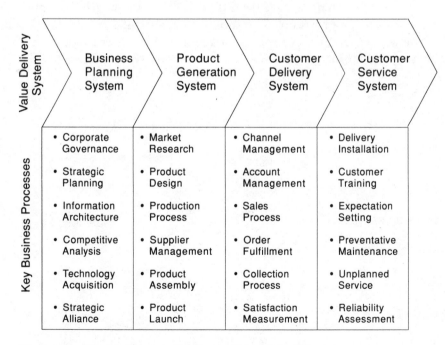

Figure 3–2. A Generic Business Enterprise Model

customer: business planning system, product generation system, customer delivery system, and customer service system. Each of these systems is composed of key business processes that contribute together to generate value at that phase in the value delivery system.

Value is delivered in a particular sequence of activities. Value from the associates (I will use this term instead of the alternatives—see discussion in the "customer" highlight box for my reasons) within the business is added to the value contributed by supplier-partners to produce the total value delivered to the customer. The value perceived by the customer, relative to the value offered by competitors, drives purchase decisions, and therefore drives the market share. As the relative value perceived by the customer becomes higher, so the ownership value to the stockholder becomes higher. Thus, the value contributed by employees determines the value perceived by customers, which in turn provides the value realized by the owners. This three-part "evergreen" value system is embedded within the basic structure of an organization (see Figure 3–3). By understanding how an organization works together to cooperatively deliver value, we will understand how the business enterprise operates as a system.

Organizations tend to have three different voices to which they must respond. The emphasis on the response to a particular voice is similar to the way a mother uses a special voice for notifying her children that (finally) she means It—it is really time to come home when she calls

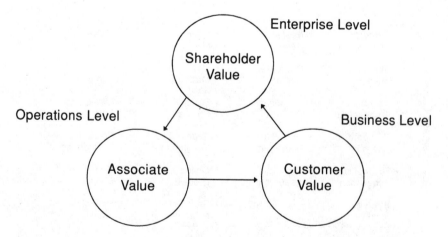

Figure 3–3.   The Evergreen Value Chain

using that voice (and, of course, being bright children, that is the only tone of voice that they are *really* on the alert to hear!). Organizations are, in a manner of speaking, like children. They respond to a primary voice, even if they may hear and respond to other voices. There is one particular voice that will always get their attention. This is illustrated in Figure 3–4.

I first used this model to explain how an organization works with my quality department at Compaq Computer Corporation. One of the members of this team dubbed this model the three-ring circus. Many businesses may seem to operate as a three-ring circus unless people understand how this stimulus-organization-response model really works to capture the attention and focus of all three levels of the organization.

At the enterprise level of the organization, senior management leads the organization's response to the voice of ownership.[19] Their key measures tend to reflect the (primarily) financial concerns with the organization producing "value for the shareholder": return on assets, profit before taxes, earnings per share, stock market share price, market share, and revenue per employee. The work that gets accomplished at this level tends to be cross-business planning to distribute capital investments in a way that will maximize the return on the total business. This level of the organization continually seeks breakthrough improvement in key business processes, and its most appropriate change management vehicle is business systems engineering.

The second level of the organization is the business level where

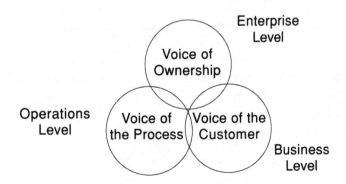

Figure 3–4.   The Atomic Structure of Organizations

products are produced and services are delivered. This level listens primarily to the voice of the customer to understand their needs and expectations as well as their perceptions as to the performance of the business relative to their competitors. The business level operates the key functional business processes of each particular strategic business unit. The key primary measures at this level of the organization tend to be relationship oriented: market share, customer repurchase rate, win-loss proposal ratio (these first three measure customer loyalty), customer satisfaction performance (relative to competitors), employee satisfaction performance (a predictor and driver of customer satisfaction), and response time (to all major customer events for both the customer delivery system and customer service system). Of course, this second level also records and manages using the same financial information that is required to be reported by product line to the enterprise level. This measurement congruence with the enterprise level provides an ability to gain alignment between these two levels on a coherent business plan. The work that gets accomplished at this level of the organization tends to be cross-functional with an emphasis on generating and delivering products to customers and servicing the product once it has been successfully installed at the customer's site. The change focus of the business level of the organization focuses on both breakthrough improvement and continuous improvement using either a systems engineering or a quality improvement (*kaizen*) approach to realize improvement.

The third level of the organization most clearly listens to the voice of the process. The principal work of this level of the organization is to reliably maintain the flow of both products and services to customers. The people in these processes do not tend to have direct "line-of-sight" to the customer and tend to use process-related measures as their surrogate for customer-centric measures. Their job is to maintain the reliability of the product and dependability of the service production process. (Note that reliability is the demonstration of quality over time, while dependability is the demonstration of reliability across product lines—if both reliability and dependability are known to the customer, then they will produce goodwill, which is recognized through loyal purchasing patterns.) The principal measures at this level are defect rates, processing cycle time, value-to-cost performance of each activity required to make the output, safety of operations, and environmental standards performance. The primary change focus of the operations level of the organization is on either maintaining standards of performance (for instance, consistently following an ISO 9000 quality system standard or a procedure for controlling hazardous materials) or on the continuous improvement of these internal effectiveness and efficiency measures (for instance, they may emphasize reducing cycle time, process waste, and processing cost). The work that is accomplished at this level tends to be tied to specific functional work processes, and work is accomplished either by individual contributors or by teams of employees. The principal tools for change management are: process documentation, problem solving, and quality improvement methods.

It is important to understand this "three-ring" model from the perspective of the maturing of an organization's understanding and practice of business process improvement (this journey toward quality maturity is described in a previous book[20]). As organizations mature, the process is usually initiated from the bottom up. The operations level tends to take the initiative for business process improvement because it has the most pressing need and can see its most immediate benefit. The level begins its focus with classic product quality emphasis on inspecting quality and then, when that is not sufficient, by controlling quality at the source (these are the first two levels of quality maturity that I described in *Strategic Benchmarking*). At this first level, work teams partner among associates to use problem-solving processes, basic statistical tools, management by fact, root cause analysis, work process documentation, standards and measures, and meeting management techniques to maintain performance or continuously improve. These teams were able to build awareness, establish documented processes, learn how to use basic statistical tools, develop effective behaviors that facilitate teamwork, and use measurement to manage their daily work processes. Unfortunately, they found that the level of improvements did not affect the system's core processes and that it was possible to lose ground and reverse the change by changing personnel or the focus of the team. A more permanent approach was needed to get away from constantly finding and fixing problems. But, this is where the first barrier was encountered (see Figure 3–5).

The first barrier for the development of a "total quality" focus was the inability to get management's attention and penetrate into the business level. The perspective of the early adopters of "total quality" was not appreciated at this level until they learned the magic word—"customer"—and were able to agree that product quality or "little q" should expand in emphasis to include a customer focus. This birthed

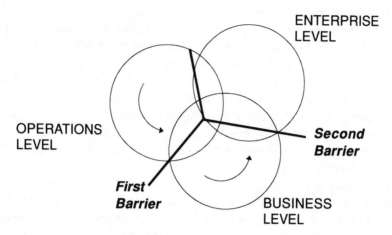

Figure 3-5.   Overcoming Organizational Barriers

the commonly accepted framework for total quality or "big Q." The extension of the language included both the inclusion of the customer focus as the primary emphasis of business and the need to develop an approach to assure (provide quality assurance) of meeting the customer's expectations (requiring the measurement of both the customer's expectations and perceptions). Quality managers learned how to integrate customer expectations and requirements into product planning using Quality Function Deployment. They learned how to build customer requirements into business processes using quality improvement processes. They learned how to extend the process capabilities of their internal teams by including suppliers as "partners" in their work processes. They learned how to influence and manage customer expectations using structured communication plans, product guarantees, and customer service standards. They learned how to listen to the customer by developing customer survey systems and closed-loop complaint management systems. With all of this emphasis on the customer, "total quality" by then had evolved into the customer-centered means to achieving the business-centered end of productivity through cycle time reduction and cost reduction, which were aimed at bringing improved performance to root causes of customer dissatisfaction (high cost and poor responsiveness). (At Compaq I defined quality as: "The value of Compaq products and services as perceived by our customers.") Inspired leadership was the catalyst to encourage this transformation—

managing the transition from one paradigm to another. The difference comes from bringing to bear all of the forces for positive process improvement through a working partnership between suppliers and associates—all dedicated to delighting the customer (this is the third level of quality maturity that I described in *Strategic Benchmarking*).

Today, quality professionals are facing a second barrier to the effective deployment of their message. They do not participate in the boardroom discussions on how to listen to the voice of ownership. However, the tools that have been successful for improving both work processes and business processes can also be applied to the entire enterprise as a system. These tools form a necessary contribution, although not a sufficient contribution to participation in change at this level. It is imperative that all of the cross-functional change agents band together in a nonpartisan, cross-functional partnership dedicated to change. This means that information systems analysts, human resource managers, controllers, and quality managers must work in unison to drive systemic improvement as a cohesive, united force. This team can overcome the barrier to the boardroom-level problems only by changing their vocabulary again—by learning the magical language of "business." This shift will produce systemic changes that are not reversible because the entire system and model for doing business will transform. The focus on change as this second barrier is vaulted will be on building integration among business elements, learning systemic relationships, developing a culture that adapts to both internal and external forces, erasing functional barriers and lines of authority, and planning for the needs of organizational core competence and process capability through a balanced strategic planning process that relies on external strategic benchmarking, internal business assessment, and coordinated deployment of change strategies (using *hoshin kanri* or policy deployment) in a way that builds consensus throughout the entire organization and makes it easy to manage these strategic change initiatives. The successful application of business systems engineering will result in overcoming this second barrier and achieving a mature level of business performance. (This is the fourth level of quality maturity from *Strategic Benchmarking*—at this level, maturity is no longer labeled "quality" but has transitioned into a holistic business focus and may be better labeled as "sustained business success.") Only when this transformation occurs will an organization achieve a truly mature level of quality management.

Reengineering Compared with Total Quality Management

Several of the purveyors of Business Process Reengineering position it as the worthy successor to Total Quality Management. I, for one, think that they have missed the boat and not fully appreciated what the true distinctions between these methodologies are. Much of the basic operational context for this process change management approach comes from the contribution of the statisticians and quality engineers who developed TQM over the past four decades. My definition of business systems engineering blends together these elements with the notions of Business Process Reengineering to create a holistic process model for strategic change management (this is the topic of Parts II and III of this book). But, just as reengineering means many things to many people, TQM is also the subject of a variety of interpretations—from Crosby to Deming to Feigenbaum to Juran—each with a different understanding of how its elements are linked together. I prefer an eclectic approach to TQM that borrows from all schools and then positions it within the context of the particular culture of an organization. For me, TQM is all about producing organizational change and creating value—it is the combination of five core elements:

1. A behavioral model for cooperation, which is based on teams functioning in a participative environment.

2. The use of statistical tools, process analysis, and management by fact to provide analysis of process elements.

3. The focus on the customer as the driver of the business product and service requirements (see prior note on the customer).

4. The adoption of a closed-loop planning process that is consensus-based and empowering of teams because (a) it provides a participative decision framework that is based on the use of structured data analysis, internal business diagnosis, and strategic benchmarking; (b) it negotiates the setting of enterprise objectives with the allocation of resources to achieve personal objectives; (c) it links organizational performance and competence development with individual performance and competence development through a closed-loop performance appraisal and recognition system.

5. The use of project management methods to deploy change initiatives throughout the organization.

On the other hand, I view reengineering as an extension of project management to direct major strategic change initiatives that have been deployed within the context of a robust TQM system. If reengineering exists outside the context of the TQM system, then it will subvert the TQM planning and deployment process for change initiatives.[21] Consider the following comparisons between TQM and BPR (see Table 3–1).

Table 3–1. Comparison of TQM and BPR

	Total Quality Management	Business Process Reengineering
Justification	Required to compete.	Required business streamlining.
Objective	Both continuous and breakthrough improvement.	Large-scale, dramatic change.
Scope	Enterprise-wide, never-ending team effort.	Selected key business processes, one-time focused project effort.

While these differences indicate the inclusion of reengineering within the definition of TQM, consider how the similarities also indicate an association. Both reengineering and TQM share the following attributes:

♦ Emphasize business process performance as a key to competitiveness.

♦ Use teams to develop and implement new procedures and processes.

♦ Require senior management support and leadership.

♦ Focus on improved customer and supplier relationships.

♦ Empower employees to participate in the change initiatives.

Thus, reengineering is a subset of TQM, and the inverse cannot be true. When some proponents of reengineering use a more narrow definition of TQM—relating it only to continuous improvement—or they say that benchmarking is targeted only at competing businesses, they present a biased perspective that indicates their limited understanding of the interrelationship of these more advanced quality methods.

But, how does the degree of integration and coordination occur that will produce this sustained business success? The answer lies in the manner in which business diagnosis and policy deployment is managed (see Figure 3–6).

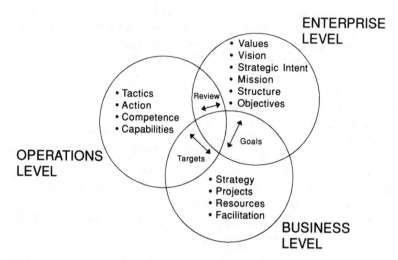

Figure 3-6.   Managing to Overcome Barriers

The work of the three levels of the organization has transformed with the change in the roles of the individuals. At the enterprise level, senior management's role becomes a strategic focus on developing the organizational values, vision, strategic intent, mission statement, structure for governance, and enterprise objectives. These are compiled into the organization's strategic plan and goals that commit to delivery of the enterprise-wide objectives, and senior management negotiates these goals with the management of the business level. The business level then deploys these goals within the context of its market environment to develop a strategy for allocation of resources, development of products and services, and facilitation of relationships with customers, suppliers, and strategic alliances among business partners in a way that has a high probability of overachieving the agreed-upon enterprise goals. The business level then deploys business objectives to teams and negotiates upon targets that will result in the achievement of specified enterprise objectives. Both of the negotiation processes must allow for modification of both the plans and the goals or targets based on the resources available for allocation and the process capability of the performing business team. At the operations level, the business objectives and targets are translated into action plans and measures for inclusion in both team and individual performance objectives. The level of both team and individual competence and skills are assessed to identify high-priority development areas that are required for the success of the plan. These developments become the focus of the organizational training and educational needs assessment, and they are the subject of a development contract between the organization and the individual. This provides a direct linkage between strategic plans and requirements for specific learning experiences of individual employees. The review process at the lowest level of the operation is the individual's performance appraisal—with individual and team performance assessed within the context of personal training contracts with management, process capability, and management resource allocation. The loop is closed by reviewing both teams and individuals for recognition based on their contributions within the context of the entire planning system. Deming, who objected to performance appraisal based on individual performance goals that were randomly chosen for work processes and that were out of the control of the employees, would be pleased.

In Chapter 4, we will examine how the entire business systems engineering model works in detail.

4

Elements of
Business Systems
Engineering

What is firmly set up can't be pulled down;
What is firmly embraced cannot slip free.
Lao Tzu, *Te-Tao Ching*

CREATING ORDER OUT OF CHAOS

Today, business exists in an environment of chaos and is being challenged by a growing need to be "lean" and "flexible" and "competitive." But what do these terms really mean? Beneath the high-sounding philosophies of leading thinkers who call for a concoction of time-based competition, values management, globalization, and the strengthening of core competencies lie the details of day-to-day operational management issues. Surely implementing all of these initiatives at once would create chaos at the nitty-gritty level of most businesses. Is there any way to simplify the structure of an organization's strategic planning and business management processes so that order can be created and form reliable ways to manage work activities? Viewing an enterprise as a business system provides an opportunity to gain congruence between such organizational philosophizing and daily operational activities.

56

VALUE CREATION IS THE FUNDAMENTAL DRIVER

Value creation is the ultimate objective of every enterprise. However, the true value is defined by the customer of that enterprise, not by its management. Value is not equal to customer satisfaction because the customers don't always know what they want until they see it delivered in added value to their business. There are at least two reasons why your customers don't know what they want. First, technology blocks their ability to know. For instance, consider the medical industry. Who would dream of attempting to understand all of the elements of medical practice just to be a consumer of a doctor's advice? In the realm of computers, many technophobics can't tell the difference between RAM, ROM, or a microprocessor—they just know that it needs to be easy and give good output. The second reason why your customers don't know what they need from you is that most of them are focused intently on their own problems—not on the possible services or products available from a supplier. How many times have you heard a customer say, "I didn't know you could do that!" The job of a successful enterprise is to diagnose its business and determine how it can deliver the most value to its customers.

The stimulus for most organizational change is the need to increase the value delivered to customers. This type of organizational change can touch such elements as values and beliefs, products or services, organization structure, management systems, business processes, information systems, technologies, and employee skills. Management is faced with a paradox. The environment where an organization lives is turbulent; however, the organization must hold on to a structure or order of the present and yet be prepared to leap to the new order when the time for transition comes.

PLANNING VALUE CREATION IN THE MIDST OF CHAOS

This ability for organizational renewal means that senior management must learn to think of their business model as an adaptive system that is a prototype rather than a finished product of "how we do business." All business processes need to be susceptible to alteration, adaptation, and adjustment to better serve the organization in its chaotic environment. For instance, planning should encourage the constant renegotiation and questioning of planning guidelines and assumptions. Therefore, planning should be evolutionary, recursive, and incremental in nature. While planning guidelines may be set for a limited time interval, they are ultimately fluid. Plans and processes are organizational prototypes that suggest how individuals will behave together to deliver value to customers. Plans and processes are like a dialog that is in progress—they must always allow for response to unexpected circumstances. Given this degree of fluidity, one can even ask if business planning and process management are possible. Strategy really represents our collective best thinking about our long-range direction at a particular point in time.

ENGINEERING A BUSINESS SYSTEM

The business systems engineering model begins with the value-creation driver and merges it with an assessment of organizational performance from the daily activity level to determine where broad-based organizational change is needed. The value chain provides the underlying structure for the enterprise model. The measurement map provides a statement of the analytical relationship of daily work processes to business processes and, therefore, to the metrics that assess the performance of the value chain that is at the top of the enterprise model. From this point on, the business systems engineering model (see Figure 4–1) is composed of a combination of the tools of Total Quality Management. Process analysis is the front-end analysis from the quality improvement process, while the process benchmarking step uses only the planning

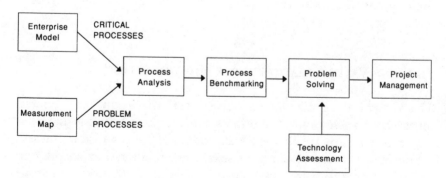

Figure 4–1.   Business Systems Engineering Model

and research aspects of the benchmarking process. These two elements are described in detail in Chapters 5 and 6. The remaining three blocks of this process—problem solving, technology assessment, and project management—are used in their full normal context and are only covered at a general level here.

In addition to the model for business systems engineering, two other factors can drive the change management process. The first factor is the use of information technology and the trends that are emerging in this field that directly influence the nature of strategic business change. This topic will be addressed in depth in Chapter 7. The second factor is the approach for developing, communicating, and reviewing strategic change initiatives through the organization's planning process. This approach is called policy deployment. While we will touch on the context of policy deployment here, it is covered in more detail in Chapter 8.

In Chapter 3, we briefly described the business systems engineering model and provided a description of the underlying organization issues. In this chapter, we will decompose each of its elements—box by box—and explain how the model functions.

THE ENTERPRISE MODEL AND MANAGEMENT CONCERNS

Historically, we describe work in terms of functional silos. Farmers use silos to isolate and store a particular type of grain until it can be consumed by its ultimate user. Silos provide isolation for a single food product that protects it from a harsh external environment. When we build silos around functional departments in an organization, we are preventing their ability to interact and resolve issues at the nitty-gritty level of work processes. The silo structure is disempowering. It forces all decisions up to the top of the organization and defocuses management from the strategic business issues regarding both customers and competitors. The use of the silo reflects a basic management belief: Managers believe that they manage functions rather than the interfaces of the value chain.

The organization chart only shows how people are administratively assigned and illustrates a convenience of communication, but it does not tell us how the work gets done in an organization. Organizations with a silo-type structure can create "islands of performance excellence" within the business, but this type of structure hinders the development of a flowing system that allows the customer value chain to operate flawlessly as it moves horizontally across the organization. The largest opportunities for business system improvement are at the "seams of the organization" where the functional departments are linked through hand-offs in the value-creation chain. Former Xerox quality executive Richard C. Palermo has observed that: "If a problem has been bothering your company and your customers for years and it resists resolution, despite your efforts, that problem is the result of a cross-functional dispute where nobody has total control of the whole process." He feels so strongly about this observation that he calls it "Palermo's law." He has also developed a corollary that describes the interpersonal dynamics of an organization where this law applies: "People who work in these different functional areas hate each other."[1] The enterprise model (Figure 4–2) resolves these issues by providing a picture that links business and work processes to the customer value chain and market segmentation model for the delivery of products and services. (Notice that the cross-functional business sup-

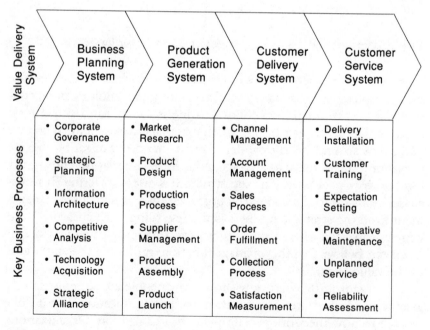

Figure 4–2. A Generic Business Enterprise Model

port processes are illustrated as horizontal processes across the flow of the value chain. The special enabling effects of the positioning of these support processes is described in Chapter 5.)

The enterprise model is constructed by illustrating the primary organizational value chain across the top of the business system structure and the supporting business processes below it.[2] The value chain tracks the development and delivery of an organization's products and services from the supplier to the customer. It is segmented into the major subsystems that create value from the perspective of the customer.[3] For instance, in Figure 4–2, the value chain shows four major subsystems in the business system. The business planning system provides value by structuring the long-term direction of the organization relative to the competition. It establishes a place for the organization within its industry and defines how it will be differentiated from the customer's perspective. This will determine the deliverables that will be available to each customer.

The second subsystem is the product generation system. It determines what specific functions and capabilities will be delivered to the customer through the design and delivery of products and services. The customer touchpoints in product development are essential to its ability to deliver a winning product. The third subsystem is called the customer delivery system. It manages the relationship with customers through the point of sale. The fourth subsystem is the customer service system, which actually delivers the physical goods or intangible services to the customer. Below each of these subsystems on the value chain are the key business processes that represent the major functionality of this part of the value chain.[4] We will return to the further decomposition of business processes into work processes when we discuss process analysis later in this chapter.

In Chapter 3, we described the three organizational levels of an enterprise as the enterprise, business, and operational levels. It will be helpful to expand on these areas to help understand how the business system fits together. Figure 4–3 describes the concerns that get management attention as a function of each organization by level. The concerns of top management are primarily focused on the financial performance and governance structure of the organization—its principal metric is return on assets. The concerns of the business management team are on market performance and process engineering to deliver that performance—its principal metrics are market share and customer satisfaction. The concerns of the operations management

Organization Level	Performance Goals	Organizational Focus	Management Attention
Enterprise	Return on Assets	Governance Structure	Fiscal Performance
Business	Market Share Customer Satisfaction	Process Engineering	Market Performance
Operations	Process Productivity Employee Satisfaction	Work Design	Process Performance

Figure 4–3.   The Attention of Organization Levels

team are focused on process performance and work design—its principal metrics are process productivity and employee satisfaction. These concerns fit within the context of an overall management system (see Figure 4–4), which may be considered the position descriptions of these three management levels. Each level of the organization structure defines, at an appropriate level of detail, how the organization operates, what it accomplishes, how it measures performance, and how it documents work activities. It is important to notice that each organizational level requires a different level of detail to perform its functions. If these levels of detail are not honored, then the organization can fall into one of two traps. First, if the senior management team works at a level of detail that is too finely tuned, then they will end up micromanaging the organization and undercutting the authority and empowerment of their employees. Second, if the operations level seeks to drive the entire enterprise, then it will be guilty of suboptimization because it lacks the overall perspective to make effective judgments about the whole organizational framework. Figure 4–4 is presented here to set the context of the organization-wide policy deployment system. Chapter 8 describes the operation of policy deployment in detail.

Organization Level	Business Definition (What to do?)	Functional Description (What to accomplish?)	Performance Determination (How is completion known?)	Documentation (How is activity recorded?)
Enterprise	Enterprise Vision Enterprise Mission	Priorities Enterprise Objectives	Metrics Benchmarks Goals	Business Strategy
Business	Business Mission	Business Objectives	Results Measures Benchmarks Targets	Operating Plan
Operations	Operations Mission Team Charter Position Description	Operations Objectives Team Objectives Personal Objectives	Process Measures Benchmarks Standards	Product Documentation Service Standards Work Procedures

Figure 4-4.   Management Systems Elements

Relative to strategic change management, there are different approaches that fit the organizational work structure of Figure 4-4. The activities of each organizational level for change management are shown in Figure 4-5. At the operations level of the organization, the performance focus is on the work process. Teams that are formed to improve work processes tend to be from the same department and are functionally oriented. Their efforts are focused on standards maintenance, process foolproofing, and work process optimization. Their primary change methodology is the problem-solving process where they seek to identify gaps in performance between the current state and desired state (these may be established by deviation from standard, deviation from plan, deviation from industry average, deviation from benchmark, or deviation from target). Problem solving is used to identify and close these performance gaps. At the business level of the organization, the performance focus is on the customer and the business processes that deliver customer value. Teams that are formed to improve business processes tend to be cross-functional (resistance to Palermo's law is built into the change mechanism) and are oriented toward improving the results or outcomes of the business processes. These teams work to develop both continuous improvements and

Organization Level	Principal Process Focus	Primary Change Method	Basic Team Structure	Performance Issue Focus
Enterprise	Strategic	Business Systems Engineering	Cross-Business	Ownership
Business	Business	Quality Improvement Process	Cross-Functional	Customer
Operations	Work	Problem Solving Process	Departmental	Process

Figure 4–5.   The Activities of Organizational Levels

breakthrough performance on these key business processes. The primary change methodology used by these teams is the quality improvement process, which is useful for process design when a process has not "been engineered in the first place." At the enterprise level of the organization, the performance improvement focus is on the set of issues that are the concerns of its ownership and the strategic focus of the business. When teams are formed to improve the strategic performance, they tend to be cross-business teams dealing with strategic changes at the highest level of the enterprise model. Such teams tend to be standing committees composed of the most senior managers and may be called the Operating Committee, Executive Team, or President's Council. The primary change mechanism that is available to them is business systems engineering within the context of the policy deployment management system.

THE MEASUREMENT MAP

One of my favorite business quotations is attributed to Bill Hewlett: "If you tell me how a person is measured, then I'll tell you how that person manages." The strength of work process measurement is so strong that Dr. Joseph M. Juran has decreed that, "If you don't measure it, then you don't manage it." How should measurements be used to direct the course of a business enterprise? To answer this question, we must differentiate between metrics and measures.

Metrics define categories of information that are accumulated into an overall quantified expression that represents a processed view of a real-world state (for example, return on assets, market share, customer satisfaction, productivity, and employee satisfaction). The focus of a metric is strategic rather than operational. On the other hand, a measure is the means by which a metric becomes operational—it represents the quantification of the metric in terms of specific, actionable activities that are observable in either business or work processes. Measures may be classified as either *P-measures* or *R-measures*. The term *P-measure* refers to process measures that quantify the in-process performance of a business or work process. *R-measures* are results measures that indicate the outcome of a business or work process in terms of quality, cost, or cycle time performance. In an aligned business system, the P-measures for a work process will predict the behavior of the R-measures—they will be highly correlated—and may be used to adjust the process to achieve improved performance in the R-measure.[5]

In Japan, the way that measures are used in day-to-day work activities is called a daily management system. Daily management is the combination of business processes, work processes, and their accompanying measurements. Daily management systems may be documented by a process map and a measurement map. The process map continues the description of process interrelationships that was begun with the business enterprise model and extends it to the business process and work process levels.[6] The measurement map illustrates the derivative relationships among metrics and measures as well as between R-measures and P-measures. Figure 4–6 illustrates the high-level transition of a measurement map from the metric level to the measurement level for return on assets (ROA). To complete this map, the results measures for each of the business processes would be illustrated and then related to the process measures that provide an interim estimation of the outcome of the R-measure for a particular performance period.[7, 8]

THE PROCESS ANALYSIS

Process analysis is one of the fundamental work activities that occurs throughout the bowels of an organization. I say this not to be disre-

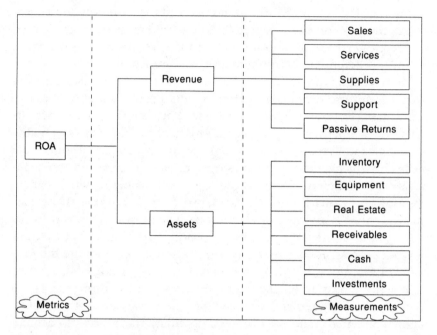

Figure 4–6. ROA Measurement Map

spectful, but to strongly indicate that it is a basic natural process that characterizes all well-managed organizations. Process analysis is the methodology for the documentation, management, and optimization of both business and work processes. The distinction between business and work processes is one of inclusion. Business processes are groups of related work processes that deliver a common outcome (see Figure 4–7). Business processes are performed by combinations of work processes, while work processes are performed by individuals acting as a team.

Each work process may be characterized in terms of its ability to:

♦ Produce quality output.

♦ Add value to the product.

♦ Add capability to the organization.

♦ Consume cost in the transformation of its output.

♦ Consume time to produce the output.

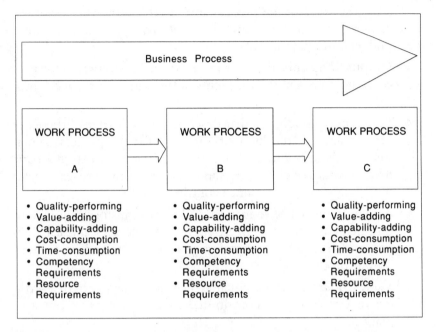

Figure 4–7.   Business Process Decomposition

◆ Build or require the development of skills and competencies to produce the output.

◆ Consume resources in the transformation of inputs into outputs.

The work process is the lowest-level group activity within the organization. It is a kernel that may be used to grow the entire organization as it is grafted onto other work processes to form business processes. Process analysis investigates these kernels by documenting their operation, managing their transformations, and optimizing their performance. To better understand how a work process functions, consider the elements of a well-formed work process documentation specification:[9]

◆ Inputs: products or services provided from a source outside the work group that are transformed into the outputs of the work process.

◆ Work Process Owner: the individual who controls the process and is responsible for its daily management. This person represents the voice of the process and has the authority to commit resources within the decision limitations of the organization's budget and operating plan.

♦ Output Recipients: the internal or external customers of the process who represent the recipients of the output of the work process.

♦ Boundaries: conditions that describe the perimeter of the work process and set the limit of authority for the process owner. Beyond these boundaries are relationships with external partners, output recipients, or suppliers where the process owner must negotiate performance contribution.

♦ Activities: the set of sequenced tasks that transform inputs into outputs, consume resources, apply competencies and capabilities, and respond to systemic signals for increased or reduced output production.

♦ Value Addition: the incremental increase in the worth of a product or service that is contributed by a work process transformation.

♦ Cost: the total value that is consumed by an activity to produce its output.

♦ Cycle Time: the unit of time that it takes to produce a single unit of output from the time its production is requested (demand generated) to the time that it is delivered to the customer (demand satisfied).

♦ Critical Success Factors: factors that make the work process successful in the eyes of its customers. These are the vital few, not the significant many, nor the trivial mass.

♦ Output: the product or service that is produced by the work process.

There is a natural process improvement sequence that occurs as companies apply TQM to their work processes. I refer to it as the elimination sequence for gap closure. This model (illustrated in Figure 4–8) is an important concept for two reasons. First, it provides a roadmap for process improvement that is generic in its application to work processes. Second, it suggests that most problems can be attacked through the application of the basic quality tools of problem solving and quality improvement processes before there is a need to automate

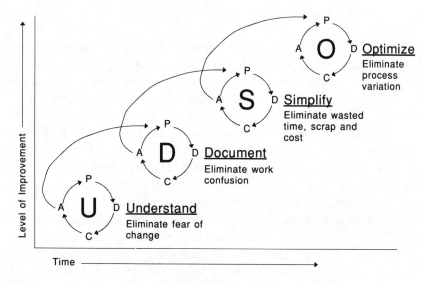

Figure 4–8.   Quality Improvement Levels

work processes or seek information technology-intensive solutions.[10] I call this model UDSO in recognition of the four levels of work process improvement that it describes (Understand-Document-Simplify-Optimize.)[11]

Change becomes a reality only when people are ready to change. The first step in the elimination sequence deals with the readiness of people to accept change. Dr. Deming said that we need to "Drive out fear." This is possible only as we study our work and understand its critical success factors, competence requirements, and capability shortfalls. This is done by applying the Plan-Do-Check-Act (or PDCA) cycle in terms of the quality improvement process (QIP) or the problem-solving process (PSP) to get a better understanding of how we produce out work outputs.[12] In the process of developing a common understanding, we eliminate fear of change. The tools required to understand the work process are the basic organizational development tools including both group dynamics and team-building skills. The fundamental question asked in this activity is around the mission or charter of the group: What are we supposed to be doing? It seeks to eliminate those things that are not essential to the mission. The first iteration of these process improvement sequences captures much of the low-hanging fruit—the obvious tasks and responsibilities that are not aligned to our primary mission—

and prepares a team to move to the second level of the elimination sequence.

At the second level of work process improvement, the focus is on the documentation of the work process. This captures the administrative improvement opportunities available in a work process that comes from a clear definition of our individual and team work process activities that deliver the results of our primary mission. By documenting the work process, a team can eliminate the confusion caused by overlapping or undefined roles and responsibilities, unaligned objectives and tasks, as well as unclear process outcome requirements. Clarified role requirements and the clear delegation of authority and responsibility build upon the common basis for understanding of the activities as developed during the first PDCA iteration. Between these two levels, a work group may reorganize and restructure itself to be more efficient and effective. The tools for completing this second level build upon the group dynamics and team skills of the first level and add the basic documentation skills required for the implementation of ISO 9000. The fundamental question of this second level is: Given our agreed-upon mission, how will we work together to accomplish our objectives? It seeks to eliminate those activities that are not focused on delivering our required output. However, these first two levels represent the limits of the "soft" skills of organizational development to deliver productive change. The first two improvement levels of the elimination sequence address the concern: Are we doing the right things? The third and fourth levels address the concern: Are we doing the right things right? To move on to the third level of improvement requires the active use of analytical skills in order to simplify the process.

The third iteration of PDCA, in the form of either QIP or PSP, focuses on the elimination of wasted time, scrap, and cost. The work team can concentrate on improving its ability to make better products, quicker and cheaper. A three-prong approach on quality (scrap reduction), cycle time reduction, and cost reduction (and value improvement) can help to drive performance improvement.[13] To achieve this result, tools are applied such as cycle time reduction, activity-based cost management, and quality foolproofing (these are described in Chapter 5). The fundamental question of the third level is: Given a well-organized work group, how can we work together to streamline our work process by improving quality, eliminating non-value-adding work, or reducing costs? This level seeks to improve productivity by eliminating those wastes, costs, and time that are easily identified and can be eliminated quickly by the work team without the support of external "statistical consultants." This third level of the elimination sequence completes the improvements that most work teams can accomplish on their own. To move on to the fourth level requires the support of a statistical consultant who can guide the team in the use of staff-level consulting statisticians who can advise work teams on how to implement statistical process control to reduce variability in each activity of their work process.

The fourth step focuses on process optimization through variability reduction. It applies the tools of experimental design, process capability studies, and statistical process control to achieve optimal process performance. The fundamental question of the fourth level is: Given that we have a streamlined process, how can we manage process variation to produce consistently reliable results? This level seeks to improve productivity through the consistent production of low-variation products through the reliable operation of low-variation work processes. The principal measure of this level is alternatively called Six Sigma or C_{pk} (process capability). Only when this fourth level of the elimination sequence has been mastered and the process variability reduction goals have been met should a process be committed to the expense of automation. The violation of this principle is the primary reason why most of the process reengineering projects have been failures.

> *The problem with most automation and information technology projects is that they have embedded ineffective or inefficient work processes that have not been defined by such a rigorous task analysis process as the elimination sequence.*

The Process Analysis step indicated in Figure 4–1 represents the completion of the first three steps of the quality improvement process (Figure 4–9). (The remaining steps are included in the rest of the business systems engineering process.) During these three steps, the following activities occur:[14]

- ◆ Identify process owner and appropriate team members.
- ◆ Select participants for the improvement project.
- ◆ Determine roles and responsibilities.

PLAN	1. Establish Process Ownership	PLAN
	2. Assess Process Performance	LEARN
DO	3. Select Improvement Opportunity	
	4. Design Work Process	
	5. Document Work Process	
CHECK	6. Determine Process Capability	
	7. Implement Improved Process	
	8. Inspect Process Performance	
	9. Evaluate Test Results	
ACT	10. Operate Work Process	IMPLEMENT
	11. Monitor Control, Streamline & Improve Work Process	

Figure 4–9. The Quality Improvement Process

♦ Obtain commitment and buy in to the need for the analysis.

♦ Identify the customer of the process.

♦ Identify customer issues, concerns, and needs.

♦ Identify process output.

♦ Develop supplier specifications to clarify process input requirements.

♦ Select process measurements—both P-measures and R-measures.

♦ Determine potential improvement opportunities among work processes.

♦ Evaluate improvement opportunities to determine priorities.

♦ Select a specific work process as the designated improvement opportunity.

Many work processes are not well defined. Either the responsibilities of individuals (and their position descriptions and work objectives) have not been well defined, or the process by which they produce their work output has not been well defined. Without the documentation of a process, there can be no real agreement on the assignment of work to individuals or teams, nor can there be an appropriate allocation of responsibility or authority to individuals. Work process documentation, the output of the quality improvement process, is a fundamental requirement for self-directed work teams or empowered work groups. The lack of such process documentation is particularly felt during downsizing when the "survivors" need to determine how to reallocate work based on those individuals remaining. How can work be reallocated if there was no agreement on the initial requirements of the work process?[15] Downsizing is not process redesign or systems engineering. Wholesale staff reduction without work process redesign is a risky proposition because, unless the fundamental work processes that the staff is a part of are changed, the productivity problem cannot be solved solely by the elimination of people. (To make the downsizing process less humane, we can refer to people in a more generic way as "head count.")[16,17] Downsizing may be the result of the redesign of a system of work processes; however, it is not a requirement of business systems engineering. One way to determine an appropriate number of people to perform a work process is to benchmark the number of people required to produce at the highest level of productivity. This is what Ford did when it discovered that the Mazda accounting office was ten times more productive.

THE BENCHMARKING STUDY

After the process analysis has identified the process for engineering and provided some basic functional description of that process, then the team needs to benchmark in order to understand what other organizations have achieved in performance and how they were able to increase productivity. Steps 1–5 of the Xerox benchmarking model illustrated in Figure 4–10 are the focus of this benchmarking effort. The benchmarking effort focuses on *measuring* other company processes to determine where excellence exists in this performance arena and then on *learning* what those companies did to produce the excellence indicated by the R-measures of the process. The completion of the last five steps in the benchmarking process is included in the remaining phases of the business systems engineering process.[18] The benchmarking process helps to define the problem statement in Step 1 of the problem-solving process—the next activity in the business systems engineering model.

PLAN	1. Identify Benchmark Topic	PLAN
	2. Identify Best Partners	
DO	3. Plan and Execute Data Collection	LEARN
	4. Determine Current Performance Levels	
	5. Project Future Performance Levels	
CHECK	6. Communicate Results of Analysis	
ACT	7. Establish Functional Goals	IMPLEMENT
	8. Develop Action Plan	
	9. Implement Plan and Monitor	
	10. Recalibrate Benchmark	

Figure 4-10. Xerox Benchmarking Model

THE PROBLEM-SOLVING PROCESS

Unfortunately, we don't live in a linear world and problems don't present themselves to us one at a time for resolution. Problems are outcomes of work processes or business processes that are different from what was expected. Stated alternatively, the existence of a problem is recognized by a gap between the current level of a process measure and the desired level of a process measure. Problem solving has a goal of eliminating this gap. A good approach to problem solving is a fundamental quality tool because it is useful at all levels of the enterprise—from the strategic planning level to the level of daily work operations. However, problems tend to present themselves as a confounded array of issues with conflicting causes and potential solutions. The need to work through this system of presenting issues is driven by our need to take action and eliminate the gap between where we are and where we want to be. This gap can't wait a long time as we sort through a myriad of possibilities to determine an optimal solution. How can we take an approach to problem solving that will get us resolution of the issue (the gap) as quickly as possible? There are two tools that can help us to sort through the process of analyzing system-level problems, identifying potential solutions, and implementing the corrective action required to resolve the issue.[19] The first is the problem-solving process (PSP) as illustrated in Figure 4–11. The second tool is the problem matrix illustrated in Figure 4–12. Taken together, these tools provide a great capability to understand and evaluate system-level problems—a key requirement for the learning organization of the future.[20, 21] The first five steps of PSP are used at this stage of the business systems engineering approach to conduct the analysis necessary to identify the potential process problems and prioritize each of the problem areas that have been generated to date by the business systems engineering activities. The problem matrix is used to record the output of these analyses until all of the presenting problems have been completely analyzed and a decision is ready to be made on which path to pursue. The practical reality of timing requires that these last three steps of the business systems engineering model (process analysis, benchmarking, and problem solving) be conducted in parallel by dedicated teams and accumulated in the problem matrix by a supervising executive-level oversight committee. To summarize the flow of the business system engineering model so far:

♦ The enterprise model has contributed critical business processes that are candidates for work process redesign.

♦ The measurement map has contributed problem business processes whose daily performance is not up to expectations and whose owners do not have the resources necessary to turn around their performance deficiency.

♦ The first three steps of the quality improvement process were used in the process analysis to define each of these candidate business processes in a way that will allow us to prioritize them for selection as the critical processes to be targeted for redesign and systems engineering.

♦ We have benchmarked each of these candidate business processes (through Step 5 of the Xerox benchmarking model) to determine how other companies have dealt with similar situations.

♦ We have used the first five steps of the PSP to prioritize business processes for redesign as part of the systems engineering effort.

PLAN	1. Identify and Select the Problem	PLAN
	2. Analyze the Problem	LEARN
	3. Generate Potential Solutions	
	4. Analyze Alternative Solutions	
DO	5. Select Priority Solution	
	6. Develop Action Plan	
	7. Implement the Solution	
CHECK	8. Evaluate the Solution	
ACT	9. Integrate the Solution	IMPLEMENT

Figure 4–11. The Problem-Solving Process

♦ The problem matrix has allowed us to understand the interactions among the various business processes that are candidates for the change.

Now we need to backtrack just a little bit. When the problem-solving process is being used to identify the specific solution for an organization to pursue as a business systems engineering breakthrough project, it has an additional input that does not typically occur when PSP is applied at the work process level—a technology assessment.

THE TECHNOLOGY ASSESSMENT

As the team engineers the business system by working through the problem-solving process, at Step 3 they will encounter the need to generate potential solutions to the identified problem. An additional input to this step in the problem-solving process is the technology assessment. Steps 1 and 2 of the problem-solving process will have identified gaps and deficiencies in the way that the process is being

Problem Statement	Measure	Current State	Desired State	Root Cause	Potential Solutions

Figure 4-12.   The Problem Matrix

followed and will have defined the principal performance issues that need to be resolved. The purpose of the technology is not to replace equipment or information systems with state-of-the-art equipment and computers, but to ensure that the technical capability of the organization will support the future business needs and deliver the business results desired in the goal statements of the organization. The technology assessment evaluates both the physical product processing and distribution requirements, as well as the information systems requirements, and takes into account the following considerations:

♦ The degree to which the current system's capability will inhibit the performance of the required business activities of the new process.

♦ The maintenance requirements of the current systems and the difficulty in keeping these systems supported by equipment hardware and software suppliers.

♦ The availability of packaged products that provide satisfactory alternative solutions in either hardware or software.

♦ The likely growth in equipment capacity and information processing needs due to projected growth in business process transactions.

♦ A productivity comparison and cost-benefit study of alternative support system designs for information processing or physical equipment processing capabilities.

The technology assessment provides an infusion of creative possibilities for the definition of the potential solutions. However, caution should be used in overrelying on technology to provide productivity growth: A lesson learned from one *Fortune* 100 company's study of its use of advanced technology applications in field sales and service productivity improvement indicated that people *expect* technology to solve their process problems, but they don't know how to use most of the technology effectively once it has been delivered because they haven't changed their work processes to accommodate the technology improvements. Blind faith in technology will not make work processes more efficient!

CHOOSING THE STRATEGIC CHANGE FOCAL POINT

The choice of a particular problem to work on—Step 5 of PSP—and the development of a team charter to engineer the chosen process will depend on applying a set of decision criteria that allows the senior management team to clearly understand their priorities. The set of criteria will differ from organization to organization; let me suggest a set of five criteria that describe the general elements of competitive advantage and may be customized to define an organization-specific set of criteria. These criteria are labeled: quality, cost, delivery, technology, and responsiveness.[22] Competitive advantage occurs when an organization develops a long-term strategy using these criteria to differentiate itself in the marketplace from its perceived competitors. These five criteria need to be interpreted from the perspective of the broad customer segments that the company is targeting. They represent a surrogate use of customer purchasing criteria. These five criteria also represent an operational definition of the "value" that you provide to your customers and that, ultimately, contributes to their success with their customers. The major decision for the senior management team will be to determine how each of these five criteria—considering your own enterprise as a supplier to your most important customers—may be used to interpret which business or work process should become the initial candidate for the redesign effort of a business systems engineering project:

♦ Quality: Quality is a value proposition to the customers. It is a combination of those performance factors that most greatly influence their own success through the use of your products and services. To some customers, quality could mean the "continuous availability of service." To other customers, it could mean "absolute reliability of the product for a specific time frame"—even if they haven't specified a time requirement! To other customers, quality could be the "form and function repeatability of a product so that each one is absolutely like the last product." No matter what emphasis a customer may put on quality, it is the responsibility of suppliers to understand that definition and operationalize it into their own work processes to ensure their reliable provision of that performance. By using the quality criteria defined in this way, the relative contribution of business and work processes may be judged by the senior management team to identify those areas where improvement leverage is greatest.

♦ Cost: For customers, this represents both the price paid initially and the total cost of ownership. Cost engineering is not just a cost reduction for parts prices, but it is the delivery of the lowest cost parts that meet the customer requirement for reliable, long-term performance. Commodity buyers beware—not all parts are created equal. In the new purchasing approach, an understanding of reliability performance will be equal in importance to an understanding of the methods of economic production. In a supplier's organization, cost must be managed at three levels: the cost of material acquisition, the cost of value-producing work process performance, and the cost of overhead for work processes. This decomposition of a supplier's activities provides a clear emphasis on the importance of internal business and work processes from the cost perspective of the customer.

♦ Delivery: Customers want products and services delivered at their convenience—if it is important to receive a product or service on a particular schedule, then that delivery schedule should be achieved. This attitude by customers requires that suppliers understand the time-based competition principles in their business. What is the customer's idea of delivery performance excellence? What do competitors seek to provide? How important is delivery relative to the other criteria? Will a focus on delivery make a difference in this business? Motorola found that delivery was the key factor available to them for competitive advantage in the pocket pager business (see Chapter 10). If delivery is the driving factor to their customers, then suppliers must seek to improve those aspects of the order fulfillment process that provide the most flexibility in delivery at the lowest possible order turnaround time (the time from taking the order from the customer to shipping the product to the customer) using the most efficient shipment means possible for delivery. Suppliers will also need to understand how the customer interprets delivery. Some customers will say that delivery has not occurred unless the product is in operation by their people. This means that delivery also includes all support services required for installation and operation of the product, as well as the arrival of the physical product itself. In the words of Dr. Joseph M. Juran, the product must also be "fit for use" by the customer when it is delivered. This extends the idea of quality to encompass both product and services that may be attached to the product. Given understanding of this perspective of the customer's expectations, a supplier should consider which of its business and work processes contribute most strongly to delivery performance and provide the competitive advantage needed for success relative to its competitors.

◆ Technology: The key issue in the consideration of technology is whether your set of customers pull high technology from your R&D organization or you push technical developments from your R&D organization onto your customers. If the customers have a pull function, then they are seeking to understand how the latest developments of the laboratory may be used to drive their success. If you are pushing your technology on customers, then your engineers are designing products that are targeted at future, unrecognized needs of customers (current or potential). The customer values a company with "pull" better than a company that "pushes." The relative relationship between the "pull-push" emphasis will determine the need for process improvement in the design and market research functions relative to other business and work processes.

♦ Responsiveness: Responsiveness represents the customer's time sensitivity and desire for dialog that occurs in areas other than the initial delivery of the product or service. Responsiveness is the willingness of the supplier to listen to the issues and concerns of the customer and to provide an acceptable response—meeting the desires of the customer for both a timely and an adequate resolution to problems, issues, or concerns. This need defines the degree of closeness that the customer either needs or expects to have with suppliers. To evaluate the requirement for responsiveness, suppliers must develop a clear understanding of their impact on the success of their customer's business and how their responsiveness can improve the competitiveness of their customers. This knowledge becomes the factor used to evaluate how significant the internal time-responsiveness of business and work support processes is for your own business and, therefore, allows the senior management team to appropriately judge its significance in terms of selecting areas for driving breakthrough process performance.

The basic principle behind these criteria is that business system improvements should be selected in a way that maximizes the customer-perceived value of doing business with your company and drives their own success in their ultimate markets. By considering these five criteria from the perspective of their importance to the customer base, and relative to the known or estimated performance of competitors, an enterprise may make better decisions about which strategic change initiative to pursue.[23] However, making the decision is not sufficient to drive the business in the right direction; follow-through or deployment of the change is the place where most companies fail—they don't execute their great ideas to achieve excellence in the long run. The best approach that I have seen to drive a major change effort is the basic project management method.

THE PROJECT MANAGEMENT METHOD

How can we drive process improvements (whether they are based on process flow streamlining, organizational restructuring, or technology improvements) into effective deployment within our organizations? This is the most significant problem that most managers face today. They are able to create good strategies and plans; however, they are frustrated by their inability to deploy their plans effectively throughout their entire organization. The short answer to this problem is that plans need to be developed and deployed with work group participation. The longer explanation requires us to describe how to make this happen through the completion of the business systems engineering process and the alignment of this process with the organization's change management system.

The project management phase of the business systems engineering model is related to the strategic planning process (which we will cover in Chapter 8 as we discuss policy deployment) and is, in reality, the completion of the three models that we have seen to date: QIP, benchmarking, and PSP. Because it represents a more complete statement of the project management process, Steps 4 through 11 of the quality improvement model (see Figure 4–9) are recommended as the steps of the project management approach.

Choosing a project for improvement and executing that project are, in reality, part of a larger process for strategic change management called policy deployment. Policy deployment begins with the development of long-term business policy such as the vision, cultural values, mission, strategic intent, and governance structure, and then defines the operational goals and strategies that will deliver this long-range state of success. The linkage between business systems engineering and policy deployment is straightforward. In the process of deploying strategies, the senior management team conducts their assessment of projects that should be pursued. Business systems engineering is the methodology the senior team uses to drive the analysis leading to their consideration of alternative projects for breakthrough business improvement. The execution of the projects or initiatives selected by the management team using this decision criteria is deployed using the cascading of objectives through the policy deployment system. This cascade provides each employee with what Xerox Corporation calls "line of sight" from the organization's strategic objectives to its personal objectives. It allows each employee to understand how he or she participates in the strategic change management process. Figure 4–13 shows how this relationship is structured between the top three levels of the organization—deployment from the senior management level

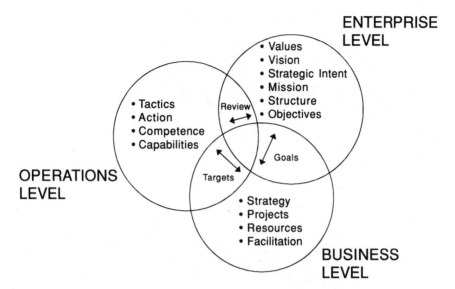

Figure 4–13.   Managing to Overcome Barriers

to the level of the individual (see the second column in Figure 4–4 for another perspective of this "line of sight" idea).

PUTTING IT TOGETHER

Some themes recur in life. For me, "Putting It Together" is one of those themes. It was the corporate theme during my tenure at both Compaq Computer Corporation and Xerox Corporation. Putting it together in the context of this chapter and this book means providing the reader with a clear picture of how the individual steps of the business systems engineering model fit together. Figure 4–14 illustrates how the development of the enterprise model and the measurement map of the daily management system drive the use of processes for quality improvement, benchmarking, and problem solving to present a decision point that is based on these process outcomes plus the technology assessment. This process completes the prework and results in the selection of one or more business processes for redesign. The redesign process is completed through the exercise of the remaining steps of the quality improvement process. All of the basic quality meth-

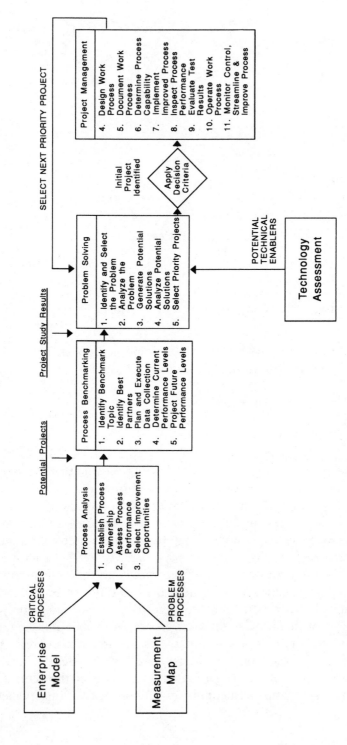

Figure 4–14. Business Systems Engineering Process Detail

ods and processes work in unison to drive business process improvement and to produce the results that can make a change in the business.[24]

THE TOOLS OF CHANGE

While this chapter has provided an overview of the process selection, analysis, and deployment processes of business systems engineering, clearly, there are tools that require further description in order to understand how to implement this system. Some of the key lessons that organizations need to consider regarding the planning and implementation of strategic change initiatives are:

- Process analysis measures performance.
- Benchmarking introduces new perspectives.
- Information technology provides enablers.
- Policy deployment fosters teamwork.

These are the topics of the next four chapters of this book.

PART III

Tools of Business Systems Engineering

5

Process Analysis Measures Performance

To know you don't know is best.
Not to know you don't know is a flaw.

Lao Tzu, *Te-Tao Ching*

PROCESS THINKING AND ACTING

Today, processes outlive products. In many industries, the life cycle of a product may be measured in months, while business processes for design, production, sales, service, and administrative functions will exist as long as the company continues in operation. This underlines the significance of process thinking and process optimization—a company may mess up a product or two, but if it messes up a process for too long it may not stay in business.

There is little disagreement about the basic premise regarding process thinking; excellence in business is the product of well-designed business and work processes, and continuous improvement of systems and processes is the key activity needed to grow a business. Over the years, I have been keeping a list of principles that relate to process. When I have shared them with audiences, these principles have struck a chord with groups as diverse as retail merchandising and health care to telecommunications and office services. The fact that a few large breakthroughs are better than many small, incremental improvements appears to be a "universal truth." This observation has led me to wonder why the debate exists in much of the reengineering literature regarding business improvement. In reality, both are necessary and may be harmonized into a single choreographed score for systemwide change. The large, breakthrough improvements tend to be managed by the senior team because of their expense and scope. The small, incremental improvements are the contribution of the work process teams who seek to continuously update their own daily management methods. As I have critiqued some people for their lack of understanding, I came to realize that this list of process principles may be something special, because I have never seen it compiled for any book or article. I believe that in order to really understand the concept of "process," one must first fully understand these fundamental quality principles. I would be pleased to provide references to the sources that spurred these thoughts; however, they have been blurred over the past seven years, and it is not possible for me to re-create the source list. This list is really the eclectic composition from quality thinkers since Frederick Taylor and is the process of the whole development of the profession of quality management. I do not claim this as my original work—I have only collated and reported the thoughts of others to create this first section of Chapter 5.

The basic tenets of process thinking read like a catechism of faith and echo *the voice of the process* in a holy hymn:[1]

- All work is composed of processes.
- All processes involve actions that can be described, measured, and studied.
- All processes have inputs from suppliers and provide outputs to customers.
- All processes that produce value have a transformation activity called work.
- All processes consume resources (cost) during their work transformation activity.
- Business productivity is directly measurable at the work process level.
- All processes can be improved by both corrective and preventive actions.
- Process improvement criteria are established to satisfy customers of the process.

- Process improvement is required just to maintain parity with competitors.
- The people closest to the process are in the best position to improve it.
- Participation of workers in process improvement commits them to implementation.
- Defect prevention should be a major activity within the work process.
- Waste elimination is an essential foundation to process improvement.
- Shortening the response time in all operations is a key improvement opportunity.
- Removing excess cost and non-value-added work improves process performance.
- Process control measures must be monitored continuously for variation.
- Process teams can modify process control parameters to eliminate the known causes of variation.
- All processes can and should be operated under statistical control.
- The best processes are transferable anywhere in the world.

These process principles imply a particular design of a process (see Figure 5–1). Every process contains these elements, and each of these elements has its own set of principles.

It is evident from these process principles and this process kernel that the customer is the true driver of the process. Also, just as the process has a set of principles that defines how it operates, the customer also has a holy litany that resounds *the voice of the customer.*

- Quality of products and services is fitness for use as defined by the customer, in the customer's workplace.
- Customer satisfaction with current products and services influences the customer's decision to make future purchases of goods and services.

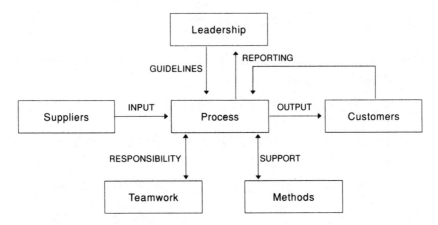

Figure 5–1 The Process Kernel

- ◆ Lack of customer satisfaction is the gap between the customer's perception of the work process output performance compared with the original expectation for that performance.

- ◆ Measurement of customer satisfaction is "perceptual benchmarking" and should indicate both the importance of each item to the customer and the performance of your organization against competitors whenever possible.

- ◆ Customer perceptions change over time and change relative to each business relationship based on either the most recent daily experiences or the influence of any enduring problems—whether resolved or not.

- ◆ Problems observed during daily operations can destroy a customer's confidence in your organization.

- ◆ Listening to customer complaints and providing a timely and effective response will eliminate most problems.

- ◆ Timely correction of the problem's root cause restores the customer's confidence.

- ◆ Activities in your business and work processes that do not satisfy customer needs are problems and must be corrected.

- ◆ The only way to know what satisfies customers is to study their behavior.

- ◆ Product and service design should be based on a thorough understanding of the needs of the customer and satisfying the current and future needs of customers should help to set future customer expectations.

♦ Customer expectations are not static—they change over time, tending to become ever more stringent and demanding as time goes by.

♦ The customers' voice must be heard often and loudly throughout the product or service development process to ensure congruence of goals and deliverables with their changing needs.

♦ Customer confidence in a product or service increases as the customer needs are more completely met and observed in the customer's daily experience—exceeding customer expectations is met with loyalty in repurchase consideration.

♦ External surveys of customer satisfaction and measures of product performance in the field must be correlated with internal measures of process performance to produce profound knowledge of actionable improvement opportunities in business operations.

Your *suppliers* are also a principal element in the process model. (It is interesting to note that this main axis of the process model represents the value chain found on the business enterprise model.) The mantra of the supplier follows this lyric:

♦ Suppliers need to understand the quality requirements of the process and work with the process owners as coproviders of the process output.

♦ Suppliers should be considered as part of the extended organization or family.

♦ Long-term relationships with suppliers provide stability that permits them to more fully engage and commit to your business without fear of losing a contract.

♦ Suppliers should be involved in the design process to fully take advantage of their contribution of core competence and process capability in the delivery of goods and services to the customer.

♦ Long-term relationships and involvement in the process output design permit a supplier to align its investments in capital equipment to better support the long-term direction of the extended value chain to the ultimate customer.

◆ Documented work processes at the supplier facility provide better assurance of a consistent practice in manufacturing—certification of supplier's compliance to ISO 9000 can provide an independent means to assess that the supplier actually performs its work processes according to the documented methods and procedures in its quality system documentation.

◆ Compliance to part specifications and delivery requirements and the reduction of variation in the part production process are the two primary product quality needs from suppliers.

◆ The final test and inspection at the supplier production facility should be equal to the incoming test of the process as this permits a performance-based elimination of the receiving inspection and a reduction in process costs.

◆ The use of value engineering to drive down the costs of parts manufacture should result in a savings that is divided between the supplier and your business, where the supplier receives relief for its investment and a reward for the consideration given to making the final product less costly.

Leadership is another driver of the process model. The leader represents the voice of the owners in the process and has its own special Gregorian chant:

◆ The principal requirements of management are to establish a shared vision and common plan, ensure resources are allocated in a way that assures success in the plan, and review and reward the progress toward achieving that plan.

◆ To influence the entire organization, quality must be driven by senior management.

◆ Management must create clear quality values and reinforce them regularly through unambiguous communication of expectations and clearly visible role model behavior.

◆ Commitment to quality improvement must be encouraged in all areas of the organization—top management should grant no exemptions to any area.

◆ The goal of all quality initiatives should be the improvement of business results and the attainment of recognized business excellence.

- All employees must be suitably trained in process improvement methods and the appropriate practices of Total Quality Management—no exemptions should be given, although different areas may be trained differently according to their assessed needs.

- Organizations need to develop both long-range strategic plans and stretch goals for their planned achievement of "role model status" in quality leadership and business performance results.

- The planning process must be "evergreen"—both flexible and rapidly adaptable to unforeseen contingencies, rather than restricted to a fixed, unchangeable direction for an unalterable period.

- Plans should be actionable, measurable, and regularly reviewed—they should not be purely philosophical or inspiring visions.

- Benchmarking is an effective approach for transferring process knowledge, setting appropriate improvement goals, and defining specific improvement plans.

- Business change initiatives should be balanced between continuous improvement and breakthrough activities, with the decision for selection based on both resource requirements and business performance needs.

- The organization's information infrastructure must support data acquisition and analysis of information at the "atomic level" of the work process.

Another element of the process model is the set of principles regarding *teamwork* that are a siren's song to the employees. If the people aren't aligned into teams where they can participate and enjoy their own personal involvement, they will not be pleased with their personal motivation and satisfaction with work:

- Individuals want to be be responsible for their work environment and the quality of their work output.

- An index of overall employee satisfaction provides a leading indicator of customer satisfaction with the provision of goods and services.

- ◆ The synergy of teamwork produces more effective results than the isolated efforts of an individual contributor.

- ◆ Team members work together, help each other, recognize and complement each other's strengths and weaknesses, and share a belief that they are responsible to each other.

- ◆ People will take more pride and interest in their work if they are allowed to make meaningful contributions for improvement of their work process and if they are able to influence decisions.

- ◆ Participation and employee involvement provide people with a vehicle for attaining personal goals and fulfilling their motivational needs.

- ◆ Self-directed teams improve both loyalty and work process productivity because empowered employee involvement builds intense commitment to business success.

- ◆ Empowerment gives teams the freedom to think and the encouragement to act.

- ◆ Empowerment operates within the framework of resource, schedule, and work process accountability boundaries.

- ◆ The transfer of decision-making authority to teams is a positive indicator of the empowerment of teams by management.

The process kernel would not be complete without a methodological foundation. Also supporting the voice of the process are the analytical *methods* and techniques of quality management that ring with a less variable tone:

- ◆ Customer confidence is maintained by the systematic management of product and service delivery processes.

- ◆ All operations and decisions that take place in an organization need to be based on facts and data, and evaluated using prudent business judgment.

- ◆ All measurements and process characteristics have variability, and both sources of variation must be considered when evaluating business data.

- ◆ Improvement often requires understanding process elements at a system level.

- Characteristics of systems can be identified and measured for study.
- Systems are composed of related processes that produce a product or service.
- Processes within a system usually interact with each other.
- Activities within processes often interact with each other.
- Assessment and review of systems and processes are part of an overall business control mechanism that also includes financial audits.
- People who study a process systematically can improve its operation.
- Processes that display statistical stability over time can be reliably improved.
- Process stability can be maintained over time.
- Reduction of variability stabilizes processes.
- Variability is either predictable or random.
- The causes of predictable variation are knowable and may be controlled.
- All variability can be reduced to a limited range.
- Waste and inefficient operations occur when variability exceeds acceptable limits.
- System simulation can provide a theoretical basis for understanding the limits of process improvement and the need for the technical development of a process.
- Either management or the process is the most likely cause of a problem, not the people who operate the process.
- Messengers of process problems should be rewarded and not reprimanded.

THE ELIMINATION SEQUENCE

Now that we recognize that a substantial set of principles underlies process thinking, what do we do with this material? The key insight I have gained from this seven-year study is that work process improvement has a natural sequence. I hope that the relationship between these principles and the sequential approach to work process optimization will be apparent to each reader. Figure 5–2 illustrates the sequence for attacking persistent problems that follow these process principles. The four levels of process improvement were described in Chapter 4; however, the objective of the more detailed description that follows is to demonstrate how the diverse tools of organizational development, quality documentation, process analysis, and statistical control may be used in harmony to improve work processes effectively. The idea behind the sequential use of these methods is to prevent problems and to optimize the process, not to find and fix problems in the process. This sequence represents a proactive approach to continuous improvement as opposed to the reactive approach used in problem solving. This does not imply that problem solving is a lesser process. Problem solving is a method for learning from mistakes and preventing their recurrence. The alternative to problem solving is to continue to make the same mistakes and accrue unwarranted costs from the repetition of embedded problems. To eliminate these types of problems, root cause analysis methods should be followed to pursue problems beyond their symptoms, reveal apparent causes, and then get to the basic reason why the problems occurred.[2]

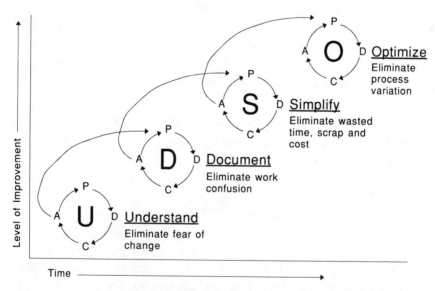

Figure 5–2.   The Elimination Sequence

Let's consider how each of the four steps in the elimination sequence applies the concept of PDCA to result in more effective process outcomes.

Step 1: Developing the Organization

Organizations are basically networks of people engaged in achieving some common set of goals or objectives. To accomplish these ends, various kinds of human processes will occur between the coworkers. Sometimes this may be a team that has not learned how to work together, an individual who has a different set of values or working principles, a lack of communication between management and the work teams so that neither understands the intentions of the other, or a fundamental work conflict that needs to be resolved. The basic work of improving organizations is the job of organizational development specialists. They work with management and teams to improve the way that a group of people work together to perform purposeful work. The body of knowledge that the organizational development specialist calls upon comes from the behavioral sciences and is usually applied to an autonomous organization such as a work group, department, division, or corporation. These specialists serve as process consultants to help their customers perceive, understand, and act upon the events of their work situation with the objective of improving the way that people work together. The primary focus of this process consultation is on changing the organization into a more effective working group. Some of the areas that process consultants will work with teams to improve may include:

◆ Interpersonal relations.
◆ Group goals and objectives.
◆ Work assignments and responsibilities.
◆ Communication and listening skills.
◆ Team building.
◆ Conflict resolution.
◆ Modifying group norms or values.
◆ Organization-wide change initiatives.

Most of the focus of this work is on how people work together and relate with one another. These interpersonal skills are the cornerstone of quality activities, because if people can't work together, then there is very little hope that the process can run in an optimized manner. It is interesting to observe that the organizational development staff specialist works across the organization in the same manner as the quality engineer, the information systems analyst, and the cost accountant (see Figure 5–3).[3] Each works as a process consultant, one who does not have the direct authority to change a process, but must find ways to coach the process owner through personal influence and guidance into making necessary changes. These staff activities actually help to facilitate the horizontal flow of products and services across the organization because they are the carriers of the corporate culture. If there is harmony among these support groups—that is, they sing from the same hymnal and use the same language about change—then the entire organization can be orchestrated like the Mormon Tabernacle Choir! The strength of this support service can be greatly increased as management works to ensure that it is using a cooperative language structure. This is one reason why an information-technology centric approach to reengineering does not work—it avoids the proper positioning of the other support elements of the organization.

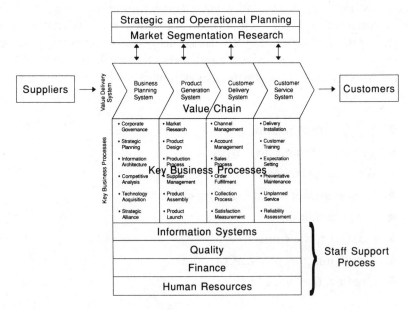

Figure 5–3.   Expanding the Core Enterprise Model

By following the elimination cycle to implement the chosen change initiative, an organization may be able to more effectively use its staff support to drive strategic change.

The direction of this strategic change effort needs to be managed by an individual who is capable of acting as the coach-facilitator and using strong interpersonal skills to engage the support of the entire team, while, at the same time, having a position of authority and commanding the respect of the entire team. Often, this may be accomplished by a senior manager supported by an organizational development specialist and the staff support of other specialists for quality, finance, and information systems. No matter how much the improvement effort of an organization progresses, the human element will always crop up as a potential issue. An organization may become mature in the use of analytical, financial, or informational technologies; however, the human factor requires constant attention throughout the change process. For this reason, I recommend that the senior management Change Master maintain a close working relationship with the organization's specialist on human interaction processes.[4, 5] Processes may become stable and predictable, but I am not so sure about human nature!

Step 2: Building the Documentation

There is an old saying among quality system auditors regarding how to implement an organization-wide quality system: If it moves, train it; if it doesn't move, calibrate it; and if it isn't recorded, then it didn't happen. Documentation records the events and decisions of the work process as well as the procedures by which work is accomplished. When *Fortune*[6] described how ISO 9000 works, it stated: "Its governing principles can be summed up in three words—documentation, documentation, documentation." The existence of process documentation means that people have agreed upon the way a process should operate and they have committed to operating the process in that manner until they agree on a need to change the process—and then they change the documentation to reflect the process adjustments. Documentation is a communication vehicle for recording team or group decisions and methods with the purpose of providing a consistent and repeatable approach to work. Documentation of work processes and standards of performance does not imply the stagnation of a work process; they are process characteristics that represent higher levels of management and communication and are necessitated as organizations grow in size and complexity. A well-managed process is adaptable to change. The documentation provides both a basis for agreement among team members as to how a process should operate and a vehicle for training as new members of the team become incorporated into the process operation.

When a company pursues ISO 9000 registration and formally faces the need for a more consistent documentation system, there is a general feeling of pain. The lack of energy and motivation of teams for documentation is Watson's first law of human energy: If a task doesn't excite a team, members will procrastinate about performing it. Of course, this has a corollary: Some of the most important tasks are considered to be boring to somebody, but they are important and fulfilling to other people. Documentation is the key to ISO 9000 registration. The documents help process workers do their jobs even better by ensuring that a consistent, repeatable process is used for the production and delivery of goods and services. ISO 9000 checks the daily operations of a business to determine:

♦ If it is designed to operate in accordance with the standard.

♦ If the documentation presents processes that follow the requirements of the standard.

♦ If daily operations are conducted in accordance with the documented processes.

♦ If daily operation performance is recorded in required records.

♦ If the daily operations are audited by an independent part of the organization to ensure compliance with the documentation.

In short, the auditor asks just three basic questions with two follow-up questions to each of these basic questions.

Basic Questions
♦ Have you documented your essential work processes?
♦ Are you doing what you describe in your documentation?
♦ Did you do it in the past?

Follow-Up Questions
♦ How do I know?
♦ By what means?

ISO 9000 implies a documentation system that matches the three organization levels identified in Chapter 3. At the enterprise level, the quality system is documented by a quality manual that describes how the value chain operates under the responsibility of management to reliably deliver products and services. At the business level, the key business processes are documented as quality procedures to describe how they coordinate the functions of the organization to produce the output described in the quality system. Then, at the operations level, the work processes are documented in the level of detail that is required for teams to operate. (This may be accomplished through differing types of work process documentation: a work process description sheet that identifies all of the elements of a work process; a written list of tasks performed in a work process; a set of photographs that illustrate a sequence of assembly operations; or the flowchart of an operation.[7])

Step 3: Improving the Efficiency

At a macro level, each enterprise must operate on a new set of time-based imperatives. These include the need to drive down the time it takes to introduce new products; reduce the number of long lead time components in products, so that the procurement lead time is abbreviated; eliminate lead time wherever possible in the customer ordering process; and work to reduce process changeover and dead times. This last imperative is the goal of process analysis—streamline the work processes. The elimination sequence seeks to keep products moving during their production and delivery processes. The third step is aimed at eliminating buffers, safety stock, and excess material from all storage locations and managing the flow of materials from the purchasing process through their disposition. The flow of production remains unbroken by stalled production or waiting lines from the initial receipt of raw materials and parts from suppliers to the shipment of finished goods to customers. This stabilization of the process flow also needs built-in flexibility to permit rapid response by the enterprise to shifting market conditions and customer demands.[8] Stabilization of the process flow occurs when deliveries are neither late nor early—they occur just when needed and in just the amount needed. This is true JIT. How is such efficiency achieved at the process level? That is the work of the third step in the elimination sequence.

Once the process has been documented (output of Step 2) and the roles and responsibilities of individual contributors have been aligned with the work group's mission (output of Step 1), work process simplification, or streamlining as it is sometimes called, can begin. This consists of the elimination of waste (non-value-added time that is consumed by the process and cost that does not produce sufficient value in the output). This step is essential before moving on to automate a business or work process.[9] The third and fourth steps of the elimination sequence attack process improvement from an internally reflecting perspective (that is, based on self-analysis and internal benchmarking). In Chapter 6 I will add the external comparison and possible lessons that may be a contribution of process benchmarking. Inputs from benchmarking studies may feed the elimination sequence at both Steps 3 and 4, when two conditions are satisfied: the process has been documented and its performance measured (by the completion of Step 2).

This focus on work process cycle time reduction can emphasize three different tactics: elimination of tasks that do not produce value; optimization or compression of tasks that add value but that take too long to perform; and concurrent processing of those tasks or activities that may be performed in parallel. A key ingredient to successful process redesign is the merging of the results from the cycle time analysis of the process with the outcome of the process value and cost consumption analysis to completely streamline the process.

This approach uses the two key external process measures (see Figure 5-4) of value produced and time consumed to mark the productivity effectiveness of the work process. In addition, two key internal process measures are 1) first pass yield—how much of the process output was produced right the first time—and 2) cost consumed by the production process. To collect these measures, the process must be designed in a way that captures data at the key points: input of materials and schedules, completion of the first pass production, test results from the internal inspection, financial transactions of the process, and the output of the process.

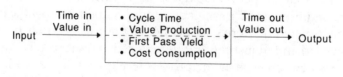

Process

Figure 5–4.   Process Measurements

The goal of the elimination process for Step 3 is clear: Compress the cycle time to complete the process; increase the value of the process output; decrease the cost of the process operation; and increase the first pass yield of the process operation. The ability to complete these goals will rely on the application of a set of decision filters:[10]

◆ Does the process add value? If yes, then continue—if no, then seek to eliminate.

◆ Can the process be time compressed? If yes, then apply time compression methods to reduce the cycle time—if no, then continue.

◆ Can the process be accomplished concurrently instead of sequentially? If yes, then perform the process in parallel to other processes—if no, then keep it as it is.

◆ Can the first pass yield be increased? If yes, then increase the yield and remove the rework cycles from the main flow of the process—if no, then keep it as it is.

◆ Can the process cost be further reduced without adversely affecting the cycle time, value production, or first pass yield? If yes, then invest in cost reduction that provides an adequate return on investment—if no, then apply continuous improvement to the cost structure.

Two primary performance indices are combined from this set of process measures: process productivity and process cost effectiveness. These equations are both illustrated in Figure 5–5.

Process productivity is a combination of three factors: the availability of the process to produce output; the ratio of the value-added production time to the total production time; and the performance of the process quality for first pass yield. Availability is reduced from 100 percent for process maintenance, operator training, and time for administration of employee communications and team activities. A planning factor used by many operations is that 85 percent to 90 percent of the actual working day is available for output production. The second factor in the productivity equation is the ratio of value-added production time to the total production time. This ratio is the output of the activity analysis for cycle time and value production.[11] This measurement is similar to the output measures used on most cycle time reduction processes. The final factor in the process productivity equa-

$$\text{Process Productivity} = \left[\frac{\text{Up Time}}{\text{Up Time + Down Time}} \right] \times \left[\frac{\text{Value-Added}}{\text{Actual}} \right] \times \left[\text{Q} \right]$$

$$\begin{array}{ccc} \text{Process} & \text{Process} & \text{First Pass} \\ \text{Availability} & \text{Cycle Time} & \text{Process Yield} \end{array}$$

$$\text{Process Cost - Effectiveness} = \left[\frac{\text{Output Value - Input Value}}{\text{Value Producing Cost - Non-Value Producing Cost}} \right]$$

Figure 5–5.   Measures of Process Productivity and Cost Effectiveness

tion is the first pass process yield. A work process is productive only for the time that it is producing good output—bad output is not productive! It is interesting to note that by combining these features, the theoretical best performance (90 percent availability, 95 percent value-added production, and 100 percent first pass yield) will result in a performance level of 85.5 percent (because these factors are multiplied to produce an overall performance level). This is a standard of excellence. Any company that can demonstrate performance averaging above 75 percent for its work processes is in the category of world-class. Yet, companies can still make money if this measure is 50 percent!

The second measure is the process cost effectiveness. This is a simple comparison of the value added by the process to the cost consumed by the process. The cost is divided into the categories of value producing and non-value producing to force the clarification of how management will deal with non-value-adding costs. Cost efficiency measurement using this methodology supports the standard approach to Activity Based Costing.[12]

When productivity increases are achieved, the direct process costs can become transferred to process overhead costs. The activity-based cost analysis approach coupled with cycle time reduction can drive down both direct costs and direct labor with the investment in appropriate technology (see Chapter 10 for an example of Motorola's use of investment to drive this third step in the elimination sequence). However, unless the overhead costs of production or service delivery are also steamlined, the savings will not be recouped but will be transferred to overhead functions instead of the bottom line. Figure 5–6 shows a classic picture of the reallocation of overhead that covers the development of a more efficient work process. The productivity paradox is that as a process becomes more productive as measured by operational measures, the associated cost reduction of the improved operation is not recouped. This is due to the evils of the accounting system that allocates overhead to value-producing work processes. Since the linkage between overhead cost allocation and the value-adding work processes is largely arbitrary, management can be led to perceptions about process performance that are based on wrong thinking. Management should ask for process cost information in two buckets: "cost due to process" and "cost assigned as overhead." The legitimacy of the overhead allocation should be subject to the same type of strenuous process improvement as the work process itself.

At this point in the elimination sequence, the direct process improvement opportunities have been captured and it is time to consider the use of statistical optimization.

Step 4: Removing Variation

By working on the first three levels of the elimination sequence, many of the root causes of variation due to special causes have become removed or controlled without resorting to statistical methods that cre-

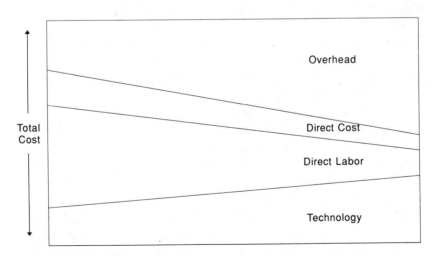

Figure 5–6.   The Productivity Paradox and Overhead

ate phobic reactions among many workers. However, you can improve a process only so much without introducing statistical methods.[13] This level of the elimination sequence focuses on the statistical process for reducing variation in work processes. The process is simple: Perform a process capability study to understand the current statistical capability of the process (at a more advanced level, this may also include an analysis of the product using the Taguchi Loss Function[14]). Conduct an experimental design to learn which process factors contribute the most to the remaining process variation. Redesign those process activities or product components that produce the excess variation to make them more stable. Continue this variation removal until the overall process stability is acceptable. Once the variation-producing factors are under control, implement statistical process control to monitor the natural drift of the process over time.

The underlying concept behind the use of this process for applying statistics is the idea of variability reduction. What is variability and why should it be reduced? The existence of variation is a law of nature: No two items in any natural category are exactly the same. Variation exists in every process and is due to a combination of the material, equipment, operator, environment, and even the inspection measurement process that is used. If two items appear to be the same and have the same measurement, then we have reached a limit in our ability to measure. The ability to measure variation is necessary before it can be controlled. (The science of precision in measurement is called metrology—an even more dismal science than economics—and, of course, an economist is a statistician with a sense of humor.) Measurement devices must be calibrated (by metrologists)—that is, evaluated and adjusted against a known measurement standard—to allow measurement equipment to precisely measure variation of an item from its specified nominal condition.

Variation may be either common cause or special cause. *Common cause variation,* also called chance or random variation, is inevitable. It is due to the small natural changes that occur due to a variety of sources in every process. Their small magnitude and the numerous sources of variation make the specific sources of common cause variation difficult to detect and identify. When only common cause variation exists in a process, it is considered to be in statistical control, which means that its performance is both stable and predictable. On the other hand, *special cause variation* is problematic. Special cause variation is also called assignable variation because its source is knowable and the total amount of variation may be attributed, or assigned, to that cause. Special cause variation is larger than common cause and is readily identifiable. The presence of special cause variation results in an "out of statistical control" condition. The control chart is used to differentiate between common cause variation (in control) and special cause variation (out of control) and to indicate when the process is being influenced by a special cause.

Process capability, the ability for a process to produce its output in a stable and reliable manner, is determined by the total variation that comes from common causes or the minimum variation that can be achieved after all special causes have been removed. Process capability, for a stable process, is the ratio of the specification limits to the variation. It represents the performance of the process itself. Since a stable process can be described by a predictable distribution of output, it is desirable to drive the process capability ratio to as high a number as possible. A process capability ratio—measured when the variation is centered at the nominal specification value—of 2.0 is the equivalent of "six sigma" performance for a process.[15] At that level of performance, management action on the common causes of process variation is not required to improve the performance of the process any further.

When variation is at an acceptable level, the work process can be placed under statistical process monitoring to recognize, identify, and then control future sources of special cause variation. After statistical process analysis, control, and monitoring has been successfully applied, the process is stable and it will take an act of management to improve the process further by attacking the common causes of process variation. To do this, the management team must reinitiate the elimination sequence by assessing the organization's performance and developing structural interventions to change the system, perhaps by attacking overhead inefficiencies identified in Step 3. In concentrating on such continuous process improvement, the team must remember one basic rule:

> *Simplifying a process at the expense of a customer requirement is not a legitimate process improvement.*

PERSONALIZING QUALITY: PROCESS THINKING AT THE TOP

The authentic test of the mastery of quality principles, methods, and practices is not in what a person says, but in what a person does. Members of management, at all levels, must become committed to becoming personal masters of appropriate skills that allow them to both manage their work processes and lead their people. The experience of senior managers who participated in the ten-year Xerox implementation of Leadership Through Quality has indicated that managers go through a three-phased transition as they absorb the practical details of process thinking.[16] In the first phase of their engagement with process thinking, managers are learners. It is up to them to take responsibility for taking the lessons out of the classroom and into the conference room. They need to learn both the academic practice and the pragmatic implementation of process analysis. The Socratic method is best for many of these managers—they need to learn what questions to ask others and how to assure that they have been given reasonable answers. After practicing process review in a variety of venues, the manager becomes recognized as one who is "serious about that process stuff." Now the manager has transitioned into the second phase of being a role model. Thus, the role model is not just one who is admired for his or her ability to be an individual problem solver, like the Lone Ranger, but is a person who can transfer this knowledge to others in addition to being able to apply it in a variety of conditions. The role model manager is a teacher and a facilitator who can teach the details of process thinking in an academic setting or can facilitate a team in the application of process analysis methods. The role model manager is a catalyst for change throughout the organization. It becomes natural for peers and even more senior managers to seek out the role model manager for advice and assistance on matters related to process effectiveness and efficiency. Now, we are observing the natural transition into a mentoring role for the manager. As a mentor, the manager gives even more personal advice—how to act and behave as a role model in order to get teams to function properly. Perhaps the mentor even needs to give some criticism about the way a "disciple" has been behaving. As a mentor, the manager learns some hard truths about the pursuit of quality. Quality improvement requires a deep, personal commitment to the pursuit of excellence; quality improvement takes a lot of hard effort in order to achieve the level of mastery;[17] quality improvement requires attention to detail in order to be able to guide the actions of others without becoming a dominant authority over them; and quality improvement takes persistence—trees don't grow up in a year or two, and neither do we.[18] However, trees can grow faster when they are fertilized and properly pruned—the same types of external growth stimulation that may come from benchmarking.

6

Benchmarking Introduces New Perspectives

To understand others is to be knowledgeable;
To understand yourself is to be wise.
To conquer others is to have strength;
To conquer yourself is to be strong.

Lao Tzu, *Te-Tao Ching*

BENCHMARKING AND PROCESS ANALYSIS

Earlier I noted that benchmarking provided a critical discovery for Ford as it sought to improve its accounting process. The performance that Mazda achieved illustrated to Ford what it could do to improve and gave Ford a real stretch goal. Benchmarking is a critical ingredient to strategic change efforts through such current programs as reengineering. Ted Richman, a Xerox manager in the Document Production Systems Division, cited four contributions that benchmarking has made to Xerox efforts in Business Process Reengineering:[1]

1. "Benchmarking helps define the context for the goals of the reengineering program.
2. "Benchmarking will give your firm clear examples of best practices that have been implemented—and even more importantly, how they were implemented.
3. "Benchmarking provides the opportunity to learn useful lessons from what has already been tried and hasn't worked.

111

4. "The ideas that benchmarking uncovers can spark new thinking."

After developing three books on benchmarking, I should be pretty well wrung out on the topic. However, this chapter will not teach teams how to benchmark (as I did in *The Benchmarking Workbook*); nor tell management how to integrate benchmarking with strategic planning concepts (the thrust of *Strategic Benchmarking*); nor provide guidance and implementation hints for quality managers (the topic of *The Benchmarking Management Guide*).[2] The purpose of this chapter is to describe how benchmarking can support process analysis and the elimination sequence, which is the fundamental tool for business improvement through process redesign. Benchmarking can occur, with differing degrees of rigor, at each level in the elimination sequence.

Benchmarking can be used to increase understanding of how organizations can be more efficiently formed, how self-directed teams and skill-based pay may be integrated to increase process effectiveness, or how management can construct a human resource system that provides reinforcement for its strategic business issues. These are all issues of the "Understand" or first level of the elimination sequence. The payback from implementing these topics is difficult to measure, in terms of cost-benefits, but case-study-like examples can convince a team of benchmarkers of the worthiness of the approach, and the strength of the analogy between the two organizations can indicate if it would be viable for their organization.[3] The result of the first step of the elimination sequence is for the work group to recognize that: "Our work is a *process*" and to gain an understanding of members' roles and responsibilities within that process.

Benchmarking can also be used in the second level of the elimination sequence to help "Document" how internal processes should be operated. Many businesses find that they have developed 20 or 30 instances of the same process without having a common process. For example, a nationwide bank may have several credit card clearing facilities or several thousand automated tellers; a rental car service may have hundreds of cleaning operations or dozens of car repair locations; a nationwide retail operation may have four regional warehouses and thousands of point-of-sale terminals; a multinational company may have 50 research laboratories and hundreds of marketing channels; and a federal government may have thousands of Social Security offices or hundreds of libraries. It doesn't matter what type of large-scale operation is considered, one conclusion is clear: It is not likely that the processes all operate alike or that the best process is known to the organization. This is a case for internal benchmarking.[4] Internal benchmarking seeks to identify the best of breed among internal processes and then to standardize the rest of the processes using that model to create *repeatable processes*. This is the ultimate goal of the documentation step.

The third step in the elimination sequence can use benchmarking to help "Simplify" work and business processes.[5] This is the traditional approach to a process benchmarking study—evaluating quality, cost, and cycle time measures of the same process at several leading companies and then seeking to understand those practices that drove the highest level of performance (while also recording interesting practices that are observed at organizations other than the leader—they may not have been implemented in a way that provides the full gain; however, they may contribute to a better practice in a different process design). The Simplify step in the elimination process seeks to optimize process "value-added" by designing an *efficient and effective repeatable process* with the fastest possible process transformation and the best first pass yield at the lowest transformation cost. By benchmarking, a company can find out how far off the mark its processes are for these key measures.

The fourth step of the elimination sequence can use global benchmarking to establish the worldwide standard of excellence for a business process. The question that begs to be answered in most benchmarking studies is: Which company has the lowest amount of variation in its process? As we saw in Chapter 4, variation reduction produces more *stable, efficient, and effective repeatable processes*. Process stability is the desirable state for most business processes because they become *reliable processes*. The use of the Plan-Do-Check-Act cycle is common between both the elimination sequence and the benchmarking process.

Benchmarking follows the basic Plan-Do-Check-Act cycle that was popularized by the late Dr. W. Edwards Deming. The four phases of this management cycle for process improvement may be stated a different way: measuring, learning, planning, and implementing. Benchmarking follows this sequence to drive business and work process improvement. The measuring phase is dedicated to understanding gaps between current state and potential states that may become the desired state of the process. The learning phase is dedicated to understanding how the "best practice" organization achieved its superiority. The planning phase is an analysis of the resource requirements and time line for implementation of the identified and selected improvements. The implementing phase follows the advice of Nike: Just Do It! Measuring and planning are two activities that management can accomplish without much encouragement. The learning and implementation phases are the tough ones. And you can't implement if you don't learn. Once an organization learns how to learn, then it can face its most difficult challenge: deployment of its plans. The first two phases of benchmarking are the precursor to planning and implementing change—these two phases, measuring and learning, focus the planning and implementation of change. Their uniqueness has led to their identification as *bench-measuring* and *bench-learning.*[6]

BENCH-MEASURING

The objective of taking measurements in benchmarking is to have an objective basis for comparison in order to identify which organization has the best practice for a particular business or work process. Measurements of this type can motivate an organization to change by providing a quantified definition of the "possible state" with a real-world proof of its existence. This leads naturally to the question: If they can, why can't we? Bench-measuring is the analytical process of gap analysis. It identifies the location and magnitude of performance gaps and builds an imperative to close the gap. To get such a convincing result from the bench-measuring process, the measurement must be right and the magnitude of the gap must be right. To make sure the measurement is right, it should be selected from an actionable level of the measurement map. The measurement map essentially has four levels. The metrics at the top of the map are global performance indicators for the entire organization (for example, return on assets). They are decomposed into functional elements (for example, revenue and assets), which are then divided into the factors that relate to them (for example, revenue due to equipment sales, due to service agreements, due to sale of supplies, or due to investment returns). Below this level, the results are stratified into the contributing factor (for example, sales by district, sales by equipment type, sales by customer type, sales by sales representative, and so forth) where the objective is to look for a factor that explains the differences. The measurement map can be translated down one further level by requiring that all data needed to conduct the stratification analysis be an element in the corporate data model that is used by the information systems analysts for designing databases. The measurement map is the missing link that most companies have not forged from the process level to the information systems level.

When a significant difference between two different processes is found through data stratification analysis at the actionable level of a work process or business process, then it indicates the potential need for some performance improvement at the lagging organization. But bench-measuring only provides an alert of the need to change, it doesn't tell where the process must change, nor does it indicate how to change the process, nor forecast how much improvement will occur by implementing the change. These types of insights come from the application of the second half of the process—learning what made the benchmark organization succeed. This is the objective of bench-learning.

BENCH-LEARNING

Bench-learning is the application of knowledge learned from other companies to your own organization. Bench-learning is the building of a social and cultural understanding of the process, technical, behavioral, and attitudinal changes that must take place in order to successfully introduce a change initiative that produces the "desired possible state." William Sandy, chairman and CEO of Sandy Corporation, has observed that some companies he has seen have "Organization charts that vaguely define roles, overlapping charters with more than one person accountable, too many decision makers, rewards not commensurate with risks, praise for activity rather than results, innovation without special nurturing. . . ." In the light of this chaotic management situation, he also noted that: "When major changes don't happen, frequently it's because people don't know why or what is expected, nor how to do it, nor do they believe the effort is worth the gain."[7]

Sandy brings up the critical point for most organizations: We are good at planning and at studying the situation, but somehow we just don't follow through. How do we bridge the gap between planning and implementation? The answer is with true learning in which the implementation team fully participates in the discovery and planning phases, develops the comparative study of performance, and then designs the improvement plan for its own organization. Such full participation eliminates the confusion about what is being done and also keeps the plan from becoming a mystery. When management does communicate its support of the given direction, people in the process don't feel fear and concern, they feel pride because of their role in the development effort. If the company is conditioned to learn, that is, senior management has moved employees in the direction where they, as Hewlett-Packard former-CEO John Young has said, "Learn to love change," then the organization can make constant improvement of its key business processes that result in better performance of the overall organization.

In essence, the company becomes a learning organization (Chapter 12 illustrates how the .United Services Automobile Association—USAA—took a 25-year journey to become a learning organization that loves change). The learning organization is one that uses action principles to define when "bench-learning" has occurred. Action principles that define when bench-learning has taken place include:

♦ The management becomes visible and clearly communicates its intent for change.

♦ The process output has measurably changed following an "improvement" effort.

♦ The team exhibits different behavior patterns when working together.

♦ The supplier contributes to planning rather than merely receiving the plan.

♦ The customer responds differently in the situation that once caused concern.

The authentic test for mastery of learning is not in what a manager says, but in what a manager does.

Just as adult learning encourages learners to take responsibility for their own education by participating fully in the education process, thereby obtaining full value from their experience, benchmarking encourages the work team to participate in all aspects of the benchmarking study so that they will understand and support decisions that may result from the benchmarking study as well as effectively implement the action plan. Adult learners learn best when they participate fully in the education experience.

BENCHMARKING TEAMS: A VEHICLE FOR PARTICIPATIVE DECISION MAKING

Benchmarking is a team activity. When benchmarking is conducted to support the improvement of a repeatable process, it is usually conducted by the team that owns the operation of that process. In such a natural work group, team members have a common language and a behavioral track record from working with each other—understanding each other's interpersonal styles and particular idiosyncrasies. However, this same group harmony does not exist for one-time, nonrepeatable projects.

When benchmarking is conducted to support a one-time strategic change project, it is usually conducted by a project management team. The difference between these two types of teams can be great. Most business systems changes involve this second type of team, which tends to involve cross-functional participation of people from many business disciplines. This means that a business language barrier may exist and that the team may need to do some interpersonal or team-building development work before it can begin the work of process improvement.

In addition to the need to learn how to work together, there is the need to learn how to talk with each other. This can become a devastating problem when there are intrafunctional dialects such as market-ese, accounting-ese, engineering-ese, and computer-ese. If each community also adds its buzzwords and acronyms to its professional vocabulary, we may have a regular Tower of Babel on our team—resulting in the same degree of confusion and lack of accomplishment of the initial shared goal as the original Tower construction team.

Discipline-specific jargon can be a barrier to organizational cooperation by encouraging team members to play games such as the "I know more than you do" game, or the "My language is more precise than your language" game. These types of attitudes and game-playing are destructive to teamwork and need to be eliminated in favor of a cultural language that is common across all the functional areas.

Some observations of the benefits from using teams to conduct benchmarking studies rather than consultants or individuals include the following:[8]

♦ Teams provide a broader perspective of the process.

♦ Teams provide a broader foundation for acceptance of the change.

♦ Teams provide a broader base for organizational learning.

♦ Teams provide a broader participation in creative contributions.

♦ Teams provide focused group activity toward a shared objective, thereby breaking down a potential barrier to implementing the change.

The increase in benchmarking team efforts has been phenomenal since 1989—especially in activities that extend beyond the company team to form cross-company benchmarking teams through sharing networks.

BENCHMARKING NETWORKS: THE GROWING TREND IN COOPERATION

Benchmarking is not a spectator sport—it is a participative sport.[9] It is not just the process of gathering measures and challenging an organization to "be better!" It is an approach to *lead* an organization to improved performance by identifying those processes that may be weak and learning how to improve and redesign them. The enablers of the redesign effort are discovered by the participants in a benchmarking study. This experience of observation is the beginning of the process improvement plan. But to obtain valuable insights on a long-term basis requires the cultivation and nurturing of a benchmarking network. A benchmarking network, ideally, will provide extended access to those organizations that have succeeded in improving those processes that your organization has targeted for process improvement. Developing a strategy for engaging these organizations in your benchmarking study project is the key to a successful large-scale business change effort. Tom Peters refers to this as the "insiderization of outsiders."[10]

This occurs when people who are outside your organization become active participants in the effort to make the improvement. There are four types of natural networks that can become "insiderized" and may form the basis of a long-term network of companies that support your change effort:

1. *Business Networks.* These intercompany connections exist in the natural framework of your business. These include: suppliers (especially preferred or critical suppliers); customers (particularly major or target accounts); service providers (consultants and technologists); strategic alliances that already exist (partners in research, distribution, manufacturing, or investment projects); and, co-owners of the business (institutional stockholders or major owners). Each of these participants in your business network has a vested interest in the performance improvement of your business. Notice that those organizations with special interests have been targeted for inclusion in the network: preferred suppliers and major accounts, for example. They are both part of your company's value chain. Preferred suppliers look to your organization as a long-term business relationship that can be improved only as both parties become stronger. Major accounts, in a similar fashion, view their suppliers as part of their own virtual corporation—they provide value that drives the long-term success of the entire business system. These business networks are dependent upon each other for long-term success, so they have a natural inclination to cooperate.

2. *Industrial Networks.* These natural networks exist to support a particular industry. They could be professional associations (American Society for Quality Control or Institute of Industrial Engineers), trade associations (American Electronics Association or Semiconductor Advanced Technology Consortium), government agencies (Department of Commerce International Trade Administration or National Academy of Engineering), or political lobbying activities (Council on Competitiveness or the Computer Business Executive Manufacturing Association). These networks use voluntary participants from their membership to staff their projects, supported by a small core of professionals. Most of these industrial networks have databases and conduct studies among their members.

3. *Commercial Networks.* These natural networks exist to provide productivity and quality information to their customer base. They could be classified as commercial databases (ABI/Inform or DRI/McGraw-Hill), benchmarking networks (American Productivity & Quality Center International Benchmarking Clearinghouse or Strategic Planning Institute Council on Benchmarking), or gateways to multiple data sources (Dialog or Compuserve).

4. *Personal Networks.* These networks grow out of individual relationships built from the life experience of an organization's management team. These networks may extend to peers and colleagues in industry, academics, former employees (alumni of your organization), consultants, and acquaintances from trade shows, seminars, and conferences. Each of us develops a network of "like souls" who may be called upon for mentoring, advice, or information about their mutual concerns. A personal network is highly informal, and its effectiveness depends on the strength of the relationships between the individuals. These personal contacts are a beginning point for establishing more formal relationships with another organization.

Any of these networks will serve the purpose of meeting with other organizations. The source of the contact becomes less important once a connection has been made. The ultimate purpose of networking is to connect organizations with problems with those organizations that have worked through solutions to the same problem. This connection creates the potential for learning. It is only by learning that change can happen. What are the signs that an organization has learned how to learn—grown to maturity in the process of benchmarking?

MOVING TOWARD MATURITY

As benchmarking has been growing in popularity, the maturity level of companies in their methods of benchmarking has also grown. In the late 1980s, there were only a handful of companies that had trained their employees in benchmarking. Today, hundreds of companies have given such training. One question that I have been asked to comment upon is: What is the end-state vision of a mature effort in benchmarking? Reflection has led me to a set of seven practices that differentiate the most robust and mature benchmarking programs:[11]

1. *Benchmarking is used as an exploratory tool for clarifying issues of strategic importance.* Benchmarking has matured from the initial efforts that examined the improvement of the "open wounds and sores" of an organization to the place where it is used for "diagnostic examination before exploratory surgery" in coping with the organization's leading edge business issues. For example, when Xerox was considering how to decentralize into a business division structure, it benchmarked those companies that it recognized for a successful transition during the 1980s: AT&T, Hewlett-Packard, and Procter & Gamble. (This application was illustrated in the previous commentary regarding the use of benchmarking in the "Understand" step of the elimination sequence.)

2. *Benchmarking influences goal-setting for the strategic plan as well as providing enablers to improve key operational business processes.* While initial benchmarking studies may provide valuable process-specific information for business improvement, organizations that are more mature in benchmarking use it as a means to set strategic goals. For instance, time-to-market is a key indicator of success in the electronics industry. Benchmarking against a time-based competitor such as Canon indicates that the average product time-to-market must decrease about 50 percent every two to three years just to stay on par with competitive performance in new product introductions. The requirement for a prolonged commitment to improvement of the product development process must be reflected in both the organization's strategic plans and its operating budget allocations to ensure long-term success. This allows an organization to build constancy of purpose across all elements of the organization and to deploy congruent objectives within the organization to align all forces (political, economic, social, and process) to achieve the desired end state.

3. *Benchmarking is used to identify both "business process" and "people process" change enablers.* There is a saying within the Xerox management team that, "The soft stuff is the hard stuff." Using benchmarks to identify and understand the approach of excellent organizations to both "soft" programs such as empowerment

or high-performing teams or performance assessment for teams, as well as "hard" areas such as product manufacturing and distribution or product development, is another indicator of the state of maturity in a benchmarking effort.

4. *Benchmarking partnerships are set up to form strategic alliances or relationships that maximize the use of natural networks, such as the network of strategic suppliers or major account customers.* Some organizations use the same partners for benchmarking studies on a multitude of subjects. In essence, they have formed a strategic information-sharing alliance about process performance that does not go over the ethical and legal lines of American antitrust laws or the arcane practices of the Federal Trade Commission in its "watchdog" role over such intercompany relations (my bias against the ineffective controls system of the federal government that limits a free market is showing). The practice of cross-company sharing makes it easier to: establish communication in setting up a focused, topical study; understand the culture of the partnering organization; adapt lessons learned from other companies; recalibrate studies on a regular basis; and simultaneously reinforce the natural network functions between companies. These functions are performed through the *keritsu* in Japanese business. (Unfortunately, the United States government restricts the free communication among similar businesses through its ill-founded and anachronistic fears of monopolistic behaviors. For many business leaders, their thoughts regarding the government's restrictions of free trade and intercompany communication are echoed by the cartoon character Pogo: We have met the enemy, and they is us! It will be impossible to compete in a global economy without a "reinventing" of our trade laws.)

5. *Organization-wide knowledge sharing processes are implemented and eliminate redundancy in benchmarking study projects across all operating units.* Mature benchmarking organizations tend to have documented processes for both conducting benchmarking studies and for sharing study results across all of the company subsidiaries and business divisions. Often, these organizations have information networks, bulletin boards, or data files of completed studies.

6. *Closed-loop business process measurement and monitoring systems are based on continuously recalibrated benchmarks for all key busi-*

ness processes. While overmeasuring business processes may be an indicator of process immaturity, appropriate measurement and use of benchmarks to calibrate business processes is a sign of process maturity. A closed-loop process that embeds corrective action with a daily management system and includes both process quality and benchmark monitoring capabilities is a best practice for the implementation of benchmarking.

7. *Benchmarking studies for their own areas are conducted by the line managers, not by a professional benchmarking staff.* In mature organizations, those people who conduct benchmarking studies are the same individuals who are most affected by their outcome. This means that senior management studies are conducted by the senior management, not by staff people on behalf of the senior management. The visible participation of line managers using benchmarking in their own work, rather than delegating this work to support staff, is a key way for the organization to reinforce the importance of benchmarking.

How can you apply these indicators of maturity? It depends on whether or not your company is benchmarking. If you are benchmarking, then your company can use these indicators to develop an operational definition of the desired state of its benchmarking maturity. Once this has been done, then conducting a self-assessment of your company's current benchmarking ability will provide a basis for estimating the gap that needs to be closed in order to reach the desired state. The criteria for this self-assessment could be further enhanced by incorporating the applicable criteria from the American Productivity & Quality Center's Benchmarking Excellence Award. If your organization is not actively benchmarking, then these seven indicators of benchmarking maturity may be used to challenge your senior management team to consider its missed opportunities. It may be that benchmarking is the missing practice that keeps your organization from becoming the recognized leader in its industry.

BENCHMARKING: NECESSARY STIMULANT FOR LEARNING AND GROWTH

What is it that drives a company with a mature benchmarking effort into becoming a recognized leader? What characteristics make a company truly outstanding? After observing the operations of over 200 companies, there are some trends that are characteristic of the leading companies—those that are the benchmark and are admired for strong performance:

♦ The company is committed to performance improvement.

♦ The company focuses consistently on its core business.

♦ The company maintains close contact with customers.

♦ The company builds strong partnerships with key suppliers.

♦ The company concurrently improves quality and productivity.

♦ The company maintains a controlled cost consciousness.

♦ The company gains competitive advantage from applications of technology.

How did these organizations get that way? How did they learn that these characteristics would lead to success? The real question is: How did they learn? The answer is that these companies tend to use all measures at their command to build awareness of change opportunities: They conduct market research; they belong to intercompany networks; they support professional associations; they belong to industry and trade associations; they monitor technical developments and patent issues in their related fields; and they benchmark. Some of the very best have tied all of these elements into a learning system—a system for sharing and recording information. In *Strategic Benchmarking*, I described the Xerox method for sharing with its BEST electronic network and benchmarking bulletin board.[12] The coordination of information from all of these sources—its collection, processing, and communication—is a key ingredient to becoming a learning organization. The use of a strategic approach to benchmarking is also the next phase that most companies who are benchmarking need to emphasize along their growth path.

Strategic benchmarking can lead to a transformational learning experience by seeking out opportunities for increased competitive advantage and by challenging the organization to increase the competence of its employees and the capability of its processes while driving the company toward solid measures of business success. Even though benchmarking may be a necessary stimulant to learning and growth, it is not an end in itself. One thing that benchmarking studies do not provide is good insight into how emerging or new technologies may be applied in process redesign. Therefore, it is important to understand how the trends in information technology are converging on the new workplace and what it will look like as they come to fruition. So, let's move on to Chapter 7.

7

Information Technology Provides Enablers

What is at rest is easy to hold;
What has not yet given a sign is easy to plan for;
The brittle is easily shattered;
The minute is easily scattered;
Act on it before it comes into being;
Order it before it turns into chaos.

Lao Tzu, *Te-Tao Ching*

INFORMATING THE WORKPLACE

"Processing information into new products is the industry of the future" and "Information is the currency of the future." These are the two conclusions that I have drawn after studying the "futurists" of the past 15 years. Interestingly enough, they appear to be right on track—especially John Naisbitt and Soshana Zuboff. While John Naisbitt taught that information has an economic value, and has forecast the ability of the "smart machine" to re-create business activities, Shoshana Zuboff has observed that knowledge has become a strategic value that has already greatly shifted the activities of the worker and the workplace.[1,2,3] As Zuboff says, the workplace has become informated—information technology has been applied in ways that not only contribute to more effective operations, but also reflect on the operating process in a way that creates a new perspective. The initial applications of information technology were on automating the work process—substituting technology for human labor to perform tasks in a more reliable, repetitive fashion. However, work process automation did not

126

provide the new insights that result from informating the workplace. Indeed, applications of the informated workplace extend the capability of individual workers to process knowledge and to apply technology that allows them to learn in wholly new and different ways. Even the meaning of knowledge has changed in the informated work environment.

KNOWLEDGE AND THE SCIENTIFIC METHOD

In a historical sense, our society has placed the value of knowledge on a hierarchical scale. For instance, scientific knowledge has been accorded the highest level of value. Scientific knowledge is a body of statistically proven and codified laws, theorems, and procedures that either have been or could be validated and verified by an independent investigator. Scientific knowledge is accepted as *TRUTH* in our society. However, we are beginning to become more suspicious and skeptical because the ultimate truth of such knowledge relies on the value system of the observer and analyst—will they be the objective investigators and reporters that we expect? Despite our concerns on the validity of some research efforts, in general, it is still the common belief that the methods of scientific research produce the best understanding of the truth in nature, according to the paradigm with which we interpret these facts.[4]

The next valuation of knowledge is the level of knowledge that comes from judgment. Judgment is a set of propositions that are widely held and accepted by a body of experts. Judgments may be made in terms of law, probability, or heuristic rules that indicate the "common beliefs" of a set of subject matter experts or even the society as a whole. Judgment interprets the meaning of data (either verbal data or analytic data). The trouble with judgment is that there are always dissenting opinions regarding interpretation. These differences can weigh heavily on the mind of some portion of the deciding body (for example, the dissenting opinion found within a ruling by a nation's high court). To deal with this problem, the idea of consensus has been introduced—we will act on the commonly held judgment and minority opinions will be heard, considered, evaluated, and even potentially followed. The fair hearing is the most important part of consensus. However, by following the consensus process, the minority agree that they will abide by and support the group outcome after they have been fairly heard.

The third level of knowledge is that of experience, where knowledge is recognized as a set of transactions or observations that may be recorded in a history of events. These events have characteristics that can be known and measured. Experience is the world of data and data analysis. It is more highly considered than the last level of knowledge—intuition. Intuition represents potential knowledge that exists as educated guesses, prophetic forecasts, or intelligent insights that may not be fully supported by observable facts. The understanding of this valuation hierarchy for knowledge is an important aspect to understanding the knowledge worker in the newly informed workplace. Also of importance is understanding the traditional sequence for planting, harvesting, storing, and distributing knowledge (sometimes called the scientific method).

The scientific method begins with the proposition of a hypothesis—a state or condition that is to be proven or disproven by an analytic procedure. The set of conditions under which the hypothesis may be proven is then determined, and a set of events is then observed, represented in an analytical form, collected for consideration, and processed by an analytical method to produce data. This data is then manipulated, presented, and interpreted to become transformed into information. Information, once tested, validated, and codified, becomes knowledge. The value system that underlies the pursuit of knowledge is procedural once the hypothesis has been formed. It is only a matter of following the steps. This means that the primary activities of the knowledge worker will be in initiating the sequence of the knowledge search—the intuitive or creative moment where the hypothesis is conceived—and the act of problem solving when the procedural search for knowledge breaks down. Thus the workplace of the future will reward the innovative worker who can create the ideas that drive this process and the problem solver who can sort through the morass of details to come up with the winning solution. The middle steps of the scientific method will become informated work processes because they lend themselves to "knowledge-ware" applications. So, what work will a knowledge worker do?

THE KNOWLEDGE WORKER

The informating of the workplace will result in a transition of work from the manual and highly functional craft-based skills to the information processing and analyzing skills of a new computer age. In so doing, the workplace will transition: Knowledge workers will become the dominant worker-type and the industrial workforce will become a minority. The effective employment of knowledge workers will become the critical success factor for increasing productivity in the knowledge-driven organization. As Naisbitt predicted: "In an information society, human resources are any organization's competitive edge."[5]

The transition from an industrial environment to an information environment means that there consequently will be a transformation in myopic activity-level work processes. The nature of work will shift from functional to cross-functional, from individual to groups, from fixed procedures to alternative paths, from structured organizations to virtual organizations, from work groups to networks of problem solvers. The entire process by which we do work will change. Why is this perspective important?

Information technology is the primary stimulant for this transformation. It is the tool of the knowledge worker—the effective integration of information technology with work processes can lead to flattened organizations, more flexible and adaptive work processes, and more reliable and responsive outputs.

This is the stimulant for most reengineering projects—they have been driven by a desire to capitalize on the promise of efficiency and effectiveness that is available through the better use of information technology. But, if information technology integration is so important, then why hasn't the automation of work processes provided a better outcome? Let's consider this question from the perspective of the value chain. The value chain has changed over time since the preinformation age. The value chain was once a sequential set of events. However, the pressure for decreased time-to-market in new product development has collapsed the value chain into a set of concurrent processes that have overlapping phases. The value chain is no longer primarily physically paced, moving as quickly as the product can be transformed from an initial breadboard device into a tested, producible, and marketable product. The physical product is becoming less important than the logical product: the drawings, the text results, the simulations, and the data analyses. Ford estimates that 70 percent of the product's value is added by the design process and less than 10 percent by the production process. A lot of nonproductive activity is built around the historical value chain: both in the timing of the product-driven activities and in the bloated overhead structure of many organizations. In addition to its focus on the production process, automation activities have also been focused on overhead functions that deliver little value. The bureaucracy of a vertical organization's hierarchy and its overhead-consuming and time-consuming functions contribute low added value for the product. Thus, the principal problem that automation has faced is its focus on the low-to-no-value-adding elements of the value chain—physical production and overhead functions— not on knowledge processing.[6]

Why is knowledge processing so important? A study by Deloitte-Touche indicated that as much as 10 percent to 30 percent of a company's information is stored on-line in databases, while the remaining 70 percent to 90 percent is stored in documents that are only read reluctantly, if at all.[7] This finding is important because, today, documents are two-dimensional conveyors of textual and graphical information that hold the majority of the company's knowledge about its customers, suppliers, employees, processes, products, and services. Documents help to clarify situations, convince decision makers, and encourage action. The production of documents consumes a lot of corporate costs (that resources are consumed throughout the entire sequence of creating, printing, distributing, storing, accessing, sorting, and evaluating documents is not often considered when we "put it in writing for the record"). Xerox has found that about 60 percent of its white collar workers spend over half of their time processing documents. The implication of this observation is that knowledge workers may be even less productive than their industrial counterparts. What do knowledge workers produce? They produce both information and documents that are consumed by the organization and its customers, suppliers, and stakeholders. But, the majority of information is not used effectively. To increase the productivity of an organization, it must increase its ability to process documents more effectively. What most organizations need is a more strategic application of information and document technology to permit knowledge workers to make better use of the full corporate knowledge base available.[8]

STRATEGIC INFORMATION SYSTEMS

In this emerging age of the knowledge worker, there will be a shift in how managers perceive the utility of information systems. A hint of this transition can be recognized in the realignment of information system labels: Some of the more systemic planning applications of *management* information systems are now labeled *strategic* information systems. These strategic information systems (SIS) refer to applications of information technology that are used to support or shape the policies and competitive strategy of an enterprise.[9] Any such SIS that seeks to deliver sustained competitive advantage must be managed as a continuous innovation process—one that keeps re-creating new advantages that drive the customer's perception of exciting quality in new product features relative to the performance of competitors.[10]

There are two linkages for the innovative management of an SIS and the process for business systems engineering. One touch point is at the start of the technology assessment where innovation is needed to discover those unique organizational attributes that can be leveraged by information technology. This implies that the information system strategy is a product or derivative of the enterprise-wide business strategy.[11] (In Chapter 8, a planning process will be presented as part of the policy deployment methodology that comprehends this requirement.) The information system strategy should focus on those business changes that achieve a significant return through the application of information technolgy and should be the result of the completion of the problem-solving process where the technology assessment is evaluated relative to the business needs. The second touch point of SIS and business systems engineering comes during the implementation process as the project team is bringing out the new work way.

While the information-systems project team can be greatly motivated by the creation of a clean-slate unconstrained implementation of technology, the team's users will typically feel threatened by the technological and sociological barrage of redesigned work processes.[12] While an unconstrained approach to strategic change is not affordable for most business organizations to swallow whole—they will need to eat the elephant one bite at a time—the human impact of such an abrupt transition should be questioned, even if it is affordable. This is because the productivity of workers is related to their higher feelings of self-esteem and worth as well as their need for security. People concerned about their personal and team security and who find their self-worth is threatened by a new work way will not be in a good place to accept new technology. For these reasons, it is an absolute imperative that the workers participate in the process redesign as well as the evaluation of the technology developments that will be implemented in their work process. One early major reengineering project at Xerox was jeopardized by this lack of involvement and communication with the people in the process who would be affected by the change. As a result, that project was never completed. United Services Automobile Association (USAA) had a similar experience. Bill Flynn, senior vice president for corporate planning and quality management, observed that: "Technology must support the employee who ultimately deals with our customers. The system must be a tool of the employee-user." If the employees do not accept the new work way or they resist the technology, then it is because the implementation touch point of business systems engineering has failed.

While this discussion would indicate that the introduction of new technology should be gradual, it should also flow as rapidly as the front line and staff employees can both assimilate the change and appreciate the benefits both to themselves and their customers. This "reasoned" approach to new technology introduction will help to make the necessary transition to the age of the knowledge worker as smooth as possible for both the workers and their customers. A side benefit to a gradual implementation of an information system change strategy is that the change can deal more effectively with incorporation of emerging technologies. This requires the technology assessment to account for the trends in technology developments and understand how these trends may benefit the long-term change roadmap of the organization.[13]

Such transitions are never easy: They are gut-wrenching to the psyche of the employee, and they require both a new way of working and a new way of looking at the job. Information technology supports this with both software (groupware, electronic mail, and relational databases) and hardware (networks and multimedia), the most exciting innovations being groupware and multimedia.

GROUPWARE AND THE NEW WORK WAY

The way that we work has changed ever since Xerox developed a capability for drawing people together on an on-line network to share information.[14] Networks first provided access for individual workers to share data and software with their local team. Networking also increased the access of problem solvers to information and to other problem solvers. However, there was still a boundary—individuals had to work as individuals and then merge their completed work together into a final product. Groupware allows teams to cross that boundary and increase the efficiency of their shared problem-solving assets by allowing these individuals to work together in the same logical space on the computer. Because the computer has become the workplace, groupware allows the virtual operation of a business team—members may be in various geographic locations and yet still share their thoughts and build their documents in a common, logical environment. Like electronic mail, groupware disrupts organizational hierarchies by permitting people to communicate with others outside their local organization. However, groupware differs from electronic mail in that electronic mail permits one-to-one or one-to-many types of communication while groupware permits many-to-many communications.

The most popular type of groupware is represented by a single product, Lotus Notes®. It combines a sophisticated messaging system with databases of work records, memoranda, and electronic documents. It changes the way that information and documents are managed in an organization. Notes operates under a different principle for communication responsibility than does electronic mail. With electronic mail, the sender of the message must identify all of the individuals who need the information contained in the message. With Lotus Notes®, the sender of the message forwards the message to a topical bulletin board, and anyone who needs information regarding that specific topic can access the bulletin board and read what associates are thinking and doing.

One industry report on this subject concluded that groupware may be an unavoidable information processing improvement. Since groupware can increase the "mind share" of the corporate knowledge worker by sharing the same logical space with coworkers in a real-time operating environment, it can provide a tremendous advantage over the more linear systems used for document processing today. This equates to improvements in white-collar productivity through both cycle time reduction and increased performance through better communication. In other words, groupware can increase competitive advantage—particularly if your competitors are not using it. This report also listed the lessons learned by various companies that have been using groupware. Some of the most significant lessons are:

◆ Groupware will change the way that businesses work.

◆ Greater access to information means that workers must take more responsibility to access the information and to contribute to the ongoing dialogs and activities on the bulletin boards that define their work.

◆ Groupware will be most adaptable to companies that have flexible cultures. Management has developed the philosophy that the best decision—improved and modified by group contribution—is the desired outcome rather than one that may be branded as the contribution of a specific manager.

◆ Groupware should be applied to specific business problems: tracking product design team progress; developing business proposals; recording and conducting work team meetings; or scheduling team calendars. There is a tendency to use groupware as a social bulletin board rather than a work bulletin board.[15]

One barrier to the implementation of groupware is the experience that many managers have with "junk E-mail"—the fact that so many other people believe that they must send this message to you. People then feel obligated to read the mail. At Compaq Computer Corporation, I would get between 30 and 80 electronic messages a day. This would be in addition to the 10 to 30 telephone calls, not to mention the 3 to 6 inches of "hard copy" mail. One fear of managers is that this situation will only get worse with the advent of groupware, which exponentially expands the available information. One way around this dilemma, however, is agent technology.

Agent technology acts like an executive secretary to help workers filter and sort through information in bulletin boards and computer files to find exactly what they need. It uses artificial intelligence and hypertext-like capabilities to identify and alert their "principal" to the presence of interesting mail. Although this capability is not currently on Lotus Notes®, you can bet that it will be soon!

Groupware will enable businesses to develop wholly new structures where the business team will be the basic building block, and the need for cross-functional knowledge and rapid response to market demands will move organizations away from fixed hierarchies and the matrix organization. These types of teams will focus on assigned objectives that require innovative solutions. Such teams operate under disciplined processes that drive for the completion of their task. Teams in this mode will operate together for a time period and then dissolve as the project has been completed. Examples of this phenomenon already exist in R&D project teams, proposal generation teams, and "tiger" teams that are charted to fix a particularly perplexing problem. Groupware helps to encourage the transition to these business teams by breaking down functional barriers through an expanded access to "function-specific" information that had not been allowed into the organization's common databases; creating a need for a shared language in order to communicate more effectively across functional boundaries; and providing the technical infrastructure that permits company-wide dialogue.[16,17,18]

INFORMATION TECHNOLOGY PUSH VS. PROCESS PULL

In this changing world, we must evaluate our motives for change: Why and how we are identifying and selecting the changes that we make? The strength of the perspective of business as a system is that it avoids engineering business processes by technology push and encourages process pull. Technology push—implementing groupware, the client-server architecture, and multimedia capability because it is there and people are talking about it—is a popularist approach to business systems management. In an organization that is driven by technology push, the impact on the bottom line is difficult to perceive. It is similar to the vast investment of General Motors in automation products that did not deliver price reductions, retained earnings, stock dividends, or increased share price. In short, the "improvements" have not been accrued in a financial sense. On the other hand, process pull—where the business process calls for the simultaneous use of differing data types and simultaneous, short-term involvement of people on project teams— requires a groupware/multimedia solution to optimize white-collar productivity.

A few weeks before writing this chapter, I was struck by a particular half-hour discussion with a colleague. As we were talking on the telephone, my colleague began to discuss an article. When he asked for an opinion on a particular paragraph, I said "fax it to me." Within a minute, the fax was spitting out the article, and I quickly scanned it and realized a more detailed response was required. I scanned the article into my word processing software, edited a response around the section, and modemed the response back to my friend. I had used all three of my telephone lines and four different kinds of electronic expressions of the same or related information. I was almost in a connected multimedia office. For the first time, I recognized the value of a single system that could accomplish all of these activities. I began to drool. I am a technophile and have always stayed up with the latest in technology (we have five computers for a two-person family), but now I could envision a more productive workspace because of a different use of this technology.

John Naisbitt has continued his prognostications about the future of the workplace. In *Global Paradox*,[19] Naisbitt discusses the power of the telecommunications industry to form strategic alliances with international partners and focus its development efforts on blended technologies that will create a global network connecting personal computers in a way that will allow groupware to more successfully create virtual economic entities without geopolitical boundaries. In this age, information technology will drive change in the same way that manufacturing technology had driven change from the mid-1800s until the late 1900s. Document imaging is one of the technologies that will influence the creation of a profoundly different workplace. Document imaging eliminates the need for sequential processing of documents—different departments can process different parts of the same document simultaneously (for example, an insurance application could be reviewed by underwriting, credit, health, and other functions without passing the paperwork back and forth). Significant changes can come to the workplace through the appropriate use of information technology.[20] Naisbitt sees the similarity between the merging of trade zones into a single worldwide economy and the merging of telecommunications networks into a single worldwide network. This "evolution in telecommunications technology is creating a revolution in information sharing."[21] When everything is linked to everything else, then the virtual business opportunities will be limited only by our imagination. What will happen as this new world order of the information society opens up new ways of working? This question needs to be evaluated in terms of the impact of this evolving technology on both work processes and the knowledge worker of the future.

BEYOND THE TECHNICAL HORIZON

How do information technology solutions fit with the systems engineering methods? Using information technology has been a critical factor in most of the published reengineering studies. It will remain a crucial factor in the systems engineering projects of tomorrow as the groupware paradigm marries with some of the capabilities of the adaptive methods and decision-making mechanisms of artificial intelligence as supported by a multimedia environment. But, what is the real contribution of information technology to business systems engineering?

In reality, the contribution of information technology comes in two distinct waves. In the first wave, the technology assessment provides enlightenment of the possible. It helps to expand the vision of potential business transformations beyond what would be discovered by looking only at the organization's past or by benchmarking other organizations that may have been restricted in their options for technology implementation. Second, during the implementation process, the team's ability to redesign a process more rapidly than it can implement the redesign creates a frustration—leading to the request to use rapid prototyping of the solution as a means to simulate how the final systems improvement will operate. These contributions were also discussed as potential roadblocks for strategic information systems. However, the momentum for change must not ignore the basic fear of the organization for the uncertain future that the change may bring. Shoshana Zuboff painted a picture of the future workplace: "Imagine this scenario: Organizational leaders recognize the new forms of skill and knowledge needed to truly exploit the potential of an intelligent technology. They direct their resouces toward creating a work force that can exercise critical judgment as it manages the surrounding machine systems. Work becomes more abstract as it depends upon understanding and manipulating information. This marks the beginning of new forms of mastery and provides an opportunity to imbue jobs with more comprehensive meaning. A new array of work tasks offer unprecedented opportunities for a wide range of employees to add value to products and services."[22] But, what will this new informated workplace mean to the knowledge worker?

THE ONCE AND FUTURE ROLE OF THE INFORMATION SPECIALIST

For many years, the staff support functions have secretly envied the financial staff. They always have the ear of the top management and their contribution is always recognized, even though they produce only overhead and provide little value-added to the customer. Of course, the financial community sees things differently. They are the troubleshooters who have to bail out the line and staff functions. They don't know how to manage in a prudent manner and need to be constrained by a "second set of eyes." I am by no means comparing myself to Martin Luther King, however, I too, have a dream. My dream is that groupware and the new information technologies will lead to the consolidation of all staff functions and the development of a new type of professional: the staff officer who can fluidly move from accounting and finance issues to human resource issues to quality and reliability issues to strategic planning and marketing research issues to information systems issues (see note 3 in Chapter 5 for supporting ideas). This vision could provide the ultimate simplicity to increase white-collar productivity among the functions of the professional staff—individuals who are cross-trained in the technologies and processes that support the line business and are capable of moving from one area to another without significant retraining.[23] Of course, this is exactly the foundation that most MBA programs provide. The synergy of actually applying this model would give a lower head count requirement for staff positions.[24] My reasoning is that most of the staff operations are driven by either the planning or the reporting calendar. This fact leaves some "quiet times" in the calendar for all of the traditional staff functional organizations. By overlapping the duties of the staff team, the staff can redesign its calendar to allow the planning and reporting functions to be more integrated (as they should be anyhow) and then create process teams (that follow the quality improvement process) to deal with the noncalendar-driven staff projects. This would focus the staff-driven special projects and also eliminate the competition that exists in the "first among the staff" game that is played in too many management teams. Combined with the information access and the white-collar productivity increases available from groupware and multimedia, the net result of this vision would be that the current specialization of business administration would, once again, become generalized. As John Naisbitt said: "We are moving from the specialist who is soon obsolete to the generalist who can adapt."[25, 26, 27]

Is it possible to consolidate all of the planning and reporting functions? Yes, the method for doing this is called policy deployment—the subject of Chapter 8.

8

Policy Deployment Fosters Teamwork

If you repeatedly accumulate Virtue, then there is nothing you can't overcome.
Lao Tzu, *Te-Tao Ching*

ALIGNMENT: IN SEARCH OF INTEGRATION

What is the major challenge of senior management? Some of today's business leaders are agreed on the need for alignment. Peter Senge says that "alignment is the necessary condition before empowering the individual will empower the whole team."[1] Senge calls alignment a "commonality of direction," the "coherent light of the laser," and a condition where "individual's energies harmonize."[2] He calls this state a precondition for team learning. Two types of alignment are necessary for an organization to be able to operate well: vertical and horizontal alignment. Vertical alignment means that the organization has a consistency of objectives from the top of the organization to the grassroots level—that people work together within their functional working groups to get their jobs done. Horizontal alignment means that the organization operates with a common language across functional boundaries—that people act as partners in a team larger than their immediate working group.

Alignment is essential to empowerment because it sets the boundary conditions within which people should act. Ask yourself some thought-provoking questions:

♦ Do your organization's key goals and strategies get appropriate focus throughout the entire organization? Have they in the past?

139

♦ Are you satisfied that your organization's goals comprehend operational work process problems that may have strategic significance?

♦ Are you convinced that the business teams are all investing their resources, time, and attention on the vital few projects that will have the most positive influence on the overall organization's performance? In other words, are we doing the right things?

♦ Are you comfortable that the results of the business team efforts will be effectively and efficiently pursued across the organization, yielding the maximum return on your investment? In other words, are we doing things right?

♦ Do all of your people in the work units understand how their personal objectives contribute to the organization as a whole? In other words, do they have line-of-sight from their position to the organization's strategic direction?

These questions help us to understand the difficulty of alignment. If we are honest with ourselves, then we had some difficulty answering all of these questions in an affirmative manner. But, achieving vertical and horizontal alignment is not the end state. The real result that we want is achieving continuous alignment. This means that the organization is capable of adapting to changing conditions because it operates within a set of common principles that allow each member to understand how to act within a framework that will make progress toward the common goals. This degree of organizational alignment is achieved through consensus and fostered by the teamwork created as the senior team works with the entire organization to develop a shared vision and value system that enable people to work together to achieve common goals. How does policy deployment help to foster the kind of teamwork that will allow the organization of today to operate in the chaos of tomorrow? Before I discuss this question, the principal topic of this chapter, I would like to provide an overview of policy deployment.

POLICY DEPLOYMENT: DAMPENING THE RISK AND DEPLOYING CHANGE

Strategic management faces the challenges of balancing an organization's need for innovation to secure its future and efficiency to control its daily operations. Management is a process of eliminating risks and ensuring a future. The challenge for the organization is how to balance the three types of risk it encounters: market risk, product risk, and process risk. To realize the future vision, we must cope with these risks.

Market risk results from intensified competition that may occur when there are swift changes in the tastes or desires of customers, or when competitors change the rules of the game. Product risk occurs when innovations fail to match the competitor's breakthroughs and your organization is caught with an inferior product and a diminishing market share. Process risk comes from failure to meet the competitor's process output levels for quality, cost, and cycle time. If your competitors are more flexible and can create an advantage by managing these three risks better, then they create a competitive advantage.

The problem with risk is that vertical organizations are encumbered by their structure and cannot deal with it well. Dealing with risk requires an organization to be flexible and make rapid decisions, implemented quickly to remain a player in a situation that has gotten out of control. Once a risk situation is detected, the organization is in a reactive and correcting mode, rather than in a proactive and coping mode. What difference does the organization structure really make? Consider what happens in a vertical organization structure: The hierarchy forces the organization to move slowly and respond only when the senior manager "buys into" the change whose need has been identified much lower in the organization where people are closer to the customer. This "vertical bureaucracy" delays decisions by lengthening the approval process. On the other hand, an empowered team can accelerate change and move fast enough to keep pace with competitors and customer trends. To deal appropriately with market trends, an organization must not create a bureaucratic planning system that has no flexibility. If the customer is always right, then the planning system cannot stray from that ever-changing customer voice. Policy deployment is a system that should allow an organization to stay much closer to its customers and will fit the empowered organization of the future. Why do I make this judgment? Policy deployment systems create a renewal of the organization through a continuing questioning and alignment process. The entire organization is involved in the process of asking questions and becoming aligned to shared directions. How does a management team work on organizational renewal so that it stays "fresh" and able to cope with the risks of business?

Policy deployment refers to a full system that includes both the strategic direction-setting process, called *hoshin kanri* in Japan, and also a daily management system for managing at the operational work process level. Taken together, these two aspects provide an integrated approach to business management. Policy deployment is a step-by-step approach to planning and implementing strategic and operational direction. It uses a systems approach for managing strategic change. The system in this case is the set of core business processes that drive the value chain of the organization.

Management must both create a vision and assess the reality. The vision helps to drive the strategic plan and establishes the direction for planned organizational change. The reality of daily performance helps to drive the operational plan. These plans overlap to form the budget—a set of decisions about how an organization will allocate today's resources to accomplish its short-term needs while striving for its long-term direction. Figure 8–1 illustrates how these two plans overlap to meet the need for considering both perspectives—long term and short term—as part of an integrated planning system.

A policy deployment system is actually a set of four interconnected processes linked together by the organization's planning calendar. These processes provide a systemic approach to managing change:

◆ *Diagnosing Progress:* The process for assessing operating results against both the prior plan and external benchmarks to determine the root cause in the gaps. Four gaps are analyzed: per-

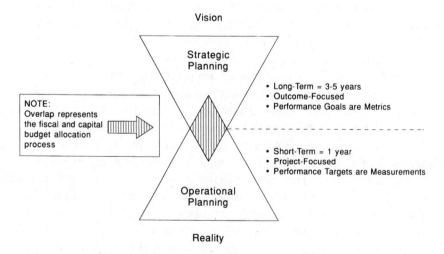

Figure 8–1. Integrated Planning Approach

formance against the standard, performance against the plan, performance against the long-term goal, and performance against the benchmark. The diagnosis also includes an assessment of the organization's process for strategic management; some companies use customized criteria from the U. S. Malcolm Baldrige National Quality Award criteria as a foundation for their process check.

◆ *Setting Direction:* The process of developing—or reviewing, confirming, and, perhaps revising—the enterprise-wide values, vision, mission, core competencies, key process capabilities, key business processes, long-term goals, and long-term strategies.

◆ *Deploying Direction:* The process of creating alignment, forming cross-functional alliances, and securing consensus on the implementation required to accomplish the desired "goal state" of the strategic direction. This also includes the linkage of the long-term plan to the annual operating plan through the resource allocation process—some dare to call it by its common name, "budgeting."

◆ *Managing Direction:* The process for doing the work that has been deployed and checking it through regular reviews of progress for each strategic change project and through daily monitoring of the business fundamentals that form the organization's daily management system.[3]

It is not the intention of this chapter to provide all of the details on policy deployment. The purpose is to demonstrate how policy deployment can foster cross-functional teamwork. I believe that this approach to strategic planning will only work if teams are actively engaged in both the planning and execution phases of the method. For readers who want to investigate this methodology in greater depth, the policy deployment methods of two companies have been shared in open literature: Hewlett-Packard, the pioneer of this method in the United States; and Florida Power & Light, another early implementer of policy deployment.[4] In addition, there is some excellent study material that provides process implementation guidance.[5]

POLICY DEPLOYMENT: FEATURES AND PROCESS

Before going into policy deployment in more detail, I should explain a little about my experience with policy deployment. I was at the Hewlett-

Packard San Diego division in the mid-1980s when *hoshin kanri* was piloted. While at the Hewlett-Packard corporate quality staff, I developed a training course for quality managers on *hoshin kanri* and then consulted to various divisions on their planning processes. I conducted a benchmarking study[6] of 15 companies to determine how they were implementing this process. I served on the GOAL/QPC research committee that studied *hoshin kanri*. I worked with the Xerox senior management team to help redefine its implementation of policy deployment. I have consulted with several organizations to establish their policy deployment systems. I mention these experiences to establish a little credibility on this topic, not as self-aggrandizement. Many people are talking about policy deployment or *hoshin kanri* today, but never have implemented a system. The information in the following paragraphs is the result of these studies, not a brainstormed list of proposals. Now, having said that, how about some beef?

The truth is that most organizations really do not know how to plan. To help managers recognize where they are on the planning development continuum, I developed the transition analysis of the planning process illustrated in Figure 8–2. The desired state represents a mature implementation of policy deployment. How far along is the development of your planning system?

But, what is a policy deployment system? There are two ways to

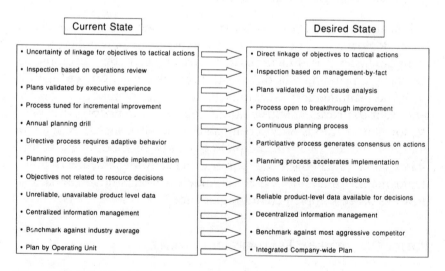

Figure 8–2.   Planning Process Transition

describe it. First, it can be seen as a set of outputs or deliverables of the planning process. Using the architecture for policy deployment processes, we can group the deliverables of a policy deployment system:

♦ *Diagnosing Progress:* Annual review, gap analysis, and root cause analysis.

♦ *Setting Direction:* Values, vision, mission, goals, strategies, objectives.

♦ *Deploying Direction:* Means and targets, cascade and catchball, daily management system, and individual and team objectives.

♦ *Managing Direction:* Implementation plan, daily control, project management, and regular reviews.

These deliverables are developed by following a basic sequence of steps that form a process model for policy deployment. This model does not exist in any one organization. It is a composite formed by combining the methods used in eight different policy deployment implementations. So far, I haven't seen one company's model that I could recommend as robust enough to be used by everyone.

Diagnosing Progress
1. Evaluate business environment—markets, technologies, competitors, etc.
2. Evaluate progress-to-plans (conduct gap analysis and root cause analysis).
3. Evaluate progress-to-benchmarks (conduct gap analysis and root cause analysis).

Setting Direction
1. Envision organizational potential opportunities.
2. Define common purpose and principle-centered values.
3. Determine the function of the business (mission statement).
4. Establish a shared vision (ten- to twenty-year horizon).
5. Assess current performance of business fundamental processes and benchmark.
6. Determine strategic change issues and strategic intent.

7. Prepare long-range goals and strategies (three- to five-year horizon).

8. Develop and communicate annual strategic change issues and direction.

Deploying Direction

1. Translate strategic directions into means and targets to satisfy the plan.

2. Cascade and catchball the plans relative to the daily management system.

3. Escalate unresolved planning issues to senior management.

4. Allocate resources in accordance with planning objectives and guidelines.

5. Translate plans into team and personal objectives.

Managing Direction

1. Deploy objectives and develop plans (Plan).

2. Implement and execute tactical actions (Do).

3. Review progress toward targets on a regular basis—monthly for process owners and quarterly for the senior management team (Check).

4. Evaluate and upgrade the planning process at least annually (Act).

In Japan, not all companies have implemented the *hoshin kanri* planning process. But the companies that have tend to be the leaders among their industry. Lessons learned from the implementation efforts of both Japanese and Western companies (I have discovered less than 40 who have implemented these methods) include:[7]

♦ Implementation of policy deployment is hard work, and it will take several cycles of the process in order to develop a planning system that is mature.

♦ If the process is conducted within an atmosphere of open and honest communications, better mutual decisions will be made. (Messengers of bad tidings should be praised, not shot. The only bad problem is the unknown problem.)

- Develop a measurement map first, then implement the strategic change process.
- Select a critical few breakthrough goals (three to five) to begin the process.
- Integrate planning systems from the beginning—do not create another planning process layer on top of what you already have in place.
- Conducting regular management reviews of progress is essential to success.
- Good data and management by fact is necessary for all reviews and diagnoses (as opposed to management by gut, executive judgment, or group brainstormed guesses).
- Standardization of solutions across similar business units is a goal of reviews.
- Review participants should all use the same methods and forms for presentation.
- Reviews are held only for direct reports or owned processes.
- Reviews are "come as you are," not glossy "dog and pony" shows.
- Reviews are for coaching teams—not for enforcement of policy.
- Reviews are exception-based, examining those areas where plans are not on track.
- During reviews, actions are taken to eliminate problems or unanticipated variables.
- Permanent solutions should be documented, standardized, and shared.

POLICY DEPLOYMENT: THE DUTY TO DIAGNOSE

Management is responsible for oversight of the implementation process. To do this, they should not just barge into an organization and ask for a "dog and pony" show. They should be prepared to probe into the functioning of key business processes by asking diagnostic questions, such as:

1. How are you addressing your customer's priorities?

2. What is your current performance against planning targets and benchmarks?

3. What is the root cause of this gap?

4. What actions have been planned to close this gap?

5. How were these "vital few" actions selected?

6. What is the expected performance outcome of these planned actions in terms of process yield, cost reduction, and cycle time?

7. How have you reallocated resources to achieve this plan, and are there any negative consequences?

POLICY DEPLOYMENT AND TEAMWORK

Now that you understand how policy deployment works, we can consider our focal point: How does it relate to teamwork? In the three-level organizational model described in Chapter 3, the output of the planning process is a harmonious organization—one that works together to design, develop, and deploy policy that is the agreed-upon strategic and operational direction of the enterprise. This is not an exercise that can be delegated. Team learning and team cooperation are essential to make it happen. The review process in policy deployment operationalizes learning for teams and builds a learning capability.

Teams function throughout the policy deployment process. At the enterprise level, the senior management team is ultimately responsible for developing and implementing the business strategy and objectives. The senior management team develops the values, vision, mission, strategic goals, and strategic objectives. The primary metrics that it uses for success are return on assets (or return on investment), market share, and customer satisfaction. This enterprise-wide focus of the senior management team joins in a dialog with the business level team to determine the annual policy of the organization (see Figure 8–3). The business team serves as an advocate for the work process inputs, which are elevated from the operations level. The operations level is responsible for the efficient, effective, and economic operation of work processes. The primary metrics of the operations level are work process productivity and employee satisfaction. The dialog that occurs—this is called catchball—debates balancing the needs of the organization's

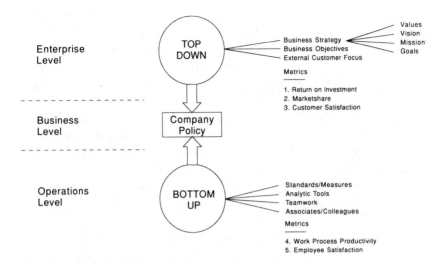

Figure 8-3. Policy Deployment Approach

strategic direction against the needs of its daily work process. Catchball means that a give-and-take process occurs until both sides reach consensus on the direction that should be mutually shared. Many companies that first hear about catchball have some problems with it. Management does not want to give up its responsibility—according to the teams, management wants to micromanage. Teams, according to managers, should stick to their knitting and focus on their work process rather than taking on the whole world for process improvement. However, I believe that the policy deployment methodology must be viewed in its proper context as an empowerment-based planning process. It is the product of the best thinking and deliberation from the entire team, and the result is their joint conclusion of the best course of action. Most companies find that they do not have such a consensus-based planning system.

However, it is an imperative to become an empowered, team-based learning organization that is capable of coping with risk and uncertainty as a daily practice. The implication of the change toward knowledge and information as the key ingredients in business has not yet been fully felt by organizations. As Peter Drucker says: "Because the modern organization consists of knowledge specialists, it has to be an organization of equals, of colleagues and associates. No knowledge ranks higher than another; each is judged by its contribution to the common task rather than by any inherent superiority or inferiority. Therefore, the modern organization cannot be an organization of boss and subordinate. It must be organized as a team."[8] This driving force for teams creates a requirement for a systematic analysis of our organization's structure that supports the team's operations. Jeffrey Pfeffer has analyzed this situation in detail, and I wholeheartedly recommend his book, *Competitive Advantage through People,*[9] as a manifesto for analysis of your own organization's preparedness for managing an empowered workforce. Another equally challenging book was developed by the SANNO Management Development Research Center in Japan, *Vision Management: Translating Strategy into Action.*[10] These two books help management understand how to deploy consensus-based teamwork in an organization.

To optimize a policy deployment system, an organization should have a team-based structure.[11] While this is not a prerequisite for implementing policy deployment, it does make the planning system work better. Team structures provide the environment where consensus and catchball can operate best. Policy deployment does foster teamwork.

PART IV

Applications of Business Systems Engineering

9

Engineering Product Design

Creating Competitiveness in the Automotive Industry

No need to leave your door to know the whole world;
No need to peer through your windows to know the Way of Heaven.
The further you go, the less you know.
Therefore the Sage knows without going,
Names without seeing,
And completes without doing a thing.

Lao Tzu, *Te-Tao Ching*

CASE STUDY HIGHLIGHTS

This case study illustrates the effect that one company's efforts at benchmarking and process redesign can have on the rest of its industry. Toyota has led the automotive industry in work process streamlining and business process integration. However, the lessons of mass production that Toyota implemented in its factories were learned from Henry Ford and Alfred Sloan. The American automotive manufacturers were initially slow to respond to the lean manufacturing revisionism of Eiji Toyoda and Taiichi Ohno, but soon Ford, Chrysler, and General Motors focused their individual efforts to increase their productivity and create more customer value in their products. The move toward lean manufacturing has spread to European manufacturers who

153

are also developing their response to the Japanese automotive industry challenge. This study of the automotive industry provides a model for the way in which businesses will compete in the future—how they will improve by watching each other and seeking the best ideas in industry for their own process improvements. This same model could be observed today in other global industries such as personal computers, consumer electronics, and photographic equipment—each watches and is influenced by the way its competitors do business.

REDUX EVERYTHING!

Engineering a business system is normally the business of one individual organization. However, in some of the most competitive industries, the actions of one firm may closely influence, and sometimes mirror, the actions of its competition. Much of the initial emphasis on reengineering has been on simplifying and streamlining business systems in order to develop a more efficient working environment. Nowhere has this been more evident than in the automotive industry, where the industry as a whole has followed the lead of Toyota Motor Company and attacked time-to-market—the ability to move a product from the concept phase to a marketable car in record time. This concerted effort on time reduction has focused on the product development processes. The interactions and learnings among the leading automobile companies illustrate the importance of both competitive analysis and benchmarking as sources of learning that allow a company to remain competitive.

THE VIPER STRIKES WITH SPEED

To me, the Dodge Viper's speed is exciting. Not just the sports car's acceleration, but the speed with which Chrysler brought the Viper to market. The Chrysler team's project managers have credited internal bureaucratic rule breaking, teamwork, and the personal involvement of craftspeople as reasons for the car's roll-out in less than three years—an unheard of cycle time for an all-new Detroit car design.

Chrysler's product development approach struck a familiar chord with me as a longtime industrial history buff. Its approach is reminiscent of a time when craft production was the predominant manufacturing type in the pre-mass-production era that Henry Ford introduced. Chrysler's Viper team returned to that model using craftspeople to design and build its product. This historical similarity raised several questions: Does the Viper project approach signal a larger trend within the American automotive industry—an industry that had elevated mass production to the throne of greatness and relegated craft production to the hobby shop? Has the industry come full circle—both figuratively and literally around the world—to relearn the lessons of its earlier days as improved by its Japanese competitors? Is Detroit attempting to regain its former industrial superiority by returning to an empowered workforce of teams? Was the U.S. automobile industry teaching, and then expecting, the 1990s cobblers of cars to work in small teams, improve their work and business processes, benchmark other manufacturers, and use information technology more advantageously, thereby outperforming their world-class competitors?

The Viper is a specialty car, and some would argue that its time-to-market performance should not be considered an omen of the American automotive industry's return to a more competitive basis, but merely another instance of "skunk works" performance by a special projects team. However, Viper is but one of many recent cases where a U.S. automaker has successfully remade itself in the face of its need for increased business competitiveness.[1] Competitiveness in the automobile industry is its Holy Grail. The Viper project appeared to combine both an efficient and effective product design with a streamlined manufacturing process. What have they done differently below the level of public relations releases?

The Chrysler designers of the Viper production line originally considered implementing a computer integrated manufacturing system with an overhead conveyor system to move frames, automated guided vehicles to deliver parts, and robots to assemble the final product. This kind of expense for a specialty car was not warranted. But, as Howard Lewis, plant manager, Viper New Mack, tells the story, the expensive little speedster was not about high-tech. It was designed with "essential technology," and the production process would be "about people and craftsmanship." So, Chrysler used teams of "craftspeople," and returned to the basics of production.[2]

This wasn't the way that engineering had been done in the past. Before, "styling did its job, and handed it off to advanced engineering. They did their job, and handed it off to product engineering, which did their job, and flipped the ball to manufacturing. We sat there fuming."[3] There would be no way that the current manufacturing processes could be used to build the car that had been through this sequential design. It wasn't even clear that the real needs of the customer would be expressed throughout this process, even if the stylist or engineer knew them in the first place!

Buyers in the 1990s demand cars that are more customized to fit their personal tastes in styles, stereos, color shades, and options. Buyers want innovation even faster than the 1980s leaders, the Japanese automakers, could drive change. Change in this market is being more strongly influenced by luxury car features moving down the car chain into the mass market product lines. To deliver today, Chrysler, Ford, General Motors, and especially Toyota-America, have enfolded, like origami, Western workplace culture with what is called lean production—a modified version of the Toyota Production System. And the resulting production process design is, in fact, transitioning U.S. automakers to a more competitive position after many years of arrogant complacency and failure to ask serious questions that would have led them to engineer their business systems in a whole new way. How did this all begin?

THE FORD FOUNDATION

The automotive industry casts a long shadow over the way we think about production. It has gone through two major transitions in this century. The first was led by Henry Ford and Alfred Sloan who mastered mass production applications in the automotive industry. The second transition was built upon the original principles of Ford to produce what is called today "lean production" and has also been termed "Just-in-Time" or *kanban,* or "the Toyota Production System"—a contribution of Eiji Toyoda and Taiichi Ohno.[4] This system contains the concepts of concurrent engineering that are the foundation of the Viper team's success. Just what was the foundation that Ford laid for the rest of the century?

Production of Henry Ford's horseless carriages followed a cookie-cutter model. For customers, having one of Ford's basic black autos was all that mattered. Initially, styling was important only in what the occupants of the motorized wagons wore. And even as General Motors worked to improve upon Ford's mass production systems, Americans wanted variety only if it was inexpensive and did not disturb the philosophy that cars were produced only to satisfy the society's need for transportation.[5]

The Ford and GM product development processes fit what consumers wanted in the 1920s through the mid-1950s. Labor was cheap, and people were hired and fired as the product demand rose and fell. Automakers felt no particular pressure to redesign basic automobile styles. Suppliers, like the workers themselves, were secondary and could be abandoned if necessary. Huge inventories could be kept on hand because business was booming. And the minimum amount of product inspection was performed, and only the more obvious defects were reworked to satisfy the customer's demand for quality.

The Ford Motor Company's River Rouge plant laid the foundation for the modern car manufacturing processes. There, management was committed to keeping the line of standardized parts and assemblies moving. Henry Ford wrote that taking work to workers was a key principle of production. Conveyors, he said, were one of many means to productivity ends.[6]

Productivity was an important focus of the Ford plant, and Ford was one of the first to evaluate it. Familiar with Frederick W. Taylor's then popular scientific management methods that were the foundation of industrial engineering,[7] Henry Ford measured every human action. Finding that with large supply rooms, for example, workers lined up at windows to check out tools, he initiated change. "That was a waste. We found it often cost us twenty-five cents' worth of a man's time (not counting overhead) to get a thirty-cent tool."[8] He also learned that waste was wrong. "Having a stock of raw material or finished goods in excess of requirements is waste—which, like every other waste, turns up in high prices and low wages. The time element in manufacturing stretches from the moment the raw material is separated from the earth to the moment when the finished product is delivered to the ultimate consumer. It involves all forms of transportation and has to be considered in every national scheme of service. It is a method of saving and serving which ranks with the application of power and the division of labor."[9]

Ford understood the absolute importance of a short product cycle time, which is why he defined it from the moment the raw materials for a Ford were extracted from the earth to the time a buyer drove away. He didn't call his process by the names of supply chain management, Just-in-Time, or lean production—however, the principles were there. Some 50 years before Toyota showed how to efficiently use Just-in-Time manufacturing, Ford knew to build a plant so that materials could be trucked to within 20 feet of the point on a production line and made available when and where they were needed.

Ford kept his parts and products standardized. That was a key principle. When the company purchased Lincoln, he apologized for its having a customized, nonstandard luxury model. He truly believed he was in the service of a society, and automobiles were the currency of change toward a better standard of living for all people. Ford said: "The true end of industry is not the bringing of people into one mold; it is not the elevating of the working man to a false position of supremacy—industry exists to serve the public of which the working man is a part. The true end of industry is to liberate the mind and body from the drudgery of existence by filling the world with well-made, low-priced products."[10]

Following Henry Ford, and improving on his ideas, could also have saved the earth much of the human ecological ravages. In 1924, Ford wrote that his plants recycled lumber from crates and packing, and replaced wooden car parts with metal to save trees. "Saving timber," he wrote, "was as much a matter for the shop as for the forest." Also: ". . . at the present rate of consumption the country's wood will hardly last beyond fifty years."[11] Americans didn't become alarmed at depletion of the first-growth forest until the 1960s.

While Ford was still active in the Ford Motor Company, successful Japanese businesspeople began traveling to the United States to study the great Ford factories, as well as those of Alfred Sloan at General Motors. One of those world travelers was inventor Sakichi Toyoda, the founder of the Toyota Motor Company. Based on what he saw, he convinced his son, Kiichiro Toyoda, to take the family enterprise into automobiles. Expanding from textiles, the Toyodas adapted mass production to their customers' needs. The Toyodas would oversee the development of an efficient and effective product design system. It was Eiji Toyoda, nephew to Kiichiro Toyoda, who would visit the Ford plant in the spring of 1950, as his uncle had done in 1925, and begin the vision of "lean production" that became the Toyota Production System.[12]

THE TOYOTA TRANSITION

While many U.S. automakers lost touch with the valuable legacy of Henry Ford's manufacturing lessons, one foreign manufacturer who didn't was Taiichi Ohno, the Toyota company's production chief and the father of what has become known as the Toyota Production System. Henry Ford provided a role model for Ohno: Ford was able to mine iron ore on Monday and produce a car using that same ore on Thursday. Ford's focus on speed and waste elimination provided the focus for Ohno. As Norm Bodek, publisher of Shingo and Ohno's English works through Productivity Press, observed: "Mr. Ohno just simply updated Henry Ford."[13]

Updating Ford was what actually produced breakthroughs for Toyota. Where production workers on the Ford assembly lines fought the mindlessness of boring and repetitive tasks, Toyota eliminated job classifications to give workers flexibility and increase their participation in the development of the product. Toyota's factory became a role model for Japanese industry—building upon the nation's response to limited natural resources and the Japanese tradition of individual craftsmanship that holistically aligned the arts with commerce.

The Toyota Production System (TPS) is a method of managing production flows to stay in tune with the demand of the customer. The TPS has been called a streamlined adaptation of Western practices for materials management. In the TPS, production is smoothed to an even flow—parts flow smoothly from "mother earth" to final production without the buffers of inventory that existed in the Ford production system. Waste, which Henry Ford called a "crime," is eliminated entirely. As is warehousing. And cycle time is greatly reduced.[14]

Although Ohno had no quarrel with Henry Ford, he was uncharacteristically critical of Ford's successors for riding the weary horsepower of a once great system, and failing to jetison the processes that didn't work. Ohno summarized Ford's successors as striving for "the larger the lot size, the better" in a market that was starting to require the opposite.[15]

The Toyota Motor Company had, by the 1960s, continually reengineered its production lines based on the drive toward a standard of process excellence. Toyota's management held to the theory that if it honed the design and production system, market share would follow. This was proven correct.[16]

Not coined until 1978, the phrase "Just-in-Time manufacturing" describes a process that Henry Ford and Taiichi Ohno had unknowingly joined hands in developing. While visiting America to benchmark the U.S. automakers, Ohno said he learned *kanban*, the communication system for Just-in-Time, from the way that American supermarkets rotate their perishable stock of fruits and vegetables.[17]

The Toyota Production System evolved out of need. Restrictions in the marketplace had caused Toyota to manufacture small quantities of many car varieties in times of low demand. The Japanese plight caused by lack of raw materials and competition against opponents with large market shares and the economies of scale due to mass production, seemed to some an impossible position. But the very difficulty of this situation was what made Toyota, and then other Japanese carmakers and industrialists, engineer production systems that would lead to future success.[18]

In the early 1970s, Toyota led the way in designing an effective and efficient product development process with the pioneering of a design method called Quality Function Deployment (QFD).[19] QFD is a methodology for analysis of customer-perceived product requirements in a way that translates them into design features and ensures that these customer requirements are carried through all the way to the production line.

As Ohno cites, the production system that would propel Toyota into business history was not widely recognized, even in Japan, until the 1973 oil crisis. Without a local supply of oil, the Japanese markets were constrained suddenly, and the effective, efficient, and economic use of all resources became even more important as Japanese growth stagnated.[20] Despite production decreases, Toyota continued to grow during this economic downturn. It succeeded by delivering a wide variety of cars in small quantities. Its production system, with every worker's relentless pursuit of waste elimination, even in a period of slow growth, was able to propel Toyota to world-class levels of productivity.

As this recognition dawned on his Japanese competitors, the respect for Taiichi Ohno grew. Just as Henry Ford had greatly influenced Taiichi Ohno by his emphasis on the elimination of waste in production, so did the Japanese business leader influence his fellow Japanese automakers in the mid-1970s when the world's economic crisis pushed Toyota's product design model to the forefront.

By the time the world had recovered from the Middle East oil embargo and worldwide petroleum supply shock, the Toyota Production System had become recognized as the premier production management system and became the benchmarking target of many industries that sought to decrease costs and increase capital turnover.[21]

Some 30 years before Chrysler developed the Viper, Toyota's management system was using individual craftspeople in self-directed work teams. Ohno saw a relationship between the Japanese approach to teamwork in sports and business. He stated that the Japanese don't compete in business and sports, rather they "seek the way and study it."[22] This Zen-like approach to teamwork can drive a company full of teams to understand their business and then to do what's right for the good of the whole organization. By cooperating through the effective use of teams, an organization can attain *wa* or the harmonious working of the individual members as a whole.

FORD EMBRACES TOYOTA'S METHODS

Ford was one of the companies that had not embraced the Toyota Production System during the 1970s.[23] However, the Ford Motor Company's billion-dollar losses in the early 1980s led to management's reevaluation of quality and the eventual reengineering of the product design system. While not giving itself over entirely to the Toyota Production System of Taiichi Ohno, Ford reinvented its production approach in the way it conceived, designed, and manufactured the Ford Taurus and Mercury Sable, which were the market successes that returned Ford to profitability in the late 1980s.

What did they do? Team Taurus benchmarked the world-leading competitors and looked for features that would "delight the customer"—they incorporated 77 percent of the 400 features that were benchmarked. It redesigned its product development process with an American version of QFD—and it listened to the voice of the customer before developing its design specifications. The result: Sales soared as the car-buying public reacted favorably to this special attention. Ford, the company that had introduced mass assembly-line automaking some 80 years earlier, was a viable industry player once again. By 1987, Ford had reversed its situation—starting the decade with a $1.5 billion dollar loss in 1980 and achieving a $4.6 billion profit in 1987—Ford had gained back 4 percent of its lost market share.[24] With Taurus, U.S. automakers had finally left Sleepy Hollow and awakened from their systemic slumber. Ford learned that it needed not to complain about the way the Japanese conducted business, it needed to focus on providing products that the customer really *did* want. Quality is the value of a product as perceived by the customer. The customers cast their votes for quality by investing from their pocketbooks. Ford learned, the others would soon follow suit.

TOYOTA TEACHES GM: THE NUMMI STORY

The Toyota-General Motors joint venture plant in America, not surprisingly, was the first user of lean production in America. At NUMMI (New United Motors Manufacturing Inc.) in Fremont, California, automaking was a blend of Ford's linear assembly line (because that's how the former GM plant was laid out) and Toyota's Just-in-Time manufacturing process using *kanban,* a card-based communication process that signaled when parts supplies should be replenished. Despite this diverse mixture of production systems, it took a scant two years (from 1984 to 1986) from pilot production for workers, operating in nontraditional (for American manufacturers) team units to become almost as productive as the sister plant in Japan, and more productive than any other GM plant in the world. The numbers of cars rolling off the production lines increased significantly, and the number of problems were decreasing due to the lean production model.[25]

A study of automakers established that the semi-lean model at NUMMI was the best for fostering organizational learning—increasing worker morale while achieving continuous process improvement.[26] Renewing the workforce through active learning is critical to successful implementation of the lean production organization. In this environment, teams have extraordinary responsibility for quality workmanship and self-determination over their manufacturing processes.[27] The by-product of this learning is increased flexibility.

Workers at NUMMI rotate tasks to avoid the mental fatigue that comes from doing repetitive work. Lean production is facilitated by the cross-training of workers in the different jobs of their team. This approach creates a great deal of flexibility in workforce assignments. For instance, when the NUMMI plant needed some very old robots rebuilt for the body shop, the high cost involved caused management to reject buying new robots or having a contractor do the work. So a team of workers was formed, trained, and put to work.[28] What does the American management team think about the use of the Toyota

Production System? Here is what Michael Dodge, vice president of manufacturing for Toyota Motor Manufacturing, U.S.A., has to say: "Today, the emphasis and respect for the individual worker are exemplified. This production system is a method for motivating our team members and assuring quality. Our people make us successful. And we have proven that America has the ability to compete on a global scale."[29]

The 1980s provided an expensive lesson for automakers on how the line worker, engineer, and supplier could together streamline their processes to rapidly transition from paper concepts to high-quality cars. General Motors spent billions through the 1980s on cost reduction by automating direct labor tasks through information technology and computer integrated manufacturing. The American automotive leaders had mistakenly focused on breakthrough improvement driven by technology in order to increase their competitiveness. But when they discovered the solution to productivity malaise, the answer was "fix the process" before even considering automation.

CHRYSLER CAPITALIZES ON FORD AND GM LESSONS

Viper was only one part of the learning process that Chrysler used to bring itself back into the competitive domain. Its LH sedans, during conception, used the same approach as Team Taurus in studying the best in class. The LH team benchmarked the Nissan Maxima for body structure, Acura Legend for engine performance, and Taurus and Chevrolet Lumina for suspension, just to name a few. The outcome: Chrysler introduced three winning models in 1993. Thus, the Dodge Intrepid, Eagle Vision, and Chrysler Concorde were born with the needs of their customers as standard equipment.[30]

An analysis of auto design in 1992 from the research and development angle led Harvard Business School's Marco Iansiti to compare production systems. The Chrysler LH platform, he said, carried the team approach toward fast cycle time the farthest. Iansiti called these new and effective worker units integration teams, and he said they had a systems-focused approach.[31]

While Ford Taurus and Sable had employed a limited team approach, and while Honda had used teams for years, Chrysler's LH cars were using concurrent production to move from concept to drive-out in three years. Chrysler's old system allowed a five-year cycle.

Reading the words of Chrysler's chief designer Thomas Gale is reminiscent of Taiichi Ohno and Henry Ford. Gale said the major changes between the Eagle Optima and the LH design were made for manufacturing efficiency. Gale commented on the redesign of the front windshield pillar of the Chrysler LH. "By drawing the cut lines (the shape of the stamping die) differently, we were able to have almost square door panels. That saves a lot on metal-stamping waste."[32] It's clear that Chrysler has received the message: Eliminate waste and reduce cycle time to become more competitive.

SATURN: A DIFFERENT KIND OF PRODUCTIVE COMPANY— IT'S AMERICAN

Saturn represents a new beginning for General Motors and also a transition from the purely automated facility to one that is a lot more Japanese-like. The Saturn project began in 1982 as a small car project that was aimed at finding a new way to design and manufacture small cars. In January 1985, the Saturn project became the Saturn Corporation, a wholly owned subsidiary of General Motors. The first Saturn cars were introduced to the market in 1990. By 1993 they had captured 2.4 percent of the domestic U.S. market.[33]

GM designed the Spring Hill, Tennessee, Saturn plant from "the ground up" to be the lean production facility that could combat the Japanese invasion of the domestic market's lower end. The Saturn plant is built on the principle of partnership—partnership between the United Automobile Workers of America (UAW) and management, as well as a GM partnership with its suppliers. These relationships were not to become adversarial—they were to take a creative approach and work as a team that would be committed to their customers. Both suppliers and employees are accountable for their work output, and customer feedback information systems provide them with information about field failures within 24 hours of their occurrence. This application of information technology provides a continuous stream of information about production problems. Suppliers, likewise, operate in a paperless ordering environment where they observe the consumption rate of their parts and replenish them as needed. Saturn has defined a lean production facility and then engineered its business around that system.

HONDA RETURNS TO ITS HERITAGE

The Accord from Honda, a product of a reengineered systems approach, was the best-selling car in America from 1989 to 1991. Then the Toyota Camry, Nissan Altima, Ford Taurus, and Chrysler LH all made strong entries into the Accord market. In 1992, the Accord lost its market share leadership to the Ford Taurus—a piece of evidence that the Ford transition toward excellence continued and that Honda had not kept up the pace. But, as Yamaha discovered in the motorcycle business, it's not safe to challenge Honda.[34]

The Honda company had risen to automaking success from its core motorcycle product lines, which it became famous for after World War II. Because Honda had an effective design capablity for small engines, it made an easy transition into slightly larger ones that were used in the small car market. The Honda business strategy was to transition its core competence from a motorcycle product line into an automotive product line.

Boston Consulting Group analysts George Stalk, Philip Evans, and Lawrence E. Shulman said that Honda had two overriding process capabilities that provided strong competitive advantages. The first was dealer management and the second was product realization. Honda's systematic management of dealers for efficiency, independence, and customer satisfaction was leveraged across all of its products—whether the product was a lawn mower, motor scooter, or automobile.[35] Honda developed enthusiastic motorcycle dealers and helped them become successful marketers and managers. When they were done, Honda's dealers knew how to use their business systems. So when Honda moved into automaking, its strong dealer channel and business systems gave it a competitive advantage over General Motors. The second capability was its ability to realize products rapidly. Honda had collapsed the traditional product design and development activities into concurrent activities. The 1994 Accord took four years from concept to showroom, but Honda's management, feeling the pressure, had started early to be certain of every decision. For the first time, the Japanese company designed for manufacturability in its American assembly and engine plants. American managers spent months with the design teams in Tokyo. Efficiency of production was stressed. For the 1994 Accord, some 50 percent of parts were carried over from the successful 1990 Accord. Honda even went so far as to ask Rockwell

International to redesign a larger cargo area for the Accord. The final designs were so steady that only a half of the $14 million design change budget was spent.[36] Honda has a reputation for "breaking the glass" and doing things in different ways. In the Honda-Yamaha wars of the early 1980s, Honda introduced or replaced 113 motorcycle models in just 18 months.[37]

With growing strength among its competitors, Honda recognized that to regain the market leadership position it had to make the 1994 Accord a success. The founder of Honda, Soichiro Honda, a technical genius in motorcycle design, broke into the car business in Japan despite the strict control on the number of Japanese producers, and was active in the business until his death in 1992. Nobuhiko Kawamoto, his successor at the helm, redesigned the entire way that Honda did business to make it more effective in the marketplace. However, by changing the way that the company operated so drastically, Kawamoto was actually honoring the memory of Soichiro Honda: "I rejected Mr. Honda's way, but that is the Honda spirit."[38] Just like Honda, a company must learn to love change if it wants to be flexible and remain ahead of its competitors.

DRIVING PRODUCTIVITY—A DIET FOR FAT-FREE MANUFACTURING

American carmaking of yesterday was characterized as the industrial revolution's nightmare. TV news producer Bill Moyers judged that the U.S. auto industry had treated humans like they were mere extensions of their machines. There was continual bickering between organized labor and management. The discord grew louder and the adversarial relationship grew stronger as the U.S. market share dwindled. Meanwhile, the manufacturing process that came to be called lean production was being honed in the Far East.

The automobile manufacturing systems that were invented by Henry Ford, refined by GM's Alfred Sloan, and adapted by Taiichi Ohno, provide the basic philosophy for lean production. This fast-moving, lean production machine contrasts greatly to the lethargic processes of mass production. Lean production eliminates the overproduction generated by the need to consume excess inventory and costs related to workers, land, and facilities needed for management of that unwarranted inventory. Mass production promotes large lot sizes and produces lots of inventory independent of the market demand. Lean production, on the other hand, uses half the quantities of mass production. "Half the human effort in the factory, half the manufacturing space, half the investment in tools, half the engineering hours to develop a new product, in half the time. Also, it requires keeping far less than half the needed inventory on site, results in many fewer defects, and produces a greater and ever growing variety of products" reported the authors of *The Machine That Changed the World*.[39]

Analyzing the downturn of American automakers, an MIT study implicated a significant technological gap. In the 1989 MIT study, *Made in America*, the authors observed that the automatic transmission was the last major automotive innovation by U.S. companies, and that was in the 1940s.[40] To return to a competitive position, U.S. automakers had to focus on effective and efficient product design and assembly.

Effective product design means an automaker's success at meeting the expressed desire of its customers. In other words, the design engineer becomes a surrogate for the customers, one who becomes closely attuned to their requirements and able to apply technology in a way that answers the end-customers' true needs. Without this close relationship, in which the engineer can predict customer needs before the customer can articulate them, success remains a crap shoot.

Efficient product design means the speed at which designs are introduced to the market. This competitive factor is the product of two related activities: rapid design development and highly efficient production operations. In most cases, this requires concurrent engineering, where both the product and the production process are simultaneously developed to coexist in harmony. One of the implications of this approach is the removal of functional barriers so that design and production engineers become more aware of one another's activity. For example, the early involvement of a manufacturing representative on the design team is an imperative to structure the car by considering manufacturability attributes from the very beginning of the development process.

The MIT study published in 1989 judged American automakers had "lessened their disadvantages" in cycle time, productivity, and product quality, but still trailed.[41] Since then, the Big Three U.S. automakers, GM, Ford, and Chrysler, have moved toward regaining the lead. In early 1994, some forecasters projected that the Big Three could outsell Japanese manufacturers worldwide during the year. Some elements of their business system improvement of the engineering design process is mentioned in every assessment of this resurgence. For example, the 1994 Chevrolet Lumina has 900 fewer parts than it did three years ago, and it takes a third as much time to build. Gains like this in time-to-market and product design efficiency are the result of renewed attention to a better engineered process for product development. Reducing the cycle time for product development, or making time-to-market decrease, while simultaneously providing a car that thrills the customer, is *The* agreed-upon model for success in the automobile industry. Streamlining the process for delivering a concept-to-car is an example of a major systems engineering effort that many different players in the industry are taking. The shift to lean production by the automobile industry will lead the way for other industries.[42] This transition will have a profound effect on human society, and it may truly change the world.

"No new idea springs from a void. Rather, new ideas emerge from a set of conditions in which old ideas no longer seem to work."[43] Perhaps Taiichi Ohno has indicated the direction. In an interview, Productivity Press publisher Norman Bodek asked Ohno: "What is Toyota doing now?" Ohno replied: "All we are doing is looking at the time line from the moment the customer gives an order to the point where we collect the cash. And we are reducing that time line by removing the non-value-added wastes."[44] Well, Ohno has got it right—that's exactly what American industry is doing today in its current reengineering efforts. However, and this is a *big however*, Ohno's reply was in 1988, the year when Toyota was working on our 1993–1994 strategic change agenda.[45, 46]

10

Engineering Manufacturing Systems

The Bandit Line at Motorola

Rigidity and power occupy the inferior position;
Suppleness, softness, weakness, and delicateness occupy the superior position.
Lao Tzu, *Te-Tao Ching*

CASE STUDY HIGHLIGHTS

This case study illustrates how one company has dedicated itself to the combination of continuous improvement and breakthrough technology. Motorola has used its quality efforts to move the company ahead on a variety of fronts. The Bandit project illustrates how the focus on the customer, new product design, breakthrough process design change, quality teamwork processes, and time-based competition have driven Motorola to the front of its industry. It also illustrates how Motorola has positioned itself to continue learning the lessons from the Bandit project by leveraging the manufacturing and design lessons into the mobile phone business.

THE MOTOROLA STORY

In 1988—the year Motorola won the Malcolm Baldrige National Quality Award—it was a $6.7 billion global electronics and commu-

169

nications business with **89,000** employees. What's particularly interesting about this statistic is the measure of progress it represents for a company that initially went into business around the turn of the century to develop automobile victrolas and, most recently, had to battle its Japanese competitors to both stay in business and gain the leadership position in its pager and cellular phone markets. (According to company folklore, the Motorola name is derived from the two core concepts of its initial product: *motor*ized vehicles with vict*rolas*.) What allowed Motorola to achieve that progress probably has to do with the company's philosophical foundation; it is based on quality principles and practices. Motorola's depth of competitiveness has forged a remarkable and indelible impact on both its industry and the entire global marketplace. The fact that it remains the only one of six American electronic pager manufacturers that were in business ten years ago adds credit to its focus on strategically developing both process and product quality improvement.

It was probably one of the company's first product prototypes that established this strong commitment to quality early in the life of the business. As the story goes, an initial prototype of the "automobile record player" sparked when it was turned on, igniting fumes from the gas tank located just forward of the passenger compartment, and consuming both the prototype product and the founder's car in flames. This event was quite literally the initial spark that ignited the young company's focus on improving quality in its product design process. It may be not only the event that fanned the spark of creativity and innovation, which has become a formula for success at Motorola, but also what fostered the need for Motorola to develop its workers into flexible individuals with both vision and tenacity. As some of its internal literature describes it, Motorola seeks to develop employees who have "the mind to imagine, the skill to do, and the determination to follow through." Employee training and development have always been a strong enabler of Motorola's quality improvement progress. How were these values embedded within the organization?

In the case of Motorola, it is clear that these traditions have their roots firmly based in the company's leadership. Consider the story of how Motorola began its remarkable comeback. One day in 1979, during a strategy meeting of the company's top executives in a Chicago hotel, a sales executive quoted a Hewlett-Packard report describing a statistically based engineering study that showed Japanese manufacturers of DRAM semiconductors (Dynamic Random Access Memory—the electronic chip technology that is so important to the production of computers) had surpassed the product quality levels of American manufacturers. He explicitly warned the management team that the Japanese competitors could bury Motorola's market with high-quality products. In response, Chairman Robert W. Galvin immediately mounted a two-pronged, company-wide drive to accelerate Motorola's new product development and improve product quality by achieving a tenfold reduction in defects by 1986. As Galvin describes it: "Everything changed after that one meeting."[1]

To carry out Galvin's demand for such massive improvement, the company began a two-year examination of virtually every aspect of its internal manufacturing operations. At the same time, teams of Motorola managers scouted plants around the world conducting benchmarking studies to look for new, advanced production techniques to adopt. This was a sharp break with the company's longtime custom of relying solely on manufacturing methods invented in-house.[2, 3]

These hunts for ideas spawned many changes. For one thing, the traditional command and control hierarchy had isolated manufacturing from other corporate functions and inhibited the interaction and cooperation required to speed up and improve performance. Realizing the need for a more broad-based team approach, Galvin set up a management training program to breach the barriers among design, purchasing, production, distribution, and marketing functions. This was only one of the traditional operating methods that had to change. Such extensive change required the understanding and support of the management team, and the flexibility of the workers who willingly participated in its implementation. "Breaking traditions is scary, but it is vital when you're trying to change an entire corporate culture," said Robert N. Weisshappel, vice president and general manager of North American cellular-telephone operations.[4]

By 1987, Motorola had achieved Galvin's first, and seemingly impossible, quality improvement goal. In response to this achievement, Galvin challenged Motorola again with another two seemingly impossible goals: achieving a hundredfold improvement in product quality by 1991, and making virtually perfect products by the end of 1992. This second goal has become widely known as achieving Six Sigma levels of quality, which means 99.9997 percent error-free performance or, alternatively stated, a defect rate of about 3 parts-per-million produced. By setting these breakthrough goals, Galvin intended that Motorola learn how to stretch itself well beyond its current way of doing business. In 1993, Galvin declared victory on this Six Sigma goal. By then Motorola had achieved an average of 5.5 Sigma across all company processes. Galvin, based strongly on the Motorola experience with the Bandit project, provided another challenge and asked his management team to seek an additional tenfold reduction in all cycle times within the next two years. By now, all employees throughout the Motorola organization have become challenged with the need for breakthrough performance and an emphasis on high-quality and rapid-response manufacturing.

Among the many other improvements Galvin has brought to the manufacturing process, one of the most impressive is Motorola's thorough retraining process for displaced workers. While many U.S. manufacturers are worried about the ability of the current industrial workforce to handle the new technology crowding onto the factory floor, Motorola has taken action. It has gone farther than most companies in solving this problem of maintaining current worker skills with a massive program to upgrade the competence of its nearly 100,000 employees. At a cost of about $50 million a year, management has set up a number of joint education and training ventures with local community colleges and developed a point system for giving salary increases to employees who learn to cope with emerging technology and develop new on-the-job skills.[5] As George M. Fisher, Motorola's former president and CEO, has said: "We find it necessary to continually train all of our workers."[6]

One of the individuals who broke the mold of old style thinking and drove these changes was George Fisher, the rising star within Motorola during this period who ultimately succeeded Galvin as CEO and then left in November 1993 to take over the helm at Eastman Kodak. In many ways, Fisher epitomized the culture of Motorola, where change is seen as a positive and necessary element. Fisher once said: "I like change because it wakes you up."[7] After joining Motorola from AT&T, Fisher's initial position was as director of quality and information systems for the communications division. In 1983, he brought charges before the International Trade Commission that Japanese competitors were dumping pagers on the U.S. market, and persuaded the Commission to levy 100 percent duties against the imports. As the leader of Motorola's paging business, however, he also realized that he did not have much time to create a competitive advantage that could be sustained beyond this tariff protection.

The Bandit story is about an American manufacturer that demonstrated how, in the rapidly growing market for electronic pagers (sometimes called "beepers" for their unique message alerting sound), to deliver "first-to-the-market" innovative products that capture market share, while simultaneously reengineering its business processes. Motorola redesigned both a new product and a new manufacturing process within 18 months. It proved that time-based competitiveness is not only possible, it is also a pragmatic imperative.[8] This response to the growing competitive environment allowed Motorola to reverse its market share decline in the pocket pager business and create a capability that would eventually be extended to its cellular mobile phone product line.

THE BANDIT PROJECT

By 1986, Asian manufacturers had knocked out every U.S. producer of electronic pagers except for Motorola. As a result of benchmarking, Motorola had recognized that its pagers took too long to build and that product quality was too erratic to compete on the same playing field as the Japanese. Upon analyzing its business situation, the company concluded that it could only achieve parity with its Japanese competitors on such product design aspects as cost, quality, technology, and features. However, because it was located closer to the U.S. market, Motorola could gain a competitive advantage by achieving increased product availability in the marketplace. To succeed, the company required far better connectivity between the customer's order and the factory's production capacity than had ever been achieved in any American manufacturing project at that time.[9, 10, 11, 12, 13] Enter the Bandit project, which took the limelight on the Motorola product development stage with a challenge to improve the order-entry-to-ship cycle time by over 85 percent in just 18 months.

Through benchmarking, the Bandit project "stole" off-the-shelf technologies from world-class manufacturers around the world. Motorola combined these "stolen" practices with its own strengths, allowing the company to develop its processes rapidly and to avoid "reinventing the wheel." This practice of unabashed "thievery" caused the design team to designate the project with an appropriate code name—Bandit. The leader of the benchmarking project, T. Scott Shamlin, noted that the team did not find any one "best" factory, but that it could combine the unique ideas of many factories into its own world-class facility.[14] This project represented a major manufacturing engineering project for Motorola. For the rest of us, it clearly shows an eminently successful linkage of benchmarking—used to identify critical enablers of performance improvement—with the process of systems engineering for both the product design and development processes and the manufacturing production development process. [15,16,17,18]

Bandit was the code name for both the new product development and the new manufacturing process. The new product would be a more streamlined addition to Motorola's pocket pager product line— the Bravo. The Bravo also presented a higher degree of complexity. The product design allowed each pager to be personalized with individualized customer codes, digital readout display, and a unique set of product options that resulted in the possibility of providing about 21 million different hardware and software combinations to the ultimate owners. With this degree of customization possible, the manufacturing system would have to be able to either schedule or manage true production lot sizes of one.[19] The design was much more efficient: The part count for the Bravo numeric display pager was 134 parts, representing a 25 percent decrease over the prior generation product.

The Bandit manufacturing process would be the key to achieving the targeted level of performance on the breakthrough order-turn-around-time goal. The Bandit production line uses a build-to-order approach rather than a fixed schedule build plan. This permits greater flexibility in the production process since specific product options are not identified for production until the last possible minute. This production feature also has some strong implications for the design team. It means that product options should be software programmable to the greatest degree possible; standard parts should be used to the maximum extent; and that suppliers must be more flexible in developing their ability to respond to shifting demands of flexible production schedules through both their own flexible manufacturing processes and JIT parts delivery capabilities. Since human operators introduce significant variability into production operations, the Bandit line had been designed to minimize the intervention of the production workers. This means that robotic machines had to do those repeatable tasks that would fatigue or bore human operators, while tasks that required a distinctly human touch—such as the final inspection from the customer's point of view—were reserved for the workers.

In addition to managing the human element created by the need to change the work content of production workers, there was a significant technical challenge. To accomplish the breakthrough goal required the coordination of two technical project elements. First, the product design had to be rationalized for adoption to a fixed manufacturing system and, second, the factory scheduling system had to be linked directly to the order processing system. This required greater connectivity between manufacturing automation systems and the Motorola mainframe business computers. This computer integrated manufacturing (CIM) approach was accomplished by automating the manufacturing facility. The factory cell design called for three levels of Hewlett-Packard shop floor computers used as production line controllers and linked to the IBM mainframe for receiving product orders. Hewlett-Packard work cell controllers and individual workstation controllers were linked to Seiko robots and Panasonic automated electrical component insertion equipment. It was a complex software system.

To carry lessons learned in the classroom out onto the plant floor, the Bandit team had been challenged to meet new, seemingly impossible, standards of quality and speed, and to do it with fewer layers of management. T. Scott Shamlin, leader of the two-year CIM benchmarking study, was chosen to direct the development of the pager manufacturing facility.

Shamlin saw the Bandit project as an exercise in culture change. He recognized that while most American companies may set a cost or customer satisfaction or quality improvement goal of 10 percent to 20 percent for the coming year, their Japanese counterparts were setting improvement goals on the order of 200 percent annually. This was the kind of thinking that he wanted the Bandit team to emulate. Shamlin described his need for breakthrough thinking and moving this project beyond incremental, continuous improvement: "We've got to stop finding mistakes, uncovering their root cause, and then correcting the environment that allowed them to happen. That kind of thinking is obsolete. Instead, we have to put an infrastructure in place that senses a situation that is beginning to go out of control, predicts when it will go out of control, and then takes preemptive corrective action while it's still within given tolerances."[20]

To do this job, Shamlin selected a 24-person team, representing all required functional specialties, to design both the production process and the new product. Shamlin's team included product designers, process developers, tooling designers, software specialists, purchasing experts, and financial analysts. Their common goal was to develop and produce the Bravo product within 18 months instead of the three to five years required for previous products.

Empowerment became a key ingredient to gaining the commitment and dedication of the entire team. For instance, within the manufacturing cell, the production line workers more or less ran the assembly operation—dramatically changing Shamlin's job as well as their own. "My role has gravitated to being a cheerleader, " he says. In this atmosphere, "people don't need a lot of (direct) management anymore. They just need leadership to keep their enthusiasm up."[21,22,23]

Even the suppliers of parts had to take on expanded roles. From the beginning the Motorola Bandit team had managed the supplier base starting with some 300 eligible suppliers. The team identified approximately 60 companies for site inspections and then, finally, selected 22 suppliers to provide the 134 parts, offering these companies sole-source contractual relationships to reward their responsiveness.

Consider what Kyocerra learned. Motorola's early supplier involvement program had provided it with an up-front look at how its parts were going to be used and how it needed to be modified to better support the manufacturing process. Kyocerra ended up developing a new product for its general market based on the Bandit requirement for robotic assembly.[24]

Hewlett-Packard's involvement in Bandit seemed to be all-encompassing. It required a collaborative effort featuring intercompany technology transfers between several of Hewlett-Packard's leading manufacturing divisions: San Diego (makers of pen plotters and color thermal inkjet printers), Roseville, California (makers of network computer systems), Vancouver, Washington (makers of personal printers), and Fort Collins, Colorado (makers of work cell and manufacturing computer systems). Since this application of its products had never been implemented outside of its own factories, Hewlett-Packard systems engineers worked together with their Motorola counterparts to develop the real-time systems required to manage the production operations of the Bandit process.[25]

These stories illustrate a strategic movement for Motorola from a traditionally adversarial vendor relationship to a more cooperative environment of supplier partnering and JIT production operations. Motorola has followed a "leadership" strategy focused on quality leadership, cost/cycle-time leadership, management leadership, and training of employees for team and self-leadership. Due to the increasing complexity of its product and process technology, as well as the decreasing market life cycle of its products, Motorola has developed strategic partnerships with its suppliers and an emphasis on taking time out of all business processes wherever practical to do so. These supplier partnerships have helped Motorola position itself in a strategic, time-based "warfare" with its competitors where supplier-partners help to focus the company's resources on engagement within the first two stages of the product life cycle: product innovation and process innovation. Nowhere has this strategy been more evident than in the Bandit project.[26]

That pretty much describes the environment that produced the Bravo pager at Motorola's Boynton Beach, Florida, plant. Stretch goals drove the team for breakthrough action—not allowing themselves to be content with incremental, continuous improvement from the prior generation's product. To summarize, the Bandit team facilitated its journey by identifying and implementing three process enablers: using cross-functional teamwork, computer integrated manufacturing, and early supplier involvement to drive its improvement process toward the stretch goal. How did the team do?

The results were worthy of an Olympic Gold medal in world-class manufacturing. In 18 months, Shamlin's Bandit team had constructed, equipped, and placed in full operation a brand new, world-class, $9 million manufacturing facility at Boynton Beach. Its factory design had delivered tremendous performance improvements:

- ◆ Order fulfillment time reduced from 3 weeks to an average of around 2 hours (the time to begin building a product after the receipt of an order is down to a best performance case of 16 minutes from receipt of the order).

- ◆ Manufacturing efficiencies improved by greater than 150 percent (production cycle time best performance is 57 minutes (averaging about 2 hours—compared to 20 days on the old assembly line).

- ◆ Defect rates reduced by over 50 percent (the mean time between failures—the measure of a product's reliability in the hands of the customer—is a phenomenal 150 years).[27]

What did the team learn? Two major lessons are seen from the perspective of time. First, there is a systemic relationship between product quality, process flexibility, cycle time performance, and automated assembly methods. These factors are interdependent and must be taken on as a system in order to realize breakthrough performance. Second, there is a need to establish partnerships with suppliers of both parts and systems to build a complete and successful system. Both the product assembled in the facility and the facility itself must be in harmony for them to operate in smooth unison.

BEYOND BANDIT

In 1989, Motorola introduced the world's smallest and lightest cellular telephone. This product, a pocket-sized phone, was dubbed the Micro Tac, and its introduction put Motorola at least a year ahead of its competitors in one of the world's fastest growing markets (by then Motorola's total annual sales for fiscal year 1989 had grown to $8.7 billion). Six months earlier, the Bandit project had been completed with the introduction of the Bravo pager. Shamlin and his team had beat their tight product introduction deadline by a few days. Interestingly, the quality of their pocket pager was so good that Motorola not only regained its domestic market share, but also grabbed a significant piece of the Japanese market. Another seeker of improved methods, Motorola's Bob Weisshappel, adopted many of the same methods used by the Bandit team to more efficiently produce the Micro Tac cellular telephone. Specific technology transfers included order fulfillment system, robotic parts placement techniques, supplier early involvement, and technical testing methods.

With the introduction of these two new personal communications products, Bravo and Micro Tac, Motorola became the most formidable competitor in its global market. The Motorola team had achieved a spectacular resurgence from its market doldrums in the early 1980s. Motorola is now the world's number-one producer of cellular telephones, a leader in two-way mobile radios, the only American company in the pager market, and the fourth ranking semiconductor manufacturer behind three Japanese firms. The challenge for Motorola will be to extend its learning process and leverage the lessons from these strategic change initiatives across the rest of its product lines.

11

Engineering Customer Service

The Compaq Response to the Attack by Dell

Correct words seem to say the reverse of what you expect them to say.

Lao Tzu, *Te-Tao Ching*

CASE STUDY HIGHLIGHTS

This case study illustrates what can happen to a company in a rapidly changing business environment. Over a two-year period, Compaq was faced with rising attacks on its products and distribution system. When the ten primary distributor chains merged into just six chains in mid-1991, they left Compaq with excess inventory that amounted to about a month's worth of product sales in its distribution pipeline. When Compaq announced this fact and adjusted its sales forecast for the fiscal year downward from $4.2 billion to about $3.6 billion, a panic of confidence erupted on the stock market. The share value plunged from the $75 range the stock had been commanding to about $50 a share. This decline and a consistent attack by rival firms, principally by Dell Computer and AST Computers, triggered a need for Compaq to reconfigure itself on four fronts: (1) The product line needed to be transitioned to the lower end of the price spectrum; (2) The channels for distribution needed to be opened up to include superstores and possibly even direct sales; (3) Compaq needed to provide customer service

179

directly to end users—not just through the dealers; and (4) Compaq needed to streamline its operations to make itself as cost effective as its leading competitor. Did Compaq make it? In 1993, Compaq booked $7.2 billion in revenue and remains in a leadership position in the personal computer industry. The stock now trades around the $100 range. Was this magic? No, this successful transition was orchestrated. It required nothing less than a complete transformation of the entire company.

COMPAQ—THE HIGH-TECHNOLOGY STAR

Compaq had been a dream company from its beginning, which occurred just after IBM introduced the personal computer in 1981. The founders of Compaq—Rod Canion, Jim Harris, and Bill Murto—worked together at Texas Instruments and became dissatisfied with the lack of support from TI management to move a portable personal computer project into the product development cycle. Their transition from TI marks the beginning of Compaq. Why did these three engineers leave TI? TI, a Dallas-based manufacturer of semiconductors and electronics, had dominated its markets by providing the latest in electronics technology and following a low-cost marketing strategy for new products (such as calculators, digital watches, printers, and computers). TI had built up a remarkable portfolio of patents, which provided a royalty stream that kept it profitable despite falling sales. TI met its sales decline by cost-cutting on the products. It followed this strategy to the point where TI products were less attractive than its competitors. TI held onto this strategy despite the market signals. When the market called for increased features, TI looked to its technology edge to provide them at the lowest cost. This cost-first structure restricted TI's competitiveness and delayed product introductions. These delays in product introduction due to TI's dysfunctional business model (in the late 1970s) led to the loss of the three engineers.[1] Canion, Harris, and Murto left TI's Houston operation in 1981 and formed Gateway Technologies, in early 1982, to produce the portable computer that could not be made for TI. Meanwhile, IBM introduced its personal computer in 1981 and met with overwhelming success. The demand was so great that the production lines at IBM couldn't keep pace. The timing for the foundation of Compaq was extraordinary.[2, 3]

No American company had ever grown as quickly as Compaq in the first five years of its existence. From 1983 when it set a $111 million sales record for its first year of business, Compaq grew at a phenomenal rate. It attained the *Fortune* 500 ranking faster than any company that preceded it—by 1985—and attained sales records for the time to achieve both the $1 billion (1987) and $2 billion (1988) sales levels. Other companies didn't make it. For instance, Osborne Computer, the maker of the first portable computer, filed for bankruptcy after the public panned its nonstandard operating system. At this time all new entrants in the personal computer business, and there were literally dozens of them, were met with skepticism by Wall Street investors.[4] So, why did Compaq succeed? The success model for Compaq could be summarized in three words: product, process, and people. Let's look at these three critical success factors in the Compaq growth formula.

THE PRODUCT ADVANTAGE

From the very beginning, Compaq understood that quality meant whatever the customer perceived it to mean. In early 1980s, it meant the availability of software, and all of the software designers—most notably Microsoft and Lotus with their breakthrough product in the Lotus 1–2–3® spreadsheet program—were developing programs for the IBM system. While other portables may have beat Compaq to the market, none of these competitors had an operating system that ran the software developed to the IBM system standard. IBM had made its personal computer design architecture public knowledge in an effort to set the software standard for the computer industry—it captured the interest of the software community and also opened the way Compaq engineers needed to design a product that had compatible software.

Guided by their venture capital investors, the Gateway Technology founders changed their company name,[5] established themselves in an austere bank-building office, and worked on the initial product design. The team focused on meeting the needs of its customers—the engineers and businesspeople who needed to use computers that could travel with them to the field. It was a no-frills environment—they even used folding chairs and packaging crates for furniture. Engineering investments were the top priority—not office furniture or the perquisites of office. Team members reverse engineered the IBM personal computer while sitting on the office's carpeted floor. Since Compaq used the IBM operating system and ran the same software, but used an advanced display and a ruggedized disc drive, it became recognized as the leading portable product on the market. When IBM followed with its own portable product, it was no match for the Compaq. Because of its aggressiveness in bringing out an IBM-compatible personal computer product, and its ability to beat IBM in the portable computer market, journalists dubbed Compaq as the IBM-killer. Compaq then brought out desktop models to face off against the IBM personal computers. By the time that Compaq delivered the first-to-market, Intel 386 chip-compatible product, it was considered to be the company to beat in the portable computer industry and the primary contender for IBM market share in the desktop personal computer industry. The Compaq DeskPro 386 product illustrated the speed-based design philosophy of the R&D team: Get the product to the market first, with the best technology, and the most reliability. Getting the right product to the market first meant that the whole team had to reach consensus on the product definition and then push it through the development process. Building in the product reliability meant that the design engineers had to anticipate the environment in which the customers would use their products. Two stories illustrate how senior management encouraged these behaviors.

Consensus management was primarily the contribution of Rod Canion. At Compaq, a story is told about the decision to move into the laptop computer market. Canion wanted Compaq to develop a laptop product as early as 1986. However, a marketing analysis of the market indicated that people were not ready to invest strongly in an under-featured laptop product. Even though Canion wanted to use a Compaq laptop product on his business trips, he was unable to convince the team that its customers had a demand for this product. He didn't overrule—he followed consensus and let the team make an investment in the 386 product development and waited until 1988, when Compaq introduced the highly successful LTE/286 laptop product, which set the standard for both display screen quality and battery operating life.[6] While Canion taught the true meaning of consensus through this example, Harris did the same thing for product reliability.

When Compaq brought out its first portable computer, the annual failure rate for desktop personal computers was around 20 percent. This was due to reliability problems in the hard disc drives. Knowing how important it was that products should last, Harris challenged his design team engineers by dropping the products onto an old wooden table to see if they would still operate. This "drop test" helped to make the product almost indestructible. However, the team was shocked when Harris tested the sole prototype of the production model just days before it would be introduced in New York City. If it failed this last test, Compaq may have to cancel the product announcement. Harris took this precious, unique machine by its handle and threw it down a hallway like one throws a bowling ball. Harris knew that this portable computer would travel on airlines and would have to endure some potentially rough treatment during baggage handling. He figured that if the computer booted up and would perform according to design after the extended "drop test," then it would handle the customer's environment. It did. Reliability of this product in the first year of production was around 95 percent per year—four times better than models of desktop computers that didn't fly on airlines.

Compaq products were known for being fully featured, possessing advanced technology, demonstrating extensive software compatability,[7] and maintaining the highest standards of quality and reliability. This was Compaq's first competitive distinction. But, it did not come inexpensively; while Compaq products were priced just under their comparative IBM product, they were still priced 10 percent to 20 percent above competing products from "second tier" producers of personal computers. Compaq viewed its principal competitor as IBM.

THE PROCESS ADVANTAGE

Compaq designed its business processes in response to the rapid speed of its industry rivals. The basic rule at Compaq was do it fast and do it well. This attitude spilled out into all areas of the company's operations, as if complacency in one area would contaminate the others. Just consider the approach that was taken for establishing the Compaq European Service Center at Stirling, Scotland (a suburb of Edinburgh in southeastern Scotland). The building had been a Wang manufacturing site and was not suitable for use in its present configuration. The Erskine, Scotland, management team was charged with converting the plant into a service center and developing a workforce. Erskine is a suburb of Glasgow in southwestern Scotland—just under a two-hour drive to Stirling. Despite this distance, the Erskine team gutted the production facility and rebuilt in its place a modern service facility; ordered the inventory of spare parts from suppliers across the globe;

and trained operators in the skills necessary to repair Compaq computers. From start to full on-line operations, the team took only 30 calendar days. A truly amazing response.

The real reason for building such an emphasis on speed is that "fast time-to-market with the most recent technology" is the success formula for personal computers. To achieve this capability, Compaq streamlined its product development cycle by overlapping process steps where possible to allow it to introduce a new model laptop computer every year (this is a blitzing average time-to-market of 12 months). The use of reliability growth as well as testing at the part and subassembly levels to find problems before assembling the whole machine allowed Compaq to trim time from the traditional system-level test-and-fix design approach.

Another process that provided competitive advantage was Compaq's use of the dealer channel for product distribution. In its early growth, from 1982 to 1985, Compaq needed to expose its name and products to as many potential customers as possible. The environment was one where consumers, who generally speaking were still neophytes in computing, needed to be coached, and sometimes required direct assistance, in setting up and using their new personal computers. The first few iterations of personal computer products were explained poorly, in overly technical language, and faced many integration problems. Within months of announcing its first portable product, Compaq decided that it would sell its computers only through the dealer channel (large dealerships like ComputerLand) in exchange for dealer loyalty and shelf space. Compaq refused to sell its computers directly to the public and, therefore, relied on the dealer distribution system to provide its primary end customer interface. Most importantly, Compaq would not compete with dealers as IBM did. IBM sold large volume sales directly to customers at deep discounts that dealers couldn't match. The computer dealers resented the competition that IBM gave for potential "big deals." The Compaq solution allowed them to go head-to-head against IBM with a less-expensive product that had a reliable reputation. Compaq referred its problems to the dealers and only dealt directly with them, not with the end user. The user's technical questions and hardware problems were for the dealer to resolve, not Compaq. So naturally, when the day came that personal computers had simplified and buyers had become more sophisticated, there was less need for the dealer channel—until the higher end of the product line is reached. Compaq stayed with its dealer channel because the loyalty worked both ways. In the end, changing the distribution process became the largest change made by Compaq. This long-term resistance to changing its dealer distribution system was the "Achilles heel" that Michael Dell skillfully exploited as he attacked Compaq.

THE PEOPLE ADVANTAGE

The third advantage that Compaq enjoyed was the culture that had become so deeply embedded in its people. Elements of the culture have already been discussed as we talked about the product advantage and the people advantage. The Compaq culture was marked by teamwork, consensus decision making, customer orientation, employee participation, time-based action, and a total commitment to quality. As Compaq went into fighting the forthcoming battle with Dell, it was halfway through a two-year effort to achieve ISO 9002 certification at all five manufacturing and service operations. This provided a basis for understanding what processes needed to change. The key lesson that Compaq was learning was the great difference between its internal customers—colleagues and teammates who work together to develop products or provide services—and its external customers who pay the bills and *must* be satisfied.

THE DELL ATTACK

Where was Compaq vulnerable to attack? It wasn't in product quality, time-to-market, or product features. The biggest vulnerability came from the Compaq loyalty to its dealers and the manner in which this loyalty manifested itself in the design of Compaq operations. What was the origin of the Dell attack? Consider the origins of Dell Computer. Michael Dell was a student at the University of Texas in Austin. He began his company by building personal computers in his dormitory room. While Compaq was expanding its markets overseas, Dell was developing a mail-order business advertising knock-off clones of the more expensive products that could be ordered over the phone. While Compaq created an architecturally outstanding "space-age" operations center in Houston at an investment of almost a billion dollars, Dell put only about $50 million into production capability housed in a patchwork of low-overhead, rented buildings. A flat worldwide economy, consolidation of the dealer channel, and the introduction of the computer superstore placed pressure on Compaq. The excess inventory in the dealer channel slowed down sales to their "customer" and meant that Compaq had excess inventory and too much production capacity. This implied the need for a reduction in force and a consolidation of its facilities to eliminate the rental cost of "expansion" space that was off the central Compaq campus. Dell had a cost advantage on the order of 25 to 35 percent due to its telephone direct distribution system, rather than the middleman of the dealer channel. Compaq could no longer afford this luxury. The Dell advertising campaign mocked the high prices of Compaq computer as "lunacy."[8] Just as Compaq had attacked IBM for disloyalty to the dealer channel, so Dell, Packard Bell, AST, CompuAdd, and others attacked Compaq for an expensive (to the customer) dedication to the dealer channel. The Compaq dedication to the dealer channel made it difficult for end customers to get consistently reliable after-sales service. Dell had expansive telephone hot lines that listened to its customers and quickly acted to resolve their issues. Dell said that the Compaq service approach was out of touch with its changing customer needs and that Dell could provide better service to both individual and corporate customers by using the telephone to buy less expensive products directly and then dealing directly with Dell on service issues (Dell did not provide direct field service, but subcontracted this through a network of providers). Compaq was losing sales and market share in the United States and only held on to its sales revenue by exploiting its advantage in Europe where the users did not yet have the same degree of sophistication as in the United States. This set of signals forced Compaq to reexamine its loyalty to the dealer channel and its way of doing business—recognizing the need to get closer to its real customers. When the European market showed that it, too, was learning how to buy and support systems without dealer support, Compaq was forced to make the change. As slow as Compaq may have appeared to be in recognizing and responding to the changing market, it used its time-to-market mentality to remake itself in just four months.

ACCEPTING THE CHALLENGE

The triggers for the Compaq change imperatives were fourfold: excess capacity; products that were designed for dealer serviceability rather than low price; distribution channels that no longer provided competitive advantage; and a management system that seemed to be too loyal to its past way of doing business.[9] In mid-October 1991, the board of directors felt that Compaq needed to make rapid changes and made a decision to replace the original management team with a new team that would more rapidly respond to the situation. By the beginning of November, Compaq had cut just over 15 percent of its excess employees and had committed to develop and implement a technical services center that would ultimately expand into a direct sales channel. In eight months, Compaq introduced a completely new line of low-cost computers that stimulated a price war in the computer industry.[10] How did management make these changes so rapidly?

The Compaq management team conducted a self-assessment and brought in external experts to provide it with a broader perspective of its competitive weaknesses. They discovered inefficiencies in several Compaq operations and the need to be more sensitive to product costs during design and to improve connectivity to the end user customers for service. In short, Compaq determined the need for a radical redefinition of its business model.

Let's examine one of these four triggers—the customer service challenge—which is the driver of the other changes to the Compaq business model.[11]

PUTTING THE CUSTOMER FIRST

The business assessment indicated that building a customer satisfaction capability, even in the face of a major employee downsizing, was a mandatory change. Without an incoming access capability to Compaq technical support, the company had to look to the outside to determine how to design such a system. Nemo Azmanian, director of technical support at Compaq, underscored the urgency of the situation. "There was no time for a full scale benchmarking effort. We had to learn-and-go. Every day that we went without direct phone support, sales were being lost to those who had this capability. A quick study was made of a few companies who successfully operated toll-free customer access lines."

Azmanian recalled that Xerox Corporation, American Express Travel Related Services, L. L. Bean, and Lands' End provided lessons on how to create a "valid foundation" for its new department. Another influence was the book by Ken Blanchard and Sheldon Bowles, *Raving Fans* (New York: William Morrow, 1993), which described the characteristic features of the most successful customer service organizations. Following the lessons learned in these studies, Compaq determined what it needed to do to build a first-rate service center.

Top management bought off on the project plan and assigned a cross-functional team to stay focused and execute the plan. Azmanian said that the plan needed to be monitored on a "minute-to-minute" basis as the team crafted a world-class system. "Taking such a broad scale systems approach to such a critical development took conviction and courage on the part of the management team and the implementation team," he commented.

The result was worth the effort. At seven in the morning on March 4, 1992, 60 fully trained and technically competent employees were seated at their intelligent workstations ready for calls that truly put the customer first. The Compaq Service Center was now doing exactly what the ten-year-old company had resisted so long and so strongly. And, this transformation took just four months.

Steering Toward the Future

Compaq relied on its cultural basis to make these changes: empowered teams, customer focus, consensus decision making, external benchmarking, and analytical tools. It also relied on its knowledge of computer systems technology to provide data "at the fingertips of the on-line service technicians." The Compaq value of rapid action and well-executed projects is also evident. What were the net effects of the entire system change?

Today, the Compaq Customer Support Center employs in excess of 300 technical representatives who service the line seven days a week, twenty-four hours a day. Compaq has introduced Just-in-Time manufacturing on all lines that link production to the ordering process. Compaq went through a second round of downsizing; another 1,000 people exited, leaving just 75 percent of the original workforce size. It has totally redesigned its product line to be cost effective as the industry price leader. It is still recognized for product quality. All of these transitions made a big change in its per unit cost—down an average of 51 percent since the prior year.

Compaq is a proud company that has learned that the past is not the prologue to the future. It reengineered one of the most successful business models in the face of adversity, and it continues its growth. Not too many companies can make that claim. But, without its culture, history, and the training and commitment of its people, Compaq may not have made the transition.

12

Engineering the Office

A Paperless Factory at USAA

Give birth to them and nourish them.
Give birth to them but don't try to own them;
Help them to grow but don't rule them.
This is called Profound Virtue.

Lao Tzu, *Te-Tao Ching*

CASE STUDY HIGHLIGHTS

This case study illustrates how a long-term change strategy may remain flexible, focused on the customer, and adapted to the changing technological environment. It is a story of senior management leadership and the power of a consistent vision, seen through to realize its implementation goals and make change a reality. It's also a story of a company that doesn't focus on reengineering as an end, but rather places its effort on efficiently serving its customers—the true end of its business.

When retired U.S. Air Force Brigadier General Robert F. McDermott came to the helm of this organization in 1969, it was a typical insurer in terms of its work processes and attitude. The general did not see it staying that way. His vision of process efficiency that could be improved through the use of appropriate technology became the driving force of this change. Over the next 25 years, he created the benchmark for efficiency in the insurance industry.

190

PURVEYOR OF INSURANCE TO THE MILITARY SERVICES

United Services Automobile Association was founded in 1922 by 25 army officers who wanted to provide each other with reciprocal auto insurance at a time when most insurance companies saw military people as risks or "transients"—due to constant reassignment and relocation—as well as living lives too risky to be profitably insurable.[1] USAA founders, however, saw just the opposite: a group of well-educated, affluent, honest, and honorable people. Thus began USAA's niche for insurance services, which today represents commissioned, warrant, retired, and former officers of the United States armed forces, their spouses, children, and grandchildren. Today, 95 percent of active-duty U.S. military officers are USAA members.[2] In addition, the company has grown beyond being just a "plain" insurance carrier to include a broad variety of financial services, which are available to the population at large.

What's so significant about USAA's history? Well, just about everything, beginning with the fact that a potential group of insurance customers who were not getting their needs met by the existing marketplace decided to start their own insurance company—now that's engineering a business system! Moreover, this proactive approach to doing business set the foundation for what has become an entrenched culture, one that is built upon the philosophical pragmatism of the military and the business practice of mutual or "reciprocal insurance," where primary policyholders (that is, current or former military officers, not their dependents) are actually owner-members. The company has no stock, shareholders, or dividends. Proceeds are shared with owner-members through reduced prices, dividends, and deposits into their share savings accounts. The owner-members also receive top-notch policy service and an inceasing number of additional services as a reward for their patronage and the company's ability to continually increase its process efficiency.

USAA's reputation wasn't always so rosy, however. When McDermott joined the company in 1968, "There was paper everywhere. We had 650,000 members at that time and 3,000 employees. Every desk in the building was covered with stacks of paper—files, claim forms, applications, correspondence . . . we had 200 to 300 young people from local colleges working nights finding files, just going around searching people's desks until they found the ones they were looking for. . . . I would often stay late and go around putting little marks on papers and files, then I'd check the next night to see if they'd been moved. A lot of people moved no paper at all."[3] By the time McDermott took over as CEO in 1969, he had already made four basic decisions:

1. Automate the policy-writing service.
2. Reduce the number of employees and do it by attrition (employee turnover was around 40 percent a year, so this wasn't a problem).
3. Develop education and training programs.
4. Decentralize the lines of business.

These decisions set a tradition of change management. "When McDermott took over we were using a physical process of paper handling that was put in place between 1931 and 1933," Bill Flynn, senior vice president of corporate planning and quality management, said. "But in 1968, the industry had changed its rules; we had the Vietnam War and we were suddenly overburdened in paper." Flynn described how a "policy deck instruction sheet" was passed along lined-up tables. Employees sitting at the tables would read the instruction sheet, either add a sheet of paper or not, according to the tick marks on the instructions, then pass it to the next table, where this process was repeated. Eventually, the complete policy would reach a table where it was stapled, then another where it was folded and put in an envelope.[4, 5, 6] "At the time our employee turnover was around over 50 percent and we had a volume of work that was driven by a 'tour of duty war' where increasing numbers of officers were going into active duty and swelling the number of eligible members." Today, turnover is 6 percent to 7 percent, and the company has a very highly educated workforce.

THE PAPERLESS POLICY

Once McDermott completed his strategic assessment of the company, he decided that he wanted to move from an atmosphere that feared change to a culture that embraced change and enriched employees. ("Enriched" was a word he'd seen on a loaf of bread, where it meant they'd added something to improve the nutrition. He wanted to add interest and challenge to USAA jobs, he said.)[7] Flynn described the way he saw McDermott's initiative: "The strategy he laid out really consisted of a few core elements: move a static culture that is resisting change to a dynamic culture with employees who embrace change; change employees from people who merely shuffle the paperwork to knowledge-based problem solvers; and finally, increase service and provide greater service production. To do this McDermott's focus was on aligning risk, becoming efficient through development of human resources and information systems, and passing savings from increased efficiency on to customers."

While the work was decentralized in terms of worker empowerment—not a buzzword in those days, but the same concept nonetheless—by pushing responsibility further down the hierarchical chain, the goal for information access was toward centralization and the creation of a paperless environment. "We worked the paper trails, discovered how to translate processes into a paperless environment, and then exploit technology in order to automate centralized data," Flynn said. By 1972, USAA had its first on-line system that maintained a database with automobile and customer information. But USAA wanted more. According to Flynn, "We wanted more than just a file in an on-line system; we wanted a system that incorporated imaging and that would produce a document that was legally viable."

"Technology supports the employee who ultimately deals with the customer. . . . The system is a tool the employee uses," Flynn said. Investment in technology is providing a tool for the worker to serve the customer. "We serve our policyholders and owner-members; there's no ambiguity about whom we work for: do we support the customer or do we pay homage to the stockholder? Because our members own the company, we have a single focal point for our attention: serve our members and give them the best quality service. That's what drives the efficiency improvements and quality output of our company. Reciprocal insurance. We have the advantage to make a long-term commitment to improving systems, for example, because we don't need to worry about paying stockholder dividends."

BANKING THE BENEFITS

What results have been accrued to date from this extended 25-year journey? As of December 31, 1993, USAA held over $32.2 billion in owned and managed assets. It has become the fifth largest insurer of private automobiles and the fourth largest household insurer in the nation. Other services within USAA's family of companies include property and casualty insurance, life and health insurance, mutual fund and real estate investments, banking services, and more to its over 2.6 million members and customers. The 1993 *Fortune* Service 500 ranks USAA 21st among the top 50 U.S. diversified financial companies in terms of assets. And what about that support system that was built to increase efficiency? Consider its performance statistics:

◆ 831 million instructions-per-second processing capability.

◆ 15.8 million computer transactions per day.

◆ 86 million voice calls per year; 343,000 calls per day.

◆ 3.8 trillion characters of information stored.

◆ 196 high-speed tape drives.

◆ 323,000 computer data tape cartridges.

◆ 19,900 + computer terminals.

◆ 2,100 offices defined on voice network; 20 international locations; 1,500 cellular telephones; 1,600 pagers.

◆ 2-second overall terminal response time (24-hour average).

◆ 14 high-speed laser printers; 2 impact printers.

◆ 104 remote laser printers; 2,300 + personal and system printers and plotters.

◆ 1.6 million printed computer output pages per day (.9m paper, .8m fiche).

◆ 30,000 + voice and data service calls and 18,600 + telephones.

Yes, USAA did make the transition that McDermott foresaw in 1969.

THE IMAGING PROJECT: APPLYING APPROPRIATE TECHNOLOGY

USAA has come to learn that it needs to fix its processes as a prelude to the application of advanced technologies. Its members want true efficiency, not just a technological facade that covers old processes. Bridging service gaps to the member-owner in an ever-more efficient manner has been the primary thrust of USAA information technology improvement projects.

Consider the customer-focused approach of George A. McCall, USAA vice president of information services. "When a member calls in it's because of an event and we must decide what we can do for that person. This may mean that we have to work with many organizations. We're always trying to provide our members with a way to deal with us as a single company with lots of services, rather than a group of individual companies. We want them to feel that they're only working with one company." McCall explained that the systems development and integration project began in the property and casualty area and has since spread throughout the entire company. "We receive 20,000 letters and mail out 60,000 documents on any given day. And yet if a customer calls to follow up on a letter he or she sent, the service rep will be able to say to that customer, quite honestly, "Yes, sir, I have your letter right in front of me," McCall said. "This is because the service representative can call up the customer's letter on his or her CRT screen; and any correspondence we sent out to the customer will likewise be available. . . . With the imaging system, when mail is opened, the document is scanned into an optical file and indexed. This indexed data entry includes instructions that will tell what needs to be done by when, and with what priority."[8]

"Using optical imaging, we have captured over 80 million documents in the system since 1988, and we have doubled the number of customers since that time," Ken Graham, executive director of image applications, said. "All papers that used to be stored in 35,000 to 40,000 square feet of prime office space are now maintained on the system. To give you an idea what that means . . . we get 86 million calls per year and we're the fourth largest mail order office in the world. We've got 1,800 WATS lines coming into our building." McCall added, "And we're still always trying to extend the access of our customers to our service. This effort includes access to voice response (telephone to on-line database for account information) as well as personal computers (direct PC link to on-line data). Our capability continues to grow. Just last month (March 1994) we serviced about 600,000 calls by voice response alone.[9]

"We have a slogan around here: Customer Convenient, Operator Efficient and Personal. That was the reason for the imaging system. We had tried several prior, aborted attempts at managing information more efficiently, like microfiche and other laborious processes, none of which provided an on-line 'picture' to the service representative—nor that allowed that person to respond to the customer immediately," McCall said. "But, today, we have an automated insurance environment. What initially took 55 steps from the time we got a letter until we issued a policy—an average of 13 days—today takes 2 to 3 days, and eliminated 22 percent of the callbacks from the customer."

The vision for the imaging project was to provide service reps with a robust environment where all customer information was right at their fingertips. For instance, when a customer sends an application and a check for a mutual fund, scanners enter the application and check into imaging so the check can go to the bank immediately. Then the system will cue the entries so that only the next most important piece of work is given to the most appropriate person, based on grade, experience, education, and credentials. The service manager makes the prioritizing decisions, but with 1,900 service reps, and about 30 representatives for each service manager, span of control could be an issue, especially considering the massive required transaction throughput. But with the imaging system, the synchronization of this amount of incoming work is truly phenomenal. Additionally, work sent to service representatives is "electronically fingerprinted." The fingerprint identifies the work that is received at each service terminal, records the time it was received, documents if the service representative needed help, and notes which underwriter received the file next. Every piece of customer information—all customer interactions, any needed historical data, any correspondence sent or received by customers—is all on the system. "With our electronic paper trail and fingerprint system, we are able to know where everything is all the time," McCall added.

"We learned that the need to package data support was significant," Graham said. "It's absolutely critical to involve the people within the business. You can't just walk into an organization and say, 'Here it is!'; you've got to involve the people in that business from the start, and you've got to have an understanding of how that business operates." It's also important to involve those who can help others within their area see the system impact. "We had policy service people who really knew the system and were able to see how they did things, how the system should work—many times taking out non-value-added steps."

Graham went on to describe what he calls the "business-first approach." "Technology does not sell itself. It's capital intensive and may get a high rate of return, but you've got to be able to explain those needs so that a businessman can turn it into the bottom line. . . . We spend a lot of time on business analysis and business processes rate of return. For instance, today we do 10 to 11 million transactions a day. At the time we did the long-range strategic plan in the early 1980s, we had 1.3 million members and 1,900 service representatives to serve those customers. Today we have 2.6 million customers and we still have the same number of service representatives. We keep applying technology to their environment. But this means having the environment to make it work . . . you have to treat each imaging opportunity as unique leverage—one size does not necessarily fit all. We focus on our [internal] customers' line of business—making information services fit the business not vice versa—and creating a business partnership. People have a lot of ownership for how what they are operating fits under a vision; this is an important consideration when trying to do something no one else has done. When you take a business-first approach, you're able to go back and add the numbers to say, 'Yeah, the vision was right.'"

Both Graham and McCall agree that they didn't plan for incremental imaging system changes over time. "Some things have to be redone as time goes on—but if you wait until optimal technology is available, you're losing time. We started with object-oriented technology with our 1982 Session Control, which we've had to redo several times. Today we're developing examples of generic modules that don't change and are reusable at the function level, if not the code level. If you can do this once, and apply it appropriately, it saves time and money."

THE CUSTOMER SERVICE QUALIFIER

It's hard to express the level of commitment to customer service at USAA. Of the people I interviewed for this chapter, just about every one began his or her response to a question with a qualifier like, "Well, that would depend on the effect it would have on customer service," or "If customer service were positively impacted . . .," or "You can't talk about that without discussing customer service." I began to wonder just how extensively this attitude was deployed. After all, USAA may be one association, but it has over 30 subsidiaries. So my question was: Just how entrenched is this focus on customer service? Do the subsidiaries respond in the same way?

We have a family friend, an old high school chum of my wife's, who has worked for the USAA Real Estate Company (RealCo) for eight years. Not only is she a credible resource, but she's also one of the most honest people I've ever met. If I really wanted an unadulterated, straight answer, Rebecca P. Cartall, analyst for the fairly new research department at RealCo, would give it to me. The question I asked her: What's the primary purpose of your job? And her answer: "The primary purpose of my job is servicing my client, although in my case it changes every day. Mostly I need to provide each client with market analyses and current market data, matching other companies' real estate requirements with RealCo's product availability. For my customers that means reliable, up-to-the-moment information delivered in the most immediate manner possible." Bingo.

REENGINEERING FOR QUALITY

USAA began a concerted effort in Business Process Reengineering (BPR) by beginning to educate and train teams within the company about two years ago. Linda Bond, senior quality advisor in the corporate quality office, has been instrumental in rolling out this process. Corporate Quality—which saw BPR as a tool that USAA would be able to use in multiple and diversified areas—combined processes already used at USAA with what they learned at other companies. They then developed a two-day training course that has been used by about a half dozen project teams. The focus of this training is on both BPR methodology and the further development of team skills. The role of Corporate Quality is to serve as a consultant or touchstone for teams as required.

"I have found that in reengineering projects, the methodology is the easy part; it's the people part that's really, really hard," Bond said. "When process meets culture, culture wins." She explains that part of the philosophy at USAA is to help people get a different perspective. "We try to get people looking at things differently and to take risks . . . encouraging them to open their minds. We've had training sessions where we use experiential exercises that help people get ready for change. The key is to have them maintain that same feeling and sense of discovery in the reality of their work process."

From training, behavior profiles, values diversity, and more, Corporate Quality tries to encourage people to work together in a non-threatening way. One example Bond shared was the PRIDE (Professionalism Results In Dedication to Excellence) Feedback Team, a corporate-wide, cross-functional effort that looked at reengineering both employee and member feedback processes in order to emphasize that both were equally necessary. "Part of change management is to let people know that it's okay to challenge things that are assumed to be off limits." To this end, Bond describes the team's success at creating a myth that became part of the company folklore. "We had invited a senior manager to attend a team meeting where all the participants were asked to come in casual dress. When the senior manager arrived, however, he was wearing a tie. I announced that we needed to do something about this, and immediately took out a pair of scissors and cut off his tie. There was an audible gasp around the room, followed by a sigh of relief when they all saw that the manager was smiling. He wore the tie like that all day. And the effect it had on the team was amazing . . . one year later I still had people saying to me, 'John must have really been committed.' Well, if you can get a senior manager to interact with a team, and to sacrifice his tie, I'd say that's a good demonstration of commitment."

Nevertheless, Bond explains that "when it comes to change leadership, we're still new at defining these roles." However, when the claims process was reengineered, three people from human resources were dedicated to the project solely for the purpose of dealing with change management issues, which reflected an integration of human resources, systems technology, and operations. "It's getting harder and harder not to embrace reengineering, teams, and empowerment," Bond said.

BUSINESS PROCESS MANAGEMENT PRINCIPLES

In all of the change, Bond observed that, "We had to look at processes as the foundation to our business. We are becoming more systematic, defining process owners and making process change more of a planned approach." Some principles that support both BPR and the USAA approach to continuous improvement include:

- ◆ Involving top management.
- ◆ Gaining the customer perspective.

- Empowering people.
- Monitoring process.
- Ongoing communication.
- Planning for change.
- Eliminating non-value-added.
- Continuously improving.

BENCHMARKING PROCESS

Benchmarking helped to provide an external focus to the reengineering efforts. Coached by Jan Johnson, until most recently the USAA benchmarking manager, teams followed the USAA process for studying other companies during the third phase of its business process management process:

- Determine what to benchmark.
- Identify key performance measures and practices.
- Measure your own performance.
- Identify the benchmark companies.
- Measure performance of benchmark companies.
- Analyze results and communicate findings.
- Develop goals and action plans.
- Implement and monitor results.

Benchmarking may target any particular company that is excellent in a process. However, as Bill Flynn remarked: "When you learn from your competitor you can really step up the action level of the teams." Measuring processes with a common family of measures, USAA has established a common way to evaluate process performance.[10] By merging the methods of reengineering with both benchmarking analysis and continuous-improvement team activities, USAA has been able to build upon its successful past projects and then leverage change for its future. The company will not stand still. It will not be content, because USAA sees business improvement as a never-ending journey.

CATCHING THE VISION

USAA had been motivated by a dynamic leader's vision of a high technology future where the picture of an office burdened by paperwork becomes replaced by a "paperless environment." Where is the vision going to take USAA in the future? General Robert T. Herres, the current chairman at USAA and successor to McDermott, is likely to keep up the push for practical applications of high technology that laid the foundation of its current capability. An engineer by training, Herres is no stranger to "star wars technology," having served in a technical support role for the Space Policy Advisory Board. And star-wars-type technology may be where they are going.

USAA has kept ahead of its competitors by using leading edge information technology better.[11] The future will continue the vision. It will merge multimedia with expert systems that leverage the expertise of staff specialists—especially for underwriting and loan approval—across the entire organization, creating a capability for the staff specialist to work on the exceptions and difficult cases, rather than the mundane ones. The company will continue to integrate information technology with benchmarking and reengineering, linked under a common umbrella of strategic planning. The focus on technology for its own sake will not be a driver—USAA is interested in technology "only if we can turn it into better service and more satisfying jobs."[12]

It seems to me that USAA has caught the vision and demonstrated that it knows how to engineer its business as a system.

PART V

Making It Happen

13

Lessons Learned from Engineering Business Systems

Thus with all things—some are increased by taking away;
While some are diminished by adding on.

Lao Tzu, *Te-Tao Ching*

SO WHAT?

What has the study of all these current projects told us about how to apply these methods to make successful changes? Let's review our learning. First, we have noted that the building blocks of business systems engineering are not new.[1] Second, we have perceived that by integrating strategic business change initiatives with continuous improvement activities we have a more robust operational definition of TQM.[2, 3] Third, we observed that cross-functional teams are a fundamental enabler for making successful organization-wide transformation happen.[4] Fourth, we have seen that strategic changes must integrate the plans and actions of the highest and lowest levels of the organization and that systematic learning can occur when we examine the resultant outcomes of our actions in light of our plans.[5] Fifth, we noticed that some of the most productive improvements have come from the appropriate use of appropriate new technologies. Finally, we have learned that management must be clear about its plans, methods, and communications in order to enlist the support of the entire organization—people can be threatened by management's expressed need for organization-wide change because it undermines their personal job security.[6]

A recent *Harvard Business Review* article concluded that successful strategic change initiatives share two factors that allow short-term projects (less than six months) to realize long-term payoffs. These two factors are breadth and depth. Breadth means that a change initiative must address a broad business issue that improves the efficiency and effectiveness of a cross-functional process that delivers customer value. Depth means that the redesigned process must penetrate to the depth of the organizational core and influence such heartland business ingredients as:

◆ Shared values and culture.

◆ Roles and responsibilities.

◆ Measurements and incentives.

◆ Organizational structure.

◆ Job skills.

◆ Information technology.[7]

These change levers have a remarkable similarity with another set of change levers. Does this indicate that a unified field theory exists for organizational change? Xerox discovered the following set of change levers while developing its Leadership Through Quality strategy to implement Total Quality Management:

◆ Standards and measurements.

◆ Recognition and rewards.

◆ Communications.

◆ Training.

◆ Organization structure and roles.[8]

How are these levers used to initiate change that yields desired strategic improvements?

Despite all of the apparent benefits of such strategic change initiatives as reengineering, TQM, or business systems engineering, these projects can create a sensationalistic fear among employees. This is because many organizations use these terms as euphemisms for any type of organizational restructuring—and, especially, for sacking employees (I guess the politically correct term for this action is downsizing). Indeed, many consultants have jumped on the bandwagon of the "sexy new name" and are busy repackaging their credentials to fit the prevailing *theory de jour*. However, as *The Economist* noted about the implementation of these strategic change projects, "One fundamental handicap is that—like many other great management theories—business process reengineering is difficult to put into practice."[9] System-wide change is never easy. It is not a panacea for all of the ills of business, and it may be used in inappropriate situations if the senior management team is not fully aware of how to apply it.

As I studied the lessons that we have learned, four imperatives became apparent to me. I believe that these imperatives summarize all of the lessons and, unless satisfied, that we would not be able to re-anything to either ourselves, our businesses, or our systems:

1. Create capacity to act.
2. Remove the complexity.
3. Build capability upon competence.
4. Integrate your actions.

Let's examine what each of these imperatives means.

1. Create Capacity to Act

The ability to make things happen—to drive change into processes, to produce results, to act on problems and implement solutions: These all come about because people are willing to act differently. They have both the necessary competence and capability, or the capacity to act. This capacity to act comes from the clear understanding of priorities that the organization has set; the skill in analysis and problem solving that allows one to have confidence in one's proposed solution; a supportive management environment that encourages individuals or teams to make choices on behalf of the organization; and the personal or team motivation to choose a path and walk down it.

2. Remove the Complexity

One astute observer of the Japanese culture noted, around the middle of the twentieth century, that the Japanese "tend to take pragmatic attitudes and are always eager to shorten the circuit from one action to another."[10] Simple processes are better processes. This observation reinforces Tim Fuller's commentary in the *National Productivity Review*: The source of most process complexity comes from patches, tests, or work-arounds that were put in place to ensure that there would be no repeat of former failures—a process was put in place to catch them all. And, of course, what that new process change provided was non-value-added complexity.[11] Over time, nobody remembers why that extension of the process exists, and everybody assumes that it is a necessary part of the overall process. The job of most redesign efforts is to get rid of this flagrant complexity and streamline processes that are necessary to produce what the customer wants from the organization. Providing optimal value to the customer means that customers only pays for the process capability necessary to deliver their full expectations.

3. Build Capability on Competence

Process capability is truly a significant factor in developing competitive advantage. But, no matter how effective a business or work process may be, it is inconsequential unless it is supported by a team that has the competence required to capably act. This means that a team should meet the following guidelines for success. The team should be structured properly with the right skills and adequate cross-training. The team should have a meaningful charter that is supported by management. The team should have specific targets that it is seeking to achieve as well as a clear process for operating together (both a communication process and a problem-solving process are basics). Finally the team should have a sense of its mutual accountability for the results of its process.[12] The building block of the team is the individual. Just as tribes in aboriginal cultures retain their verbal history, so teams capture the record of their process-related activities in their individual memories. Each contributor to the tribe gives as he or she is able. Each individual must be developed to the extent of his or her willingness to grow in order to extend the individual's ability to contribute. This means that people should be coached in their attitudes about work, nurtured in their skills required for job performance, and mentored in their ability to apply their experiential knowledge in new directions. The investment in educating the individual is the one investment that will make a continuing return for the organization and society—all others will depreciate over time.

4. Integrate Your Actions

Systems represent only one type of action that an organization must orchestrate. In our discussions, we have talked about the need for congruency by: mapping measures from the level of organization-wide goals to the personal performance measure; aligning plans from the strategic plan to the individual workers' daily objectives; rationalizing missions from the organization-wide vision to the position description of each person; and linking the core competencies required in the organization to the current skills and development plans for each member of the entire team. Information systems and the organization staff must support this structure by becoming the flexible facilitators of this networked group, using new technologies like groupware and multimedia to facilitate the desired state of performance.

MOVING AHEAD

The questions that these four imperatives successfully beg is: How do we begin this journey and where should we start? More about that as we conclude this book.

14

An Invitation to Engineer Your Business System

The highest propriety takes action, and when no one responds to it,
Then it angrily rolls up its sleeves and forces people to comply.

Lao Tzu, *Te-Tao Ching*

IS IT TIME TO REDUX YOUR ORGANIZATION: REDISCOVER, RETHINK, REINVENT, REDESIGN, RESTRUCTURE, REVAMP, OR REENGINEER?

These days it seems like everybody is doing "re-something" to their business. However, "reengineering is becoming a euphemism for jobs that are going away and not coming back" according to New York State Lieutenant Governor Stan Lundine. Don't we want our business changes to stick—and make a bottom-line difference? Reengineering and these other strategic change approaches are relatively advanced mechanisms that imply a grassroots capability to accept change and to manage within a turbulent environment. Is this true of your organization? Many times people will want to do a strategic change effort simply because it is in vogue at the moment, not because their process is calling for that degree of redesign. The cost is great; the effort is great; the payoff, according to Mike Hammer's statistics, is not ensured by just doing it.[1] So, the prudent management team will take care in introducing these changes. The prudent manager will ask the hard question: Does our organization really have the capacity to act? Does it have the ability, training, resources, information, and motivation to

210

do things differently? Does it suffer from some "ghosts of the past"—people who are holdouts of the old way of doing things and who haunt today's activities with the voices of yesterday? Are we ready to make the journey to a new work way—or should we clean up some old issues first?

Change Requires a Foundation of Mutual Respect—Trust

All mangers want to create a learning organization—one that innovates constantly and nurtures productivity growth in its workforce. This type of organization does not just happen. It cannot be wished into existence—it must be worked into existence. In order to have an environment that grows productive change, a fundamental set of conditions must be satisfied. These conditions can make change effective:

- ◆ Managers are sensitive to the feelings and emotions of their workforce.
- ◆ Managers encourage change rather than dictate change.
- ◆ Managers effectively communicate the need for and objectives of change.
- ◆ People who are affected by the change are involved in the process.
- ◆ Everyone respects the fact that it takes time for major changes to be accepted.
- ◆ The implementation is carefully planned—it won't just happen by itself.[2]

Where should a manager start? The three drivers of successful organizational change are: management's empathy for the feelings of the workers; management's communication with the workforce about the change motivation and direction; and worker participation in the change activities. This builds trust. The answer to where to start is: Start by building trust. Trust is built from four ingredients: a common direction, shared values, consensus decision making, and a participative workforce. Dr. Frank La Fasto of Baxter Healthcare defines empowerment as: "the freedom to think and the encouragement to act." How does management encourage action? Consider the basis for action that was built into Honda.

Soichiro Honda believed that trust was an essential ingredient of the "manager's sacred duty." To build trust, a manager has four sacred duties. The manager's first duty is to create a vision that clearly identifies the direction of the organization. The second sacred duty of managers is to develop a small set of clear objectives (four or five) that will attain the vision. The third sacred management duty is to translate the objectives into everyone's work and provide the resources that are required to achieve success. The fourth sacred duty of management is to review the actions of employees and provide fair and honest feedback. By satisfying these sacred duties, management has accomplished its role of establishing principles and giving guidance, while relying on the employees to act. This structure has set up the environment of empowerment. As Rosabeth Moss Kanter says: "True 'freedom' is not the absence of structure—letting the employees go off and do whatever they want—but rather a clear structure which enables people to work within established boundaries in an autonomous and creative way."[3] By fulfilling the constraints of its "sacred duty" management has provided its workforce with the necessary ingredients to act. How should they work together to accomplish strategic change?

BUILDING CAPACITY TO ACT: RULES FOR PROCESS CHANGE

There are some principles and rules of the "common wisdom" for strategic change that may be used as decision guidelines throughout the implementation process. These guidelines are divided into two categories. The first category presents a set of principles for business process redesign. The second category provides a set of rules for process change. The principles of redesign are based largely on the sayings of Michael Hammer and supplemented by the insights of some business analysts who have observed projects or assessed approaches used for business process redesign (or reengineering). I have consolidated several lists and come up with the following principles regarding strategic change initiatives:[4]

- ◆ The objective of redesign is to create truly differentiated competitive advantage that will achieve your organization's agreed-upon strategic direction.

♦ Start redesign efforts from the desired future state and work backwards—not constrained by today's way, but considering lessons learned—do not repeat the past.

♦ Structure strategic change around core business processes and customer outcomes.

♦ Build partnerships with suppliers and customers—let customer needs drive the redesign process and supplier capability supplement your work processes.

♦ Flatten the organization hierarchy and use teams to manage work processes.

♦ Create "one-stop" work cells rather than sequential processes.

♦ Outsource noncore business processes that don't provide competitive advantage.

♦ Treat geographically separated business units as though they were centralized.

♦ Capture information once—at its source—and preserve it in a way that allows all future users to manipulate it according to their needs.

♦ Charge those who use the process output with performing the process work.

♦ Link parallel activities instead of integrating their results.

♦ Put the decision points at the place where work is performed and build control into the process.

These principles of process redesign focus on how to restructure the systems of work. They represent the approach that a team should take as it reduxes the process. They set the boundary conditions for the redesign effort. In contrast, the following rules for process change describe the way that the project management team should work to implement strategic change initiatives—the work of the redesign team once the decision has been made to go ahead with a piloted redesign project. These rules were derived in the same way that the principles of process thinking and acting were (as I described at the beginning of Chapter 5). These rules can apply to both the strategic and operational levels of business change. They may seem to be common sense— I guess that makes them uncommon wisdom. (Note: A companion to these rules is the process thinking and philosophy that is the topic of Chapter 5.)

1. Change the organization's structure to facilitate communication around the new work process.
2. Simplify the process first before automating or informating it.
3. Provide skills-based training for all of the process workers and cross-train them as much as possible.
4. Document the new process and implement a measurement system for assessing its performance capability.
5. Measure all elements of process performance: quality, cost, and cycle time.
6. Regularly review process improvement progress by asking diagnostic questions that probe into the detail of in-process performance rather than just results performance.
7. Recognize and reward the improvement activities of the organization through some form of gain-sharing.

Now that the ground rules and underlying principles have been described, it is time to consider the main issue: What is the overall process that these principles and rules support? How does one engineer a business system? Let's start at the basics of building trust through shared values and then work forward.

MAKING CHANGE HAPPEN: THE IMPLEMENTATION PROCESS

The new age of management calls for leaders who manage by principles—a clear set of core beliefs that the entire work group accepts and tries to follow. Today's management environment shares responsibility with its teams. The job of the manager is to teach the teams "correct principles" and then let them govern themselves. One set of correct principles is a description of the way that an individual can work in a team environment:

♦ Treat all viewpoints, opinions, and ideas as valuable contributions.

♦ Focus on the problem, issue, or behavior, not on the person.

◆ Listen to everyone's comments, ideas, suggestions, input—then seek consensus.

◆ Maintain constructive relationships with all group members.

◆ Value the self-confidence and self-esteem of each group member.

◆ Take the initiative to act in ways that will improve every situation.

◆ Lead by example—be a role model.

This set of principles is the precursor to the ability to implement strategic change. Such principles establish trust, which is the basis for all positive relationships—both personal and interpersonal. Now, the real meat of the process comes in. The actual approach for implementing this method is the six-step process for business systems engineering that was introduced in Chapter 4 (Figure 4–14):

1. Analyze the business situation: Develop both an enterprise model to evaluate where strategic concerns should be focused and a measurement map to determine where operational issues may be out of control and need improvement.

2. Identify the customer requirements and analyze the performance for each process that was "at issue" in Step 1.

3. Benchmark the current process performance against both internal and external organizations to establish improvement goals and learn how others have dealt with similar problems.

4. Simultaneously, perform Step 4—conduct a technology assessment to show how technology can contribute enabling solutions to improve the situation.

5. Evaluate the data collected to pinpoint problem areas and decide on the performance requirements and goals.

6. Implement the identified improvement: Manage the project, redesign the process, and implement the solution.

This model is a reasonable approach—at least four reengineering practitioners recommend very similar models.[5, 6, 7, 8] The primary distinction between this business systems model and their models is that the systems model incorporates current quality tools to perform each of these steps rather than seeking to reinvent, reengineer, redesign, rediscover, or re-anything else when fundamental quality tools will work, that is, the quality improvement process, benchmarking process, and problem-solving process. Improvement teams should spend their efforts working at improvement, not inventing new tools. While creating new tools may be a personal challenge and fun, it displaces the time that we need for taking action to improve.

CREATING CAPACITY TO ACT BY APPLYING LEARNING-THROUGH-ACTION

As we approach a complex, gradually unfolding, new environment for work, we need to both act and learn at the same time. The paradox is that learning is a consequence of action, but we have not yet learned how to act, so we must learn how to learn-as-we-go. As coparticipants in the learning organization, we need to communicate and function together in order to evolve solutions to unknown situations. This means that we must take responsibility for our own decisions and actions—not be dependent on the authority figure to tell us the "school solution" for the case study of our real-life situation. There is no school solution, only the one that we create for ourselves. In the end, we must learn to cooperate and learn from each other. But, what sort of objectives should we set so that we can create an environment where each of us, in our roles as individuals, team members, and company people, can learn in a more effective way? Here is a checklist of things to think about that will improve our capacity to know, which, in turn, increases our capacity to act:

- ◆ We should create opportunities for open communication with each other.
- ◆ We should make our own opinions explicit and seek mutual understanding.
- ◆ We should subject our own ideas to criticism, seeking to improve their quality.
- ◆ We should analyze our previous experiences to seek new applications.
- ◆ We should discover acceptable solutions cooperatively.

♦ We should select the most appropriate solutions, no matter who contributed them.

♦ We should act and then inspect the outcomes of our actions, seeking new lessons.

These are the tough changes to make because it means that we must start with our own personal attitudes and behaviors. True quality begins on the inside as a set of personal principles and beliefs and then it is radiated out. This means that we will need to add a new way to our work style—leader and coach. But, we must also recognize that there may be a time for the more autocratic style when the system does not respond. The talent of the new manager will be to learn how to balance these styles so that people believe their behavior is authentic in both types of situations—ones that call for participation and ones that call for direction. Remember the words of Rosabeth Moss Kanter regarding empowerment and management's role: "Delegating responsibility to other people does not mean abdicating managerial responsibilities for monitoring and supporting the process . . . the manager stays involved, available to support employees, reviewing results, redirecting and reorienting the team as necessary."[9]

THE NEW WORK OF MANAGEMENT

The challenge for management is to become the role model for facilitating change: coach, leader, team member, and mentor. This call to improvement starts within. Yes, we need to assess our organization for its business improvement performance. We also need to assess our teams for their performance. But, in the long run, we must evaluate ourselves—are we contributing to the increased quality of our own life? How can we engineer ourselves to become better managers, citizens, and family members? The goal that we should accept is personal mastery so that we become walking role models of quality in action. The authentic test of our quality leadership then will not be how many speeches we give on the subject of quality—not what we say, but what we do—what actions we take. Whether we are quality professionals or not, we should reconsider the statement of an old Jewish challenge: "If not me, then who? If not this, then what? If not now, then when?"

Chapter Notes

Chapter 1

1. Robert C. Stemple quoted from a speech that was produced in videotape by the American Society for Quality Control of Quality Forum IX, *Empowering People with Technology*, October 18, 1993.

2. Malcolm Knowles, *The Adult Learner: A Neglected Species*, fourth edition (Houston: Gulf Publishing Company, 1993), p. 179.

3. Michael Hammer and James Champy, *Reengineering the Corporation* (New York: HarperBusiness, 1993), p. 32.

4. Ibid., p. 3.

5. Thomas H. Davenport, *Process Innovation: Reengineering Work Through Information Technology* (Boston: Harvard Business School Press, 1993). Davenport's book describes the methodology used by Ernst & Young for Business Process Reengineering.

6. Gregory H. Watson, *Strategic Benchmarking* (New York: John Wiley & Sons, 1993), p. 149.

7. Hammer and Champy, op. cit., p. 40.

8. Henry J. Johansson, Patrick McHugh, A. John Pendlebury, and William A. Wheeler III, *Business Process Reengineering: Breakpoint Strategies for Market Dominance* (London: John Wiley & Sons, 1993). Johansson et al. describe the approach that Coopers & Lybrand apply for Business Process Reengineering.

9. Daniel Morris and Joel Brandon, *Reengineering Your Business* (New York: Mc-Graw-Hill, 1993).

10. V. Daniel Hunt, *Reengineering: Leveraging the Power of Integrated Product Development* (Essex Junction, VT: Oliver Wight Publications, 1993).

11. A. Richard Shores, *Reengineering the Factory: A Primer for World-Class Manufacturing* (Milwaukee, WI: ASQC Quality Press, 1994).

12. Lon Roberts, *Process Reengineering: The Key to Achieving Breakthrough Success* (Milwaukee,WI: ASQC Quality Press, 1994).

13. Jeffrey N. Lowenthal, *Reengineering the Organization: A Step-by-Step Approach to Corporate Revitalization* (Milwaukee, WI: ASQC Quality Press, 1994).

14. David Osborne and Ted Gaebler, *Reinventing Government: How the Entrepreneurial Spirit Is Transforming the Public Sector* (New York: Penguin Books, 1992).

219

15. Darrel Rigby's article "The Secret History of Process Reengineering" (*Planning Review*, March–April 1993, pp. 24–27) describes the historical development of reengineering.

16. Hammer and Champy, op. cit., p. 216.

17. Ibid., p. 200.

18. The preacher of old who authored the biblical book of Ecclesiastes captured this thought some 1,000 years before Christ: "The thing that hath been, it is that which shall be; and that which is done is that which shall be done: and there is no new thing under the sun. Is there any thing whereof it may be said, See, this is new? It hath been already of old time, which was before us. There is no remembrance of former things; neither shall there be any remembrance of things that are to come with those that shall come after." (Ecclesiastes 1: 9–11)

19. Rosabeth Moss Kanter, *The Change Masters: Innovation & Entrepreneurship in the American Corporation* (New York: Simon & Schuster, 1983).

20. Joseph A. Schumpeter, *Capitalism, Socialism and Democracy* (New York: Harper, 1942).

21. Peter Drucker, "The New Society of Organizations," Robert Howard, editor, *The Learning Imperative: Managing People for Continuous Improvement* (Cambridge, MA: Harvard University Press, 1993), p. 6.

22. Ibid.

23. Peter A. Phyrr, *Zero Based Budgeting* (New York: John Wiley & Sons, 1973).

24. Jay W. Forrester, *Industrial Dynamics* (Cambridge, MA: Productivity Press, 1961).

25. Thomas J. Peters and Robert H. Waterman, Jr., *In Search of Excellence* (New York: Harper & Row, 1982).

26. John Naisbitt and Patricia Aburdene, *Re-inventing the Corporation: Transforming Your Job and Your Company for the New Information Society* (New York: Warner Books, 1985).

27. Shoshana Zuboff, *In the Age of the Smart Machine: The Future of Work and Power* (New York: Basic Books, 1988), p. 395.

28. Peter Senge, *The Fifth Discipline: The Art and Science of the Learning Organization* (New York: Doubleday, 1990), p. 14.

29. Ibid., p. 139.

30. Peter Drucker, op. cit., p. 11.

31. Ibid., p. 13.

32. Malcolm Knowles, op. cit., pp. 54–63.

33. Margaret Wheatley, *Leadership and the New Science* (San Francisco: Berrett-Koehler Publishers, 1992), p. 20.

34. Ibid., p. 94.

35. Taichi Ohno, *Workplace Management* (Cambridge, MA: Productivity Press, 1988), pp. 67–70.

36. Ryuji Fukuda, *Managerial Engineering: Techniques for Improving Quality and Productivity in the Workplace* (Cambridge, MA: Productivity Press, 1984).

37. In particular, Joseph M. Juran's book *Managerial Breakthrough* (New York: McGraw-Hill, 1964) introduced the concept of the manager's job as providing a systematic approach to improving business system performance. This book greatly influenced the Japanese development of *hoshin kanri* and *kaizen:* policy deployment and continuous improvement. The term *kaizen* was popularized by Masaaki Imai in his book *Kaizen: The Key to Japan's Competitive Success* (New York: Random House, 1986).

38. Three books on policy deployment describe its basic functions: Yoji Akao, editor, *Hoshin Kanri: Policy Deployment for Successful TQM* (Cambridge, MA: Productivity Press, 1991); Brendan Collins and Ernest Huge, *Management by Policy: How Companies Focus Their Total Quality Efforts to Achieve Competitive Advantage* (Milwaukee, WI: ASQC Quality Press, 1993); and Bruce M. Sheridan, *Policy Deployment: The TQM Approach to Long-Range Planning* (Milwaukee, WI: ASQC Quality Press, 1993).

39. Rosabeth Moss Kanter, op. cit., p. 283.

40. Ibid., p. 279.

41. John Briggs and F. David Peat, *Turbulent Mirror: An Illustrated Guide to Chaos Theory and the Science of Wholeness* (New York: Harper & Row, 1989), p. 145.

42. Edgar H. Schein, *Process Consultation*, Volumes I and II (New York: Addison-Wesley, 1987 and 1988).

Chapter 2

1. As a note to readers who are in businesses that deliver a service (or services), I would like to express that I have observed all businesses have products. In a service business, the product is, in fact, the service that is delivered to the customer. The innovative design of the service product can lead to market differentiation and improved competitive position just as surely as it does for a hardware-producing manufacturer. Therefore, product innovation is as applicable to the design of services as it is for the design of durable consumer products.

2. W. Edwards Deming, *Out of the Crisis* (Cambridge, MA: Massachusetts Institute of Technology Center for Advanced Engineering Study, 1982). Deming discovered the relationship of quality and productivity in his early work with Japanese senior management (p. 3). Briefly stated, this relationship implies that improved quality reduces cost because there is less rework and scrap and fewer delays in the final delivery to the customer of acceptable products or services. This means that time spent on rework can be translated into increased productivity, which allows an opportunity to reduce price because of the advantage of decreased costs and the improved economies of scale due to increased production volume available since the process is not halted to correct problems. The opportunity to reduce prices thus provides an opportunity to gain market share over less "competitive" competitors. He continues this discussion to link his thoughts on quality, pro-

ductivity, and competitiveness with innovation. In his elaboration of the 14 points for management, which Deming cites as the basis for the transformation of American industry, Deming leads his discussion of the first point ("create constancy of purpose for improvement of product and service") by discussing the need for innovation (see pp. 23–26). Deming believes that: "Innovation, the foundation of the future, cannot thrive unless the top management have declared unshakable commitment to quality and productivity" (p. 25). Deming often acted the role of the "Quality Curmudgeon" as he berated management to act properly to fix their business system. He believed that most of the problems that influence business should be laid at the feet of the senior management team, and that it is their responsibility to remove the road blocks that inhibit the workers from making process improvement. Despite his unique style of communication, which alienated many in his intended audience, Deming's ideas have significant merit and form the foundation for much of the conceptual basis that drives business systems engineering.

3. C. Jackson Grayson, Jr., and Carla O'Dell, *American Business: A Two-Minute Warning* (New York: The Free Press, 1988), pp. 30–48, provides an in-depth analysis of international productivity and the historical position of the United States.

4. Ibid., pp. 82–89.

5. Ibid., pp. 94–97.

6. Ibid., p. 122.

7. James C. Morgan and J. Jeffrey Morgan, *Cracking the Japanese Market: Strategies for Success in the New Global Economy* (New York: The Free Press, 1991), p. 29.

8. James C. Abegglen and George Stalk, Jr., *Kaisha, The Japanese Corporation* (New York: Basic Books, 1985), p. 125.

9. Ibid., p. 279.

10. James C. Morgan and J. Jeffrey Morgan, op. cit., p. 7.

11. T. W. Kang, *Gaishi: The Foreign Company in Japan* (New York: HarperCollins, 1990), p. 226.

12. Shintaro Ishihara, *The Japan That Can Say No: Why Japan Will Be First Among Equals* (New York: Simon & Schuster, 1989), pp. 37–38.

13. David J. Lu, *Inside Corporate Japan: The Art of Fumble-Free Management* (Cambridge, MA: Productivity Press, 1987), p. 7.

14. Daniel Burstein, *Turning the Tables: A Machiavellian Strategy for Dealing with Japan* (New York: Simon & Schuster, 1993), p. 115.

15. Ibid., p. 117.

16. James C. Abegglen and George Stalk, Jr., op. cit., p. 146. Their observation of trends among *kaisha* are most insightful. They believe that *kaisha* share four key perceptions regarding competitiveness: (1) market share is the key indicator of performance—especially in a high-growth environment; (2) investment in facilities must pace the growth of the market despite any impact that this investment would have on short-term profits; (3) price is the principal competitive weapon

for dominating the market share battle; and (4) new products must be constantly introduced to continue the cycle of investment, cost reduction, price reduction, and market share (p. 34). These perceptions have shaped the fundamental business approach to competitiveness by the *kaisha*: a bias toward growth, a preoccupation with the business actions of competitors, creation and ruthless exploitation of competitive advantage, and choice of personnel and financial policies that are economically consistent with these principles (p. 5). It seems that the Japanese have internalized and improved upon the teaching of Dr. Deming on his competitiveness cycle!

17. James C. Morgan and J. Jeffrey Morgan, op. cit., p. 8.

18. James C. Abegglen and George Stalk, Jr., op. cit., p. 10.

19. Akio Morita, *Made in Japan* (New York: E. P. Dutton, 1986), p. 257. Akio Morita is a pragmatic businessman who has developed Sony from a postwar start-up company into an internationally respected industrial giant. Creativity and innovation are two of the principal characteristics of the Sony brand identity. Morita also pointed out that imitation is often the first step in a child's learning process and that the original meaning of the Japanese word for learning (*manabu*) is to imitate (*manebu*) (p. 161). Morita's own definition of the preconditions for creativity are that "creativity requires . . . human thought, spontaneous intuition, and a lot of courage" (p. 83). Morita also validates the distinction between the Western emphasis on Nobel Prizes and the Japanese emphasis on patents: "We set out to make special, innovative products, not to indulge in pure science" (p. 167).

20. Sheridan M. Tatsuno, *Created in Japan: From Imitators to World-Class Innovators* (New York: Harper & Row, 1990). While Tatsuno's book focuses on creativity in Japanese society, other books amplify this topic and relate it to innovation in business. As the interest in the subject of creativity grows, so does the literature. Michael Ray and Rochelle Meyers's book *Creativity in Business* (Garden City, NY: Doubleday, 1986) provided an overview of the material from their Stanford University business school course. William Miller, also an instructor in that course, who managed the Values and Lifestyles program for understanding consumer behavior at the Stanford Research Institute, wrote *The Creative Edge* (New York: Addison-Wesley, 1987). Miller's new book, *Quantum Quality: Quality Improvement Through Innovation, Learning and Creativity* (White Plains, NY: Quality Resources, 1993), expands upon his earlier work and connects to the message of Margaret Wheatley's *Leadership and the New Science* (see note 21 from Chapter 1). Edward De Bono has built his research into creativity from investigations into how the human brain works as a self-organizing system (described in his first book, *The Mechanism of the Mind*, New York: Simon & Schuster, 1969). De Bono's *Serious Creativity* (New York: HarperCollins, 1992) provides a systematic approach to producing creativity on demand, a significant extension of his earlier works. Other authors such as Arthur B. VanGundy (*Training Your Creative Mind*, Englewood Cliffs, NJ: Prentice-Hall, 1982) have focused on creativity within the context of problem solving and group meeting processes (see also VanGundy's *Managing Group Creativity: A Modular Approach to Problem Solving*, New York: AMACOM American Management Association, 1984). R. Donald Gamache and Robert L.

Kuhn (*The Creativity Infusion: How Managers Can Start and Sustain Creativity and Innovation,* New York: Harper & Row, 1989) take the position that the manager's role is to be a facilitator of the creative process and believe that by proper management of group activities a team may be led to creative solutions to their problems or be able to generate creative opportunities for the future.

21. Sheridan M. Tatsuno, op. cit., pp. 15–25.

22. Akio Morita, op. cit., p. 163.

23. Sheridan M. Tatsuno, op. cit., p. 57.

24. David J. Lu, op. cit., p. 86.

25. Daniel Burstein, op. cit., p. 92.

26. Ibid., p. 108.

27. Peter Drucker, "Japan: New Strategies for a New Reality," *The Wall Street Journal,* October 2, 1991.

28. James C. Morgan and J. Jeffrey Morgan, op. cit., p. 214.

Chapter 3

1. The historical context of Business Process Reengineering has its roots in many of the business management discussions of the past century: the scientific study of management by Frederick Taylor (1856–1915); the organizational structure of business by Henri Fayol (1841–1901) and Alfred P. Sloan, Jr. (1875–1966); information and measurement systems relationships described by Georg Siemens (1839–1901); and the focus on "customers" by Robert E. Wood (1879–1969). (See note eight in this chapter for a detailed description of the history relating systems thinking to Business Process Reengineering.) The emergence of Business Process Reengineering (BPR) as a contemporary discussion topic may be traced through the articles that preceded the latest flurry of book releases. The earliest discussions related to this topic really have their roots in some articles in *Harvard Business Review* that illustrate the ability to "think outside of the box" regarding business process. Theodore Levitt wrote about the analogy between production and service at a time when service was where manufacturing sent its washed-out engineers ("Production-Line Approach to Service," *Harvard Business Review,* September-October 1972). Levitt argued that service deserves equal footing with manufacturing, which complements the pleas of that time by the manufacturing engineering community for equal standing with their design engineer counterparts. David Davis introduced the term "reengineer" in the context of product development in his article "New Products: Beware of False Economies" (*Harvard Business Review,* March-April 1985); however, its usage was limited to the context of reengineering the product design. Arnold O. Putnam brought a lot of interest to the topic of streamlining the product design process with his article "A Redesign for Engineering" (*Harvard Business Review,* May–June 1985) and initiated many of the first reengineering efforts targeted on a specific cross-functional process—the product design process. Richard B. Chase and David A. Garvin extended the thinking to include business support service processes as worthy of

treatment with the same degree of consideration as the "major business processes" in their article "The Service Factory" (*Harvard Business Review*, July–August 1989). C. K. Prahalad, in a 1989 speech to The Carnegie Council on Ethics & International Affairs, pointed out that competition is basically about ideas, not technology or regulation. It is the middle manager who must act as "the engine of change," which instills the necessary competency in the organization, which becomes the source of ideas that shape the future ("The Changing Nature of World Competition: Reversing the United State's Decline," *Vital Speeches*, April 1, 1990). In 1990, Michael Hammer introduced the term "Business Process Reengineering" in his article "Reengineering Work: Don't Automate, Obliterate" (*Harvard Business Review*, July-August 1990), which then became the basis for his book. Thomas H. Davenport and James E. Short wrote "The New Industrial Engineering: Information Technology and Business Process Redesign" (*Sloan Management Review*, Summer 1990), which preceded Davenport's book. Harold Sirkin and George Stalk, Jr., described the need for an in-depth, four-loop problem-solving process that not only solved problems, but prevented them in the future by discovering root cause and anticipating future conditions where the problem could rise again. ("Fix the Process, Not the Problem," *Harvard Business Review*, July-August, 1990). Many quality engineers and managers will recognize this as thinking that is related to that of Dr. W. Edwards Deming and Dr. Joseph M. Juran in the 1950s with their emphasis on the use of measurement and statistics to prevent future causes of problems. However, the mainstream literature did not pick up on this theme until much later, and the timely appearance of this article by Sirkin and Stalk helped to position this thinking within the framework of reengineering. Tom Terez wrote "A Manager's Guidelines for Implementing Successful Operational Changes" (it appeared in *Industrial Management*, July-August 1990), which presented nine guidelines for change management of major systemic changes that were being introduced to an organization. However, Terez did not include one guideline that many of the BPR efforts were learning at this time: For change to be effective, it must involve the people who perform the process—a lesson that Alan Mogenson had been preaching in the first half of the 1900s. About 20 articles were written during 1991 and 1992 about Business Process Reengineering. It became the primary focus of special editions of *Information Week* and *National Productivity Review*. During 1993, about 30 articles were published with special emphasis occurring in *Industrial Engineering* (a series of case studies published as a 1994 book), *Fortune* (featured a cover story on how reengineering works—and doesn't—in the August 23, 1993, edition); even *USA Today* got into the picture with a feature story by John Hillkirk on November 9, 1993 ("Changing the Status Quo Is Now in Vogue"). Two articles deserve special attention. Darrel Rigby wrote "The Secret History of Process Reengineering (*Planning Review*, March-April 1993), which provided a context for BPR within the history of industrial thinking. A focus on the bottom line results of BPR came in an article by Gene Hall, Jim Rosenthal, and Judy Wade: "How to Make Reengineering Really Work" (*Harvard Business Review*, November-December 1993). As this book is being completed, more articles were being published in early 1994: *Quality Progress* is publishing a three-part series by Jeffrey N. Lowenthal, which is a synopsis of his book on the subject, in the January, February, and March editions, and *Quality Digest* published "A Reengineering Primer" in its January 1994 edition. It is clear from the set of articles and publications that a diverse set of professions is focusing their interest on the subject of reengineering: information technologists, industrial engineers, quality managers, business planners, and general managers. This is a healthy situation because it provides a neutral ground for these professions to develop a common language that they can use together to help their companies become more effective. A collection containing many of these early BPR articles was published by the Institute for Industrial Engineers (*Business Process Reengineering: Current Issues and Applications,* Norcross, GA: Institute of Industrial Engineers, 1993) and may be ordered through their professional association at (404) 449–0460.

2. Alfred P. Sloan, Jr., *My Years with General Motors* (New York: Doubleday, 1963, 1990), p. 49. Sloan managed the world's largest business and had a definite bias toward growth. "Growth, or striving for it, is, I believe, essential to the good health of an enterprise. Deliberately to stop growing is to suffocate. . . . Growth and progress are related, for there is no resting place for an enterprise in a competitive economy" (p. xx).

3. In *Strategic Benchmarking,* I described the basic factors that companies need to compete: "Quality *beyond* competitors, technology *before* competitors, and costs *below* competitors" (see the discussion on p. 9). To these I would add "organizations that are aligned to work *better* than competitors." This idea of working better leads to the criteria for what it takes to make one company a stronger competitor than another. I summarized these criteria for leadership in the race for world-class competition as follows—The winning company: (1) knows its processes better; (2) knows the industry competitors better; (3) knows its customers better; (4) responds more rapidly to customer behavior; (5) uses employees more effectively; and (6) competes for market share on a customer-by-customer basis (p. 34).

4. Peter Drucker says that the most important questions that a business can ask itself are: What is our business, who is our customer, and what does the customer consider value?

   Drucker's first two questions are the starting point of most TQM initiatives. His addition of the question relating to customer value goes beyond most TQM surveys of customer requirements. If our contribution to value creation on behalf of our customers really does drive the success of both their business and our business, then we should be particularly concerned about the productivity of our customer. We should know what drives the customer's productivity as well as the strategic direction and tactical operations of our customers for managing productivity.

5. John Guasparini, *The Customer Connection* (New York: AMACOM, 1988), p. 196.

6. Jay W. Forrester, *Principles of Systems* (Cambridge, MA: Productivity Press, 1968), p. 1–1. Systems thinking and the development of structured theories around change management are not new, but rather represent an evolutionary develop-

ment. The history of systems thinking is rooted in the analysis activities of the Operations Evaluation Group in World War II and matured at The RAND Corporation during the 1950s. Perhaps the most well known group of individuals who applied systems thinking and statistical analysis to business methods were the "Whiz Kids"—the ten Air Force officers who applied their knowledge to help shore up the management systems at Ford Motor Company. Robert S. McNamara, the most famous of this group, became the Secretary of Defense under President John F. Kennedy. He subsequently hired Charles Hitch and Daniel Ellsberg to support the restructuring of the Pentagon around more "businesslike" methods. The story of *The Whiz Kids* is well told by John A. Byrne (New York: Currency Doubleday, 1993). During the war, similar groups of analytical staff officers had created mathematical models for force level planning as well as tactical operations such as search and screening. They had applied systems thinking and statistical methods to the art of warfare and, in the process, created the science of operations research. [Consider some of the works of military operations research that evolved between World War II and my college years: Melvin Dresher, *Games of Strategy: Theory and Applications* (Santa Monica, CA: The RAND Corporation, 1961); Charles J. Hitch and Roland N. McKean, *The Economics of Defense in a Nuclear Age* (Santa Monica, CA: The RAND Corporation, 1960); J. P. Large, editor, *Concepts and Procedures of Cost Analysis* (Santa Monica, CA: The RAND Corporation, 1963); R. Duncan Luce and Howard Raiffa, *Games and Decisions* (New York: John Wiley & Sons, 1957); David M. Miller and Martin K. Starr, *Executive Decisions and Operations Research* (Englewood Cliffs, NJ: Prentice-Hall, 1960); Philip M. Morse and George E. Kimball, *Methods of Operations Research* (Cambridge, MA: MIT Press, 1951); E. S. Quade, *Analysis for Military Decisions* (Santa Monica, CA: The RAND Corporation, 1964); E. S. Quade and W. I. Boucher, *Systems Analysis and Policy Planning: Applications in Defense* (New York: Elsevier, 1968); John Von Neumann and Oskar Morgenstern, *Theory of Games and Economic Behavior* (Princeton, NJ: Princeton University Press, 1944).] After World War II, many of the "Whiz Kids" who applied mathematical techniques to operations planning were scooped up by the U.S. automotive industry to create their own strategic planning capability. Robert McNamara and his group at Ford are the most visible of this group. When McNamara, in response to the lure of John F. Kennedy's "Camelot," brought his crew of analysts to the Department of Defense, he brought with him a rich tradition of systems thinking that he transferred into the military planning system. This increased visibility of analytical methods and systems thinking in the mid-1960s created a broad exposure for these methods. In response, people began to investigate systems thinking for applications in a variety of fields. This evolutionary development of systems-based, analytical, change management thinking has four related historical developments: (1) general systems theory, (2) organizational development, (3) field theory, and (4) group methods and dynamics. In the first development, systems theories provide a conceptual framework for the evaluation of all types of complex organizations as socio-technical systems that have interacting subsystems. [Cf. D. Cleland, editor, *Systems, Organization Analysis, Management* (New York: McGraw-Hill, 1969); Jay W. Forrester, *Principles of Systems* (Cambridge, MA: MIT Press, 1968); Jay W. Forrester, *Industrial Dynamics* (Cambridge, MA: MIT

Press, 1961); F. E. Kast and J. E. Rosenzweig, *Organization and Management: A Systems Approach* (New York: McGraw-Hill, 1970); T. Parsons, *The Social System* (New York: The Free Press, 1951); J. A. Seilor, *Systems Analysis in Organizational Behavior* (Homewood, IL: Irwin and Dorsey, 1967); Ludwig Von Bertalanffy, *General System Theory* (New York: Braziller, 1968); and L. Zadeh, *Systems Theory* (New York: McGraw-Hill, 1969).] The second development—the field of organizational development—has applied tools and procedures that use systems theory to conduct organizational diagnosis of the need for change, use data for feedback into systems for renewal, and use data to more precisely plan for future directions. [Cf. F. W. Baughart, *Educational Systems Analysis* (New York: Macmillan, 1969); D. Bushnell and D. Rappaport, *Planned Change in Education: A Systems Approach* (New York: Harcourt Brace Jovanovich, 1972); R. C. Davis, *Planning Human Resource Development* (Chicago: Rand-McNally, 1966); H. W. Handy and K. M. Hussain, *Networked Analysis for Educational Management* (Englewood Cliffs, NJ: Prentice-Hall, 1968); Van Court Hare, Jr., *Systems Analysis: A Diagnostic Approach* (New York: Harcourt, Brace, and World, 1967); H. J. Hartley, *Educational Planning–Programming–Budgeting: A Systems Approach* (Englewood Cliffs, NJ: Prentice-Hall, 1968); R. Kaufman, *Educational System Planning* (Englewood Cliffs, NJ: Prentice-Hall, 1972); James M. Lyneis, *Corporate Planning and Policy Design: A System Dynamics Approach* (Cambridge, MA: Pugh, Roberts Associates, Inc., 1980); S. Optner, *Systems Analysis for Business and Industrial Problem Solving* (Englewood Cliffs, NJ: Prentice-Hall, 1965); Edward B. Roberts, *Managerial Applications of System Dynamics* (Cambridge, MA: MIT Press, 1976); and B. H. Rudwick, *Systems Analysis for Effective Planning* (New York: John Wiley & Sons, 1969).] The third development focuses on the role and aspects of organizational change. Organizational change theorists have built upon the field-theory concepts of Kurt Lewin and have focused their attention on a related set of topics: planning for change, organizational development, the role of the change agent, resistance to change, management of conflict, and the development of intervention theory. [Cf. Chris Argyris, *Interpersonal Competence and Organizational Effectiveness* (Homewood, IL: Corsey, 1962); Chris Argyris, *Integrating the Individual and the Organization* (New York: John Wiley & Sons, 1964); Chris Argyris, *Intervention Theory and Method: A Behavioral Science View* (Reading, MA: Addison-Wesley, 1970); Chris Argyris, *Increasing Leadership Effectiveness* (New York: John Wiley & Sons, 1976); Warren G. Bennis, *Changing Organizations* (New York: McGraw-Hill, 1966); Warren G. Bennis, *Organization Development: Its Nature, Origins, and Prospects* (Reading, MA: Addison-Wesley, 1969); W. G. Bennis, K. D. Benne, and R. Chin, *The Planning of Change* (New York: Holt, Reinhart and Winston, 1968); Robert R. Blake and Jane S. Mouton, *The Managerial Grid: Key Orientations for Achieving Production Through People* (Houston, TX: Gulf Publishing Company, 1964); D. E. Grenier, editor, *Organizational Change and Development* (Homewood, IL: Irwin, 1971); Kurt Lewin, *Field Theory in Social Science* (New York: Harper, 1951); Gordon Lippitt, *Organizational Renewal* (New York: Appleton-Century-Crofts, 1969); Gordon Lippitt, *Visualizing Change* (New York: John Wiley & Sons, 1978); and Edar Schein, *Process Consultation: Its Role in Organization Development* (Reading, MA: Addison-Wesley, 1969).] The final development is on the use of groups to implement organizational change. [Cf. L. P. Bradford, K. D. Bene, and J. R. Gibb, *T-Group Theory and Laboratory Method* (New York: John Wiley & Sons, 1964); Paul Hare, *Handbook of Small Group Research* (New York: The Free Press, 1962); Paul Hare, *Small Group Process* (New York: Macmillan, 1969); D. Jacques, *Learning in Groups* (Dover, NH: Croom Helm, 1984); Edgar Schein and Warren G. Bennis, *Personal and Organizational Change Through Group Methods* (New York: John Wiley & Sons, 1965); L. Solomon and B. Berzon, *New Perspectives in Encounter Groups* (San Francisco: Jossey-Bass, 1972); L. A. Zander, *Groups at Work* (San Francisco: Jossey-Bass, 1977); and L. A. Zander, *Making Groups Effective* (San Francisco: Jossey-Bass, 1982).]

7. Peter M. Senge, op. cit., p. 7.

8. Citations from Webster's dictionary are from the *New Webster's Dictionary of the English Language* (New York: Delair Publishing Company, 1981).

9. Frederick W. Taylor, *Scientific Management* (reprinted by Weston, CT: Greenwood Publishing Group, 1972).

10. The shadow box in this chapter describes the distinction between Total Quality Management and Business Process Reengineering. Business systems engineering takes a broad perspective, as does TQM, to the management of change. Perhaps, the most significant distinction between systems engineering and process reengineering is that of scope. In order to reengineer a process, a thorough understanding of the business is not required—only of a business process. However, in order to engineer a business system, the architect of change must consider all of the elements of the business and not be restricted to a singular process. This is why the engineering of an entire business system requires a cross-functional approach and also why the participation of the three major cross-functional support groups must be coordinated: quality, human resources, and information systems.

11. Strategic thinking is really the art of seeing differently. This theme is common between both Henry Mintzberg and Peter Senge. Mintzberg defines seven complementary dimensions of seeing that result in a strategy. Developing strategy takes: (1) Seeing ahead—constructs a future from events of the past, forecasting from discontinuities toward future possibilities; (2) seeing behind—looking at history to provide an interpretive understanding of the possibilities for the future; (3) seeing above—getting the big picture or macro-level perspective from 60,000 feet; (4) seeing below—sorting through the details to understand the micro-level perspective of the business that supports the macro-level perspective; (5) seeing beside—seeing laterally or in a creative way that challenges the conventional wisdom; (6) seeing beyond—constructing creative ideas into a world of possibilities that it invents; and (7) seeing it through—taking action to follow through on the strategic thinking. (See Mintzberg's article "Strategic Thinking as Seeing" in the compendium edited by Juha Nasi—*Arenas of Strategic Thinking*, Helsinki: Foundation for Economic Research, 1991, pp. 21–25.) Peter Senge notes that each of us has a "learning horizon," a period of time in which we can learn from our own direct experience. He observes also that we have a learning dilemma: "We learn best from experience but we never directly experience the consequences of many of our most important decisions" (Peter Senge, *The Fifth Discipline*, p. 23). Senge

believes that a paradigm shift is needed in our way of seeing to recognize under-lying patterns in our experience. This requires a shift:

From:	To:
Seeing parts.	Seeing the whole.
Seeing things.	Seeing interrelationships.
Seeing linear cause-and-effect chains.	Seeing interrelationships.
Seeing static snapshots.	Seeing patterns and processes of change.
Seeing people as helpless reactors.	Seeing people as active participants.
Reacting to the present.	Creating the future.

12. In this adaptive environment, new tools will be needed to create a learning environment. In particular, the systems analysts' tools of business simulation and gaming can be used to generate alternative worlds for future potential states. These tools would permit a more friendly "creative destruction" of competency and capabilities based on more contingencies than we will encounter in the real world. These tools would also help to alleviate Senge's learning dilemma (see the previous footnote). For the most flexible performance, the tools of simulation and gaming should be based on the business' real-world management information system. Such an innovative information system would provide great value to a firm. It would be difficult for competitors to imitate and also provide the rare opportunity for training and development of both senior managers and a new generation of managers who will follow at the helm of the business.

13. I distinguished between core competence and process capability in *Strategic Benchmarking* (New York: John Wiley & Sons, 1993, see pp. 29–33). For additional reading on this subject see the following articles: Gary Hamel and C. K. Prahalad, "Strategic Intent," *Harvard Business Review*, May–June 1989; C. K. Prahalad and Gary Hamel, "The Core Competence of the Corporation," *Harvard Business Review*, May–June 1990; and George Stalk, Philip Evans, and Lawrence E. Shulman, "Competing on Capabilities: The New Rules for Corporate Strategy," *Harvard Business Review*, March-April 1992.

14. Proverbs 29:18.

15. Noel M. Tichy and Stratford Sherman, *Control Your Destiny or Someone Else Will* (New York: Currency Doubleday, 1993), p. 7.

16. American Quality Foundation, *The Stuff Americans Are Made Of* SM: *An American Strategy for Quality Improvement* (Milwaukee: ASQC, 1993), pp. 16–17. The survey also asked if the most meaningful changes or improvements occurred through gradual progress or all of a sudden. Of the sample, 55 percent stated gradual progress was more significant, while 45 percent stated sudden improvements were more significant. However, when both groups were asked how they interpreted "sudden" and "gradual," 57 percent of those who selected gradual improvement identified that to mean "within several months" and 87 percent of those who selected sudden improvement meant "within several months." It's

clear that we like to see our change occur quickly whether we label the time period as either sudden or gradual.

17. Brian L. Joiner, *Fourth Generation Management: The New Business Consciousness* (New York: McGraw-Hill, 1994), pp. 27–28.

18. Much of the better thinking on organizational-level structure has its roots in the late 1970s when McKinsey & Company conducted research on the seven S's of the organization, which led to the publication of *In Search of Excellence* by Peters and Waterman. Kenichi Ohmae, the managing director of the McKinsey Tokyo Office, in his book *Triad Power: The Coming Shape of Global Competition* (New York: The Free Press, 1985), lists the seven S's: "shared values, strategy, style, skills, staff, structure, and systems" (p. 67). Ohmae also presents a generic version of the business system model, which McKinsey & Company use to base its organizational analysis (see p. 34 of his book). The latest thinking from McKinsey's organization that has been exposed to the public is its ten-step model for horizontal restructuring of a company. As described in the May 18, 1992, *Fortune* article titled "The Search for the Organization of Tomorrow" by Rahul Jacob, this ten-point blueprint includes the following organizational imperatives: (1) Organize primarily around processes, not task; (2) flatten the hierarchy by minimizing the subdivision of processes; (3) give senior leaders charge of processes and process performance; (4) link performance objectives and evaluation of all activities to customer satisfaction; (5) make teams, not individuals, the focus of organization performance and design; (6) combine managerial and nonmanagerial activities as often as possible; (7) emphasize that each employee should develop several competencies; (8) inform and train people on a just-in-time, need-to-perform basis; (9) maximize supplier and customer contact with everyone in the organization; and (10) reward individual skill development and team performance instead of individual performance alone. In the current stream of articles on the topic of Business Process Reengineering, one McKinsey article stands out: Robert B. Kaplan and Laura Murdock, "Rethinking the Corporation: Core Process Redesign," *The McKinsey Quarterly*, Number 2, 1991, pp. 27–43. They point out the distinction between analyzing core processes and the traditional value chain approach to the company (pp. 28–29). The systems model that I present in this book merges these ideas together and calls it a "value chain" even though the chain is incomplete because it focuses on the core processes. I justify this in my mind by thinking that this approach focuses management attention on the vital few processes in the value chain that are perceivable to external customers and make a difference in the way that each of the segments of the organization's stakeholders perceives the organization's performance. In addition, the model that they illustrate (Exhibit 1 of their article) would be more difficult to incorporate in the graphic that I use in Chapters 3 and 4.

19. Too many people have sought to distinguish between the characteristics of leadership and management for me to make this subject a major theme in this book. However, I have a belief that I wish to share. People tend to operate on a continuum scale of "executive behaviors" where one limit is labeled leadership and the opposite limit is called management. The distinctions between these two limits is how an individual tends to look at his or her immediate situation. As a person

is promoted in an organization to the higher levels, a broadening of capability is required as one's role transitions from the management side of the continuum to the leadership side. This requires the development of expanded ways of thinking:

From Management:	To Leadership:
Short-range thinking.	Long-range thinking.
Control of individuals.	Empowerment of teams.
Compliance with direction.	Ownership of planning.
Risk avoidance.	Risk management.
Management decision making.	Participative decision making.

One lesson that seasoned executives have learned is that becoming a leader does not mean that one is no longer a manager. There is a time for directive management, just as there is a time for participative leadership. Leaders must learn to operate within this continuum scale between these behaviors as is dictated by the situation that they face. While this scenario seems to harbor all of the ills of a very subjective or relativistic approach, it actually recognizes the chaotic environment of today's businesses. This is what Margaret Wheatley calls the interweaving of processes that reflect the order of things—"not rigid, but a dynamic energy swirling around us" (op. cit., pp. 117–119).

20. Gregory H. Watson, op. cit., pp. 41–45.

21. TQM is not without its detractions. When TQM is implemented in Western organizations, it has an insidious failure mechanism built in. Kaplan and Murdock (see note 18 for the citation) have recognized that the functional specialization of Western businesses has yielded a functional implementation pattern for TQM: "Corporate-wide improvement initiatives (like total quality management) tend to happen within functions led by managers who are generally functional specialists" (p. 27). But, an implementation of TQM can reach a point of diminishing returns if it is not implemented properly as a cross-functional and cross-organizational initiative. Kaplan and Murdock note that TQM can be a failure because of the way that it is applied: "within functions or departments, while the causes of the problems are unfortunately often outside the scope of those departments or functions" (p. 33). If TQM is "focused at the functional activity level," then it may be "unable to recognize the larger and more meaningful information issues: Lack of integration between the quotation and order-entry systems and poor integration between sales office and factory." Thus, "linkages between functional systems [may] never become a systems development priority" (p. 34). However, these observations do not represent errors in the philosophy of TQM or its methods. They do represent errors in the implementation of TQM. This comes down to human problems. To get past the functional viewpoint, the staff function needs to be rethought. Chapter 7 will describe some of the initiatives that can help to get around an organization's central staff "functionality." The team structure may not break down functional oranizations as many claim. There is still room for functional teams in the organization of the future. However, the staff support organizations can behave in a very different manner to help transcend the func-

tional barriers—this behavior can help compensate for the need to retain functional teams in parts of the organization and can be a catalyst to align the thinking of these functional teams with a cross-functional perspective.

Chapter 4

1. Palermo's law and other aphorisms regarding quality are the product of the witty mind of Richard C. Palermo, Sr. Dick, as the co-editor of *The World of Quality: A Timeless Passport* (Milwaukee, WI: ASQC Quality Press, 1993), preserved several more of his unique sayings in the chapter seven on lessons learned over the ten-year Xerox quality journey. A version of Palermo's law was quoted by Thomas A. Stewart in his May 18, 1992, *Fortune* article titled "The Search for the Organization of Tomorrow."

2. A helpful variant of this enterprise model would show the major customer interfaces for each subsystem on the value chain and also depict the major segments for suppliers and customers on the generating and delivery sides of the chain.

3. The sequential nature of most business processes is the result of the fact that information was passed around by paper, and that paper could be in only one place at one time. This is why Xerox focuses on document tracking as it evaluates organization performance during a process reengineering effort.

4. I described a methodology for evaluating key business processes in a previous book, *The Benchmarking Workbook* (Cambridge, MA: Productivity Press, 1992), pp. 18–22.

5. There are two ways to look at measurements: (1) as "hard" analytical methods that are used to indicate definitive measures of performance, or (2) as more subjective methods that are used to understand trends in opinion. In the analytical categories, benchmarking is one way to cover a subject in depth to determine specifically "what performance occurs where" in a process at a particular organization or set of organizations. It should be complemented by a survey that can illustrate the breadth of application for the trend information discovered through the benchmarking process. Subjective data are more difficult to deal with; however, they can be moved from the realm of anecdotal data to a more generic understanding of trend data by integrating two techniques. The first technique is to ask the expert—also called the Delphi technique. If a group of experts agrees on a particular content item, then it must be close to "truth." This should be supplemented by a focus group, where we "ask the customer." If customers and experts agree, then subjective methods have guided us to a better understanding of the "hard to quantify" types of information that are also needed to guide an organization.

6. A well-structured approach for process mapping among business and work processes is the IDEF methodology developed in the late 1970s as a systems definition language for manufacturing processes. IDEF stands for the Integrated Computer Assisted Manufacturing (or ICAM for short) DEFinition language. It includes three levels of complexity. The top level is the process description language or IDEF0. The second level is the data-modeling methodology that defines the in-

formation system data elements that are required to support the processes. This data entity-relationship model is called IDEF1. The third level is a simulation language that allows the sequential timing of processes and measurements to be used—called IDEF2. In my opinion, the IDEF design team missed a step in its decomposition—the mapping of processes to measures as illustrated in a measurement map. The data model then becomes a methodology for delivering the measurement map on a management information system.

7. One way that many companies predict interperiod performance is through a financial outlook process whereby they have established P-measures of financial performance that will reliably predict the end-of-quarter results. As the company approaches the midpoint of its reporting quarter, it projects the performance of these P-measures using seasonally adjusted historical information to determine if it will have an overachievement of its plan (three cheers for management) or an underachievement of the plan (the economy is no good). If a shortfall in the plan is projected, the management team still has time to make a shortfall recovery by escalating the attention of the entire team to the performance issue.

8. The tool to perform a measurement map is a tree diagram. The tree diagram decomposes the metric into its component parts and then divides these into actionable measurements. Once the measures are actionable, then statistical stratification analysis can be performed to seek areas to be changed or identify areas for improvement.

9. ISO 9000, the international quality system standard, describes an approach to managing work process documentation. It builds a documentation hierarchy that starts with a quality manual and its supporting procedure documents, which describe the major aspects of the quality system, and inspects the flow of requirements down to the work process level.

10. I owe many of the insights for this model to a group of seven Hewlett-Packard managers from the Roseville, California, operation who called themselves "the simple seven." They first coined the acronym UDSA (Understand, Document, Simplify, then Automate—only if necessary), which was an essential breakthrough in my thinking about how to apply automation to work processes. This group was responsible for the reengineering of the printed circuit board assembly operations into a leading example of process simplification with the appropriate degree of automation.

11. While many people have said that the quality community does not have any value-added output, I beg to disagree. I believe that we are guilty of producing at least two significant types of outputs—books and acronyms. UDSO is such an ugly acronym that it may even be memorable!

12. QIP and PSP were designed to be used at the work process level for work process design (the application of QIP) or for problem solving (the application of PSP). QIP may be considered to have two major phases. The first three steps are used to define the work process, while the remaining steps are actually a project management process for change implementation and the assurance of process control. While both the QIP and PSP models will be illustrated first as individual or stand-alone models that may have a variety of applications as individual work process

level tools, their real strength lies in combination with parts of the benchmarking model and formation into a business systems engineering tool as will be illustrated in Figure 4–14.

13. In Japan, this three-pronged focus is the heart of their daily management system. Their *kaizen* emphasis is called the "Five S Movement" in Japan. Perhaps the best spokesperson of that movement is Masaaki Imai, author of *Kaizen: The Key to Japan's Competitive Success* (New York: Random House, 1986). The Five S Movement takes its name from the five words starting with the letter S that focus the entire organization on continuous improvement. The first S is *seiro*, which means "to straighten up" by defining things that are necessary and eliminating things that are not. This means that a work process would eliminate things that are not necessary or not aligned with its output. The second S is *seiton*, meaning "to put things in order" and focuses on providing an orderly layout of tools and equipment so that it is ready for use when it is needed. (This conflicts with the learning that most of us received from our childhood, where we were told to store things away when we are done using them. The storage place used by the Japanese worker is "on the line" at the point of use.) The third S is *seiso*, which means to keep the workplace clean. The fourth S is *seiketsu*, which means that the habit of cleanliness must begin with each individual and that we have a responsibility to keep ourselves clean. The fifth S is *shitsuke*, which means to follow the procedures of the work process. In *kaizen* activities, the worker is seeking to eliminate three factors that represent the need for improvement. These are called the "3 Mu" checklist because each term begins with *mu* in Japanese. The focus in *kaizen* is on both recognizing and eliminating *muda* (any type of waste in resources—time, cost, or scrap— or the wasted movement of inefficient operations by workers), *muri* (the strain caused by equipment operating near its rated capacity or people operating in nonergonomic conditions), and *mura* (the types of work process discrepancies that come from not following the procedure for an optimized work activity). (See Imai, op. cit., pp. 231–234.) Shigeo Shingo, the late and venerated developer of the engineering concepts behind the Toyota Production System, wrote a book on the idea of *poka-yoke* or the process of making work processes safe from failure by developing equipment that will lead to no mistakes in the workplace. Shingo's book, *Zero Quality Control: Source Inspection and the Poka-yoke System* (Cambridge, MA: Productivity Press, 1986), provides a good complement to Imai's book for understanding the deployment of *kaizen* to a manufacturing environment.

14. The quality improvement process is based on some of the basic principles of Total Quality Management and is aimed at providing customer-focused process improvement. It is used to develop a new process or significantly redesign an existing process. It is differentiated from the problem-solving process in application, and the problem-solving process is evoked in the quality improvement process for gap closure during Steps 6, 8, and 11 of the model presented in Figure 4–9. The principles that the quality improvement process embody include: Customer needs drive the process development; process should be based on prevention of problems; problems identified in process design should be "managed by fact" and eliminated at the root cause level; process design should be continuous covering

the entire flow from input through output; all work activities can be represented as processes and all processes can be documented; process simplification reduces the opportunity for waste, errors, and rework; and all processes should be measured for results and in-process control.

15. Downsizing usually follows a relatively standard approach: first, analyze the business process to determine what are the essential products and services (as well as support resources) that will be provided in the future; second, identify those individuals who are required for conducting the essential business of the future; third, restructure the organization by flattening the hierarchy and eliminating as much middle management as possible—using team structures as the basic building block of the organization; and fourth, implement and manage the workforce reductions. Robert M. Tomasko, *Downsizing: Reshaping the Corporation for the Future* (New York: AMACOM, 1987), pp. 27–39, describes some of the ways to downsize an organization. He quotes some interesting older statistics: In 1980, 10 percent of the U.S. industrial workforce was in middle management positions. Comparing this with other countries, we are clearly in an uncompetitive position: Japan 4.4 percent, West Germany 3 percent, and Sweden 2.4 percent. Much of the emphasis on downsizing would be focused on the middle management group. *Demassing* is the word Tomasko coined to characterize the removal of large chunks of managers and professionals from their organizations; some characteristics of demassing include: relatively large reductions, 5 to 15 percent and more, of the middle management workforce; widespread cutbacks that affect many, if not all, divisions and departments; deep reductions that usually cover several levels of the organization; priority on lowering costs by lowering head count; and emphasis on completing the program as quickly as possible.

Many companies use stock price as their key indicator of performance. This "value-based planning" approach has led to decisions to break down large conglomerates because the price-earnings multiple of their stock is depressed by one or two underachieving divisions. Some call this industry restructuring that results in the divestiture by spin-off or buyout of these unproductive divisions or business units. The paradox of such a move is that by divesting itself of the unproductive unit, management must now downsize because there is a smaller revenue base to support the corporate overhead. Head count reduction, RIF or reduction in force (sometimes preceded by "V" for voluntary RIF—as in an early retirement program—or "I" for involuntary RIF—the outright form of severance), and demassing are neutral words used to describe an emotional event that influences both the departed and the survivors.

16. Downsizing can destroy team empowerment. When a company is growing and hiring people, it is recruiting for a purpose—to expand the team in a way that shapes its competence to perform its work processes. When skills or competencies are missing from an organization, there are only three possible approaches to realign the capabilities of the current workforce without hiring new employees. First, individual "excess" employees may be retrained in new vocational skills and assigned to fill the gap. Second, team members may be cross-trained so that each member can perform the jobs of the other team members. This skill-based training concept is at the heart of many company programs for self-directed work groups. With this option, management has more flexibility in reassigning people and work

because the organization has greater competence and does not rely on a single person's knowledge or skill to get the job done. The third option is to delegate management responsibilities down to self-directed teams to reduce the need for middle management. Team capabilities may be expanded to include tasks normally done by managers: scheduling, budgeting, and decision making. When management does downsize, it should take into account who will take on the objectives of those individuals who are taken out of the organization. If these objectives are assigned to the team, then each person bears a larger burden than before—which, if not properly analyzed, could result in a "punitive workload" for the survivors of the downsizing. Core competence is embedded within employees, and retraining and reallocation of objectives should be considered in the redesign process to ensure the smooth transition. Here are five lessons from the 1980s experience with downsizing: (1) Don't grow too large in the first place; (2) prepare for the down side; (3) use a targeted approach to eliminate unprofitable units or unproductive individuals, rather than cutting across the board; (4) continually manage the growth and structure of the organization so that it doesn't get out of hand in the first place; (5) don't just cut costs and jobs—focus on the other half of the productivity equation also and go for more growth in revenue and market share.

17. Jack Welch of General Electric stated his concern this way: "For a long time our actions muddied communications. We were taking out lots of people. We were taking out layers of management. We were selling off businesses. We were impacting people's lives." Welch was quoted in the book by Noel M. Tichy and Stratford Sherman, *Control Your Destiny or Someone Else Will* (New York: Currency Doubleday, 1993), p. 10.

18. For more information on benchmarking, see two previous books by the author: *The Benchmarking Workbook* (Cambridge, MA: Productivity Press, 1992) and *Strategic Benchmarking* (New York: John Wiley & Sons, 1993).

19. Another way to differentiate between QIP and PSP is that QIP primarily addresses the design of preventive measures in anticipation of what could go wrong in a work process, while PSP addresses corrective action to deal with issues that are not going right in a work process.

20. David Garvin's article on learning in *Harvard Business Review* cited the Xerox PSP as a learning method. He defines the learning organization as, "an organization skilled at creating, acquiring, and at modifying its behavior to reflect new knowledge and insights"—great insight! Garvin presents the Xerox PSP as an illustration of a way to modify its behavior. I would add that benchmarking provides a means to *acquire* new knowledge, while the quality improvement process provides a means to *create* new knowledge (for details on Garvin's thesis, see his article "Building a Learning Organization," *Harvard Business Review*, July-August 1993, pp. 78–91).

21. Dick Leo of Xerox Quality Solutions is the developer of the problem matrix for assessment of systemwide problems.

22. In Michael Porter's work on competitive advantage, he focuses on two differentiators: price and quality. By expanding this to include three additional competi-

tive differentiators, we can have a broader perspective of the competitive battlefield without making it overly complex so that we can't determine a clear focus.

23. The use of such multiple criteria for evaluating alternatives is an appropriate application of the Analytic Hierarchy Process (AHP). AHP is a methodology for taking customer perceived rankings of importance (determined by customer survey) and evaluating the importance of a fixed set of criteria (the five criteria for selection of strategic change processes), which may then be applied to a list of projects being considered. For specific information regarding the use of AHP for making such complex decisions, see Thomas J. Saaty, *Multicriteria Decision Making: The Analytic Hierarchy Process* (Pittsburgh: RWS Publications, 1991) and Bruce L. Golden, Patrick T. Harker, and Edward A. Wasil, *The Analytic Hierarchy Process: Applications and Studies* (New York: Springer-Verlag, 1989). An example of the use of AHP for evaluating decisions for production automation at the IBM Rochester, Minnesota, operation was presented in Gerald J. Baim's book *Benchmarking: A Practitioner's Guide for Becoming and Staying Best of the Best* (Schaumburg, IL: Quality and Productivity Management Association, QPMA Press, 1992).

24. What a business does with its resulting windfall from productivity improvements is a matter of how the senior management team sets its priorities. Savings from waste elimination and the increased efficiency of business processes produce returns that compete for distribution through a variety of alternatives. For instance, financial business results may be allocated in terms of: increased share price, which reflects retained earnings and reinvestment in the business; increased dividends to the shareholders as a reward for their contribution of capital to create and sustain the business; reduced prices of products and services, which are passed on to customers in order to realize additional growth in the market or to maintain market position; or profit sharing and bonuses for the employees in recognition of their contribution in producing the goods and services that are provided to customers.

Each of these allocations of financial returns is based on how the business defines success in its basic business strategy. Therefore, it is an error to judge each business as if the senior management team made equivalent decisions regarding the allocation of its windfall profits and savings. The sole measure of stock price or earnings per share—currently the market's favored, one-dimensional litmus test of business success—is a flawed measure since it does not take into account the management team's intention to distribute these productivity earnings.

Chapter 5

1. H. James Harrington has presented a set of fallacies regarding business process in his book *Business Process Improvement: The Breakthrough Strategy for Total Quality, Productivity, and Competitiveness* (New York: McGraw-Hill, 1991), pp. 17–18. I prefer to think of these as the myths of business process that are held by quality managers who are not empowered to influence their organization's business processes. We should also recognize that a set of similar mythologies surrounding the work process is held by information managers who are driving the

reengineering efforts for business processes at some companies without gaining the participation of the work process level. Indeed, the same set of mythologies prevails—try playing the following game to see what happens. The directions are: Ineffective (business or work—choose one) processes do not cost the organization as much money as ineffective (work or business—choose the other) processes. Therefore, there is little to be gained by spending limited improvement energy and effort by improving (business or work—choose the same one, for consistency sake, as the previous first choice) processes. The organization can focus its efficiencies on (business or work—stay consistent in your choices!) processes and finesse the interactions with (work or business—stay alert now, you want to choose the opposite here) processes. (Business or Work—choose the perspective of your set of myths) processes are relatively unimportant when compared to (work or business—choose the opposite here) processes. By focusing on (business or work—choose your favorite) processes, we can control (work or business—choose the opposite) processes. The key to enlightenment of process thinking is that business processes and work processes are part of a continuum and cannot be separated as a focus for continuous improvement.

2. A most outstanding book on the subject of root cause analysis is by Paul F. Wilson, Larry D. Dell, and Gaylord F. Anderson, *Root Cause Analysis: A Tool for Total Quality Management* (Milwaukee, WI: ASQC Quality Press, 1993). Root cause analysis is a basic tool that is used within the first three steps of the problem-solving process. It is one of the most essential techniques of the quality profession.

3. Looking at these four business support processes (finance, quality, information systems, and human resources) and seeing their common characteristics suggest some major changes. Just think about the implications at IBM Credit where the work of several different staff specialists was combined into a single job (see *Reengineering the Corporation* by Hammer and Champy, op. cit., p. 51). There is a potential to take each of the four types of support staff functions illustrated on the expanded enterprise model and develop a cross-trained support staff. There is probably as much similarity in their jobs as between diverse production workers who are cross-trained. At least the staff members all have the same basic approach to their customers—process consultant, process influencer, coach, and advisor. The technical skills of finance, systems, statistics, and employee relations are capable of mastery by MBA-type training. Why not build greater flexibility into the staff functions? This proposition would solve the question: How do you develop and grow the different staff functions? Such cross-training would provide competence broadening to support the growth of staff process capability in an environment of organizational flattening.

4. When organizational development people speak about process consulting, they are referring to the act of consulting with people about personal and organizational behavior change. A good place to begin reading about this is Edgar H. Schein's book *Process Consultation*, which was previously cited along with other practitioners of organization development in note 6 of Chapter 3. Two additional books with a quality orientation are David W. Hutton, *The Change Agents' Handbook: A Survival Guide for Quality Improvement Champions* (Milwaukee, WI:

ASQC Quality Press, 1994) and David Hutchins, *In Pursuit of Quality: Participative Techniques for Quality Improvement* (London: Pittman Publishing, 1990).

5. At its highest level, organizational development is about the management of structural change within complex organizations. Professor Gordon Donaldson, of the Harvard Business School, has written a book that provides invaluable case studies for this high-level intervention in the governance of organizations. It is highly recommended: *Corporate Restructuring: Managing the Change Process from Within* (Boston, MA: Harvard Business School Press, 1994).

6. This *Fortune* quotation was cited by Gerald Paradis of Information Mapping, Inc., at the 50th Rochester ASQC Section Conference, June 28, 1993.

7. Currently, ISO 9000 is as hot a book topic as Business Process Reengineering. Some registrars estimate that the number of firms registered according to this standard will grow by over tenfold by the end of this decade—surpassing a half million firms. With this much activity, it is clear that a market exists for describing the ISO 9000 standard and providing guidance on how to implement a quality system that is in compliance with ISO 9000. The following bibliography on ISO 9000 may help to answer quality system implementation questions, concerns, or issues: Richard Barrett Clements, *Quality Manager's Complete Guide to ISO 9000* (Englewood Cliffs, NJ: Prentice-Hall, 1993); Ronald J. Cottman, *A Guidebook to ISO 9000 and ANSI/ASQC Q90* (Milwaukee, WI: ASQC Quality Press, 1993); Greg Hutchins, *ISO 9000: A Comprehensive Guide to Registration, Audit Guidelines, and Successful Certification* (Essex Junction, VT: Oliver Wight Publications, 1993); Perry L. Johnson, *ISO 9000: Meeting the New International Standards* (New York: McGraw-Hill, 1993); James L. Lamprecht, *ISO 9000: Preparing for Registration* (New York: Marcel Dekker, 1992); Robert W. Peach, editor, *The ISO 9000 Handbook* (Fairfax, VA: CEEM Information Services, 1992); John T. Rabbitt and Peter A. Bergh, *The ISO 9000 Book: A Global Competitor's Guide to Compliance and Certification* (White Plains, NY: Quality Resources, 1993); and Frank Voehl, Peter Jackson, and David Ashton, *ISO 9000: An Implementation Guide for Small to Mid-Sized Businesses* (Delray Beach, FL: St. Lucie Press, 1994).

8. Production scheduling is fascinating. While serving as the production scheduling manager for the San Diego Division of Hewlett-Packard I noticed that the long-range sales forecasts were invariably in error. In fact, the accuracy of the marketing group's forecast was really quite predictable. They could forecast sales for the next month within 5 percent accuracy—this could certainly be covered by safety stock for long lead time items and allowing the production lines to ramp up or down their production volumes according to the demand. However, at a two-month horizon, the accuracy of the forecast to the actual orders was on the order of about 20 percent. This is at the outer limits of acceptability for purchased material and parts whose lead times were four to eight weeks. By placing extra materials in the supplier's production pipeline, this contingency could be covered. However, the story just got worse. At the three-month horizon, the forecast accuracy averaged just under 50 percent. You could almost flip a coin to determine a forecast—indeed, marketing may have. For parts with greater than an eight-week lead time, there was only one option—work as hard as possible to reduce the lead time to under eight weeks. What was the root cause of this situation? Well, if you

map the sales process to the forecast accuracy, you would find that the sales representatives know very accurately what sales they will close within a month. They have a fairly good idea how qualified and ready to order their prospects are within the two-month window. As for month three and beyond—well, you might as well flip a coin. . . .

9. Michael Hammer resists the notion that automating processes is the way to manage change. Hammer states: "But speeding up those processes cannot address their fundamental performance deficiencies. Many of our job designs, work flows, control mechanisms, and organizational structures came from an age in a very different competitive environment and before the advent of the computer. They are geared toward efficiency and control. Yet the watchwords of the new decade are innovation and speed, service and quality. It is time to stop paving the cow paths. Instead of embedding outdated processes in silicon and software, we should obliterate them and start over. We should 'reengineer' our businesses: use the power of modern information technology to radically redesign business processes in order to achieve dramatic improvements in their performance" (from "Reengineering Work: Don't Automate, Obliterate," op. cit., p. 104).

10. I first discussed the use of these decision filters with Mohan Kharbanda, a former colleague from Xerox and currently vice president of Service and Market Development at Honeywell, during a project planning meeting with the Society of Management Accountants of Canada. The project was to develop a management accounting guideline on time-based competition for certified management accountants. This version is more developed than the one that we shared in that meeting.

11. Just as a bibliography was presented for ISO 9000, each of the more specific elements of the process analysis methods used during the elimination sequence will have a detailed reference listing to allow readers to further investigate this material. The current emphasis on cycle time reduction came from the Japanese emphasis on Just-in-Time manufacturing and their emphasis on time as a critical dimension of customer satisfaction (see note 9 of Chapter 10 for a more complete history). Two additional books that help to position the managerial emphasis on cycle time management are Christopher Meyer, *Fast Cycle Time: How to Align Purpose, Strategy, and Structure for Speed* (New York: The Free Press, 1993) and Daryl R. Conner, *Managing at the Speed of Change: How Resilient Managers Succeed and Prosper Where Others Fail* (New York: Villard Books, 1993). The application of cycle time management is found within the context of business process analysis as described by Jim Harrington (see note 1 of this chapter) and Roger Slater's *Integrated Process Management: A Quality Model* (New York: McGraw-Hill, 1991). In conducting process analysis to improve both cycle time and the cost of activities, it is important to identify where process bottlenecks occur. A leading thinker on the subject of flow analysis is Eliyahu M. Goldratt whose latest book, *The Theory of Constraints* (Croton-on-Hudson, NY: North River Press, Inc., 1990), describes how to look at work process constraints as a way to identify what must change in the process. Itzik Kostika's book *Flow Management Technology: Breaking out of the Box* (Milford, CT: Business Technology Management, 1989) describes a flow management system to supplement a JIT

materials manufacturing process. Carol J. Lick and Pam Peterson describe the approach that Digital Equipment Corporation developed and Xerox modified called "A delta T" in their book *Theoretical Time: The Industrial Renaissance* (Colorado Springs, CO: Air Academy Press, 1990). Philip R. Thomas, chairman and CEO of The Thomas Group, Inc., an Irving, Texas, consulting firm specializing in cycle time reduction, has written three books on this topic: *Competitiveness Through Total Cycle Time: An Overview for CEO's* (New York: McGraw-Hill, 1990); *Getting Competitive: Middle Managers and the Cycle Time Ethic* (New York: McGraw-Hill, 1991); and *Time Warrior: Using the Total Cycle Time System to Boost Personal Competitiveness* (New York: McGraw-Hill, 1992). Others also take an industrial engineer's approach to this topic: Ryuji Fukuda, *Managerial Engineering: Techniques for Improving Quality and Productivity in the Workplace* (Cambridge, MA: Productivity Press, 1983) and Shigeo Shingo, founder of the shop-floor control methods at Toyota, *The Sayings of Shigeo Shingo: Key Strategies for Plant Improvement* (Cambridge, MA: Productivity Press, 1987). Shingo also led the manufacturing industry into the practice of foolproofing—making all of their production processes error-free: Shigeo Shingo, *Zero Quality Control: Source Inspection and the Poka-yoke System* (Cambridge, MA: Productivity Press, 1986) and Nikkan Kogyo Shimbun, Ltd./Factory Magazine, with an overview by Hiroyuki Hirano, *Poka-yoke: Improving Product Quality by Preventing Defects* (Cambridge, MA: Productivity Press, 1988).

12. The literature on Activity Based Costing can be divided into three categories: critique of the current system of management accounting, application of Total Quality Management methods and principles to accounting, and the implementation of Activity Based Cost Management. The best statement of the irrelevance of current accounting methods is contained in a book by H. Thomas Johnson and Robert S. Kaplan, *Relevance Lost: The Rise and Fall of Management Accounting* (Boston: Harvard Business School Press, 1987). Three books describe the Japanese use of total quality methods in accounting practices: Yasuhiro Monden and Michiharu Sakurai, editors, *Japanese Management Accounting: A World Class Approach to Profit Management* (Cambridge, MA: Productivity Press, 1989); Takashi Kanatsu, *TQC for Accounting: A New Role in Companywide Improvement* (Cambridge, MA: Productivity Press, 1990); and Zenzaburo Katayama, *Cost Reduction: How to Cut Costs Without Cutting Corners* (New York: PHP Institute, 1992). Four books trace the development of Activity Based Costing from its origins in 1986 at Computer Aided Manufacturing–International to the present: Callie Berliner and James A. Brimson, *Cost Management for Today's Advanced Manufacturing: The CAM-I Conceptual Design* (Boston: Harvard Business School Press, 1988); James A. Brimson, *Activity Accounting: An Activity-Based Costing Approach* (New York: John Wiley & Sons, 1991); Michael C. O'Guin, *The Complete Guide to Activity Based Costing* (Englewood Cliffs, NJ: Prentice-Hall, 1991); and Mike Morrow, editor, *Activity-Based Management: New Approaches to Measuring Performance and Managing Costs* (London: Woodhead-Faulkner, 1992).

13. There are so many books on the topic of statistics and such a wide variation (here is that word again!) in the ability of people to deal with mathematical and statistical

concepts, that it is difficult to select just a few books that may help any particular reader. John Allen Paulos has developed a best-seller that provides people with an ability to deal with their mathematical illiteracy—or innumeracy as Paulos calls it: *Innumeracy: Mathematical Illiteracy and Its Consequences* (New York: Random House, 1988). Also at the same level of application is the classic book by Darrell Huff, *How to Lie with Statistics* (New York: W. W. Norton & Company, 1954). Two other books that help in statistical thinking are John L. Phillips, Jr. *How to Think About Statistics* (New York: W. H. Freeman and Company, 1992) and David S. Moore, *Statistics: Concepts and Controversies*, second edition (New York: W. H. Freeman and Company, 1985). Theodore M. Porter traces *The Rise of Statistical Thinking 1820–1900* (Princeton, NJ: Princeton University Press, 1986) at its pre-twentieth-century roots. Four classic books on the application of statistical methods helped to increase the application of statistics toward the middle of this century: Walter A. Shewhard, *Economic Control of Quality of Manufactured Product* (New York: Van Nostrand Company, 1931); Edwin L. Crow, Frances A. Davis, and Margaret W. Maxfield, *Statistics Manual* (New York: Dover Publications, 1948, 1960); Eugene L. Grant and Richard S. Leavenworth, *Statistical Quality Control*, sixth edition (New York: McGraw-Hill, 1952, 1988); *AT&T Statistical Quality Control Handbook* (Indianapolis, IN: Western Electric Company, 1956). In addition to these books, I have found two books to be most helpful in my own preparation to take the examination as a certified quality engineer from the American Society for Quality Control: Dale E. Besterfield, *Quality Control*, fourth edition (Englewood Cliffs, NJ: Prentice-Hall, 1994) and Victor E. Kane, *Defect Prevention: Use of Simple Statistical Tools* (New York: Marcel Dekker, 1989).

14. The Taguchi Loss Function is named after its developer, Dr. Genichi Taguchi. Taguchi's method has two basic principles: (1) Poor quality in a product or process is measurable as a loss to society. Taguchi measures this loss in terms of the trade-off between cost and specification limits for a product, and he calls this measure the loss function. The reduction in variation (or alternatively, the improvement in quality) of a product or process represents a lower loss to society. The Taguchi Loss Function is a mathematical way to quantify cost as a function of product or process variation and to answer the question whether further reduction of variation will reduce costs. (2) The proper product development strategy can intentionally reduce variation. Taguchi's method for this is an engineer's approach to design of experiments that is based on the concept of signal-to-noise ratio and the use of orthogonal arrays for performing the design of experiments. These two principles form the basis of Taguchi's approach to experimental design. In his book *Quality Is Free* (New York: McGraw-Hill, 1979), Philip B. Crosby supports the idea that if a product is produced within the permitted tolerance limits of its design, then that product is of high quality because quality is "conformance to requirements." However, a new product may meet the blueprint specifications, but if the print does not reflect the customer's true requirements, then the customer will not be convinced that quality is truly present. According to the Crosby view, any value within the specified tolerance limits is equally acceptable. This view represents quality as an internal measure using the cost of nonconformance (poor quality) but does not consider the ramifications of poor

quality from the perspective of the customer. But the customer is the final arbitrator of what is meant by quality. The design engineers have built quality into their specification by considering how the customer will react to performance changes in critical parameters of the product. For example, the design may have a nominal value where the product performs the best from the customer's viewpoint. The manufacturer has added a tolerance band (this actually represents the customer's tolerance for distinguishing performance differences from the nominal level) to this value in order to improve its ability to manufacture the product at the lowest cost. This situation represents a potential conflict in desires: The customer always wants the best performance (performance at the nominal value), while the producer wants to allow the product to vary within the tolerance specification (at the lowest internal cost of production). The Taguchi Loss Function seeks to reconcile these two opposing positions. The Taguchi Loss Function recognizes both the customer's desire to have products and services that are consistent (the same performance level measured part-to-part for products or experience-to-experience for services) and reliable (lasts a long time) and the producer's desire to reduce the cost of production to the lowest possible level (this allows for the greatest margin and, therefore, highest profit possible). The Taguchi Loss Function estimates the costs of ownership to repair or correct situations that deviate from the desired nominal performance level. When the performance deviates from the tolerance limits, the customer will complain (not tolerating performance beyond this boundary) and seek to have the process adjusted, repaired, or replaced. This will result in a cost. (Note: The Taguchi Loss Function plots the relationship between the total cost of production and service against the specification of the design for the critical parameter of that service. The cost is composed of the costs incurred in productions as well as the costs encountered during use by the customer—repair, down time, opportunity costs of lost business, etc. In order to minimize the loss to society, the product or service design strategy should be to encourage the production of uniformly produced products and services that meet the requirement of the customer while minimizing the joint costs of production and consumption.) Using specification limits implies that, within the boundaries of the performance limits, there is little apparent difference between products, but there is a major difference between products whose performance is on each side of the limit. This is because the underlying probability model of the "specification limit" approach to product design implies a uniform distribution of tolerance by the customer between the upper and lower limits. However, the reality is that the customer's tolerance is not uniformly distributed about the nominal value; it is normally distributed. At the nominal position, the customer is most satisfied with the product or service performance. The customer becomes exponentially dissatisfied as the limits of tolerance are approached and then exceeded. For specific information on how to construct and apply the Taguchi Loss Function and more detail on additional analysis methods taught and recomended by Dr. Genichi Taguchi, see the following books: Thomas B. Barker, *Quality by Experimental Design,* second edition (New York: Marcel Dekker, 1993); Lance A. Ealey, *Quality by Design: Taguchi Methods and U.S. Industry* (Dearborn, MI: ASI Press, 1989); Glenn Stuart Peace, *Taguchi Methods: A Hands-On Approach* (New York: Addison-Wesley, 1993); Madhav S. Phadke,

Quality Engineering Using Robust Design (Englewood Cliffs, NJ: Prentice-Hall, 1989); Phillip J. Ross, *Taguchi Techniques for Quality Engineering* (New York: McGraw-Hill, 1988); Ranjit Roy, *A Primer on the Taguchi Method* (New York: Van Nostrand Reinhold, 1990); Genichi Taguchi, *Introduction to Quality Engineering: Designing Quality Into Products and Processes* (Tokyo: Asian Productivity Organization, 1986); and Genichi Taguchi, *System of Experimental Design: Engineering Methods to Optimize Quality and Minimize Costs*, Volumes I and II (Dearborn, MI: ASI Press, 1987).

15. Normally, the capability index (C_p—called process capability in the text) does not measure process variation from the nominal or target value. This measure is called C_{pk}. For an excellent description of these measures and their relative performance, see note 13, Dale E. Besterfield, op. cit., pp. 107–110.

16. Two books provide case studies of the journey to recognized quality excellence. The Xerox story is the subject of a book edited by Richard C. Palermo, Sr., and Gregory H. Watson, *A World of Quality: The Timeless Passport* (Milwaukee, WI: ASQC Quality Press, 1993). It describes the strategy, implementation approach, and lessons learned along a ten-year quality journey. It clearly illustrates that "the soft stuff (human processes) is the hard stuff!" This is an excellent case study of the implementation process for a worldwide organization: It features chapters that describe in detail the successful pursuits of the Deming Prize in Japan, the Baldrige Award in the United States, and the European Quality Award. In contrast, the IBM book describes the Rochester, Minnesota, division's Baldrige effort. This second book by Joseph H. Boyett, Stephen Schwartz, Laurence Osterwise, and Roy Bauer tells how the IBM Rochester division's successful pursuit of the Baldrige Award helped to drive company-wide changes at IBM: *The Quality Journey: How Winning the Baldrige Sparked the Remaking of IBM* (New York: Dutton, 1993).

17. The analytical interpretation of process thinking appears at several different levels among the reference books in these chapter notes. However, I noticed that these notes are not complete because they do not provide sources of good overall books on process management. There are three books that span the spectrum from simple to most complex, while accurately presenting the management of process as a business activity that is essential to the entire organization. The most straightforward of these books is by Geary A. Rummler and Alan P. Brache, *Improving Performance: How to Manage the White Space on the Organization Chart* (San Francisco: Jossey-Bass, 1990). Rummler and Brache present a wonderful tool for analyzing organizations across the functional boundaries. Their flow charting methodology is a wonderful addition to the IDEF methodology discussed in note 6 of Chapter 4. The middle book for complexity and completeness is by H. James Harrington and was cited in the first note of this chapter. The most complete and complex of the three books is by another former IBM manager, Gabriel A. Pall, *Quality Process Management* (Englewood Cliffs, NJ: Prentice-Hall, 1987).

18. Professor Harry V. Roberts of the University of Chicago has challenged many on their need to improve their personal quality. In a June 1993 article in *Quality Progress* titled "Using Personal Checklists to Facilitate TQM," Roberts challenges quality professionals to master their own behaviors using SPC applied to their

personal development goals. Roberts also joined forces with Bernard F. Serges-ketter to produce a book that expands upon this subject: *Quality Is Personal: A Foundation for Total Quality Management* (New York: The Free Press, 1993).

Chapter 6

1. Theodor Richman and Charles Koontz, "How Benchmarking Can Improve Business Reengineering," *Planning Review*, November-December 1993, pp. 26 and 27.

2. These books are *The Benchmarking Workbook: Adapting Best Practices for Performance Improvement* (Cambridge, MA: Productivity Press, 1992); *Strategic Benchmarking: How to Rate Your Company Against the World's Best* (New York: John Wiley & Sons, 1993); and *The Benchmarking Management Guide* (Cambridge, MA: Productivity Press, 1993).

3. In *Strategic Benchmarking,* the General Motors case study illustrates how to apply functional benchmarking to understand how to apply Total Quality Management principles in a company.

4. In *Strategic Benchmarking,* the Hewlett-Packard case study illustrates how to apply internal benchmarking to analyze, document, and improve R&D product scheduling effectiveness.

5. In *Strategic Benchmarking,* the Ford Taurus case study illustrates how to apply competitive benchmarking to improve the effectiveness of the product design process.

6. I owe this distinction between benchmarking and bench-learning to Bengt Karlof and Svante Ostblom, who described these ideas similarly but in a more process-oriented context in their book on benchmarking, *Benchmarking: A Signpost to Excellence in Quality and Productivity* (New York: John Wiley & Sons, 1993).

7. William Sandy, "Avoiding the Breakdown Between Planning and Implementation," *Journal of Business Strategy*, September-October 1991, pp. 30–33. Sandy Corporation was the organization that conducted the General Motors cross-industry study that I cited in *Strategic Benchmarking.*

8. This section is from Gregory H. Watson, "Using Teams to Conduct Benchmarking," *Continuous Journey*, December 1992/January 1993, pp. 12–15.

9. This section is from Gregory H. Watson, "Creating a Benchmarking Network," *Continuous Journey*, February/March 1993, pp. 48–51.

10. Tom Peters, *Liberation Management* (New York: Alfred A. Knopf, 1992).

11. This list builds upon an article I wrote for the September 1993 issue of *The Quality Observer* titled "Moving Toward Maturity: Seven Key Indicators of Growth in Benchmarking Efforts," pp. 12–13.

12. Gregory H. Watson, *Strategic Benchmarking*, pp. 86–87, 166–167.

Chapter 7

1. In *Megatrends* (New York: Warner Books, 1982), John Naisbitt describes the ten trends that will transform society at the dawning of the information age. Naisbitt

extended and interpreted these trends in the light of the growing importance of the information age. His restatement of these information trends provides a basis for considering the future of the workplace. These trends are: (1) The shift in strategic resource from an industrial to an information society; (2) the coming seller's market and the new competition for the best employees; (3) the whittling away of middle management; (4) the continuing entrepreneurial revolution; (5) the emergence of the new variegated workforce; (6) the demographic revolution of working women; (7) the growing use of intuition and vision; (8) the mismatch between our education system and the needs of the new information society; (9) the rising importance of corporate health issues; and (10) the values of the baby boomers, those born between 1946 and 1964, who are now populating the ranks of management (Naisbitt and Patricia Aburdene, *Re-inventing the Corporation,* New York: Warner Books, 1985, pp. 5–6).

2. Naisbitt and Aburdene's book *Re-inventing the Corporation* provides a charter for action—what to do about the trends presented in the first book. They suggest ten considerations that should inspire and challenge organizations as they reinvent their own corporations: (1) The best and brightest people will gravitate toward those corporations that foster personal growth; (2) the manager's new role is that of coach, teacher, and mentor; (3) the best people want ownership—psychic and literal—in a company—the best companies are providing it; (4) companies will increasingly turn to third-party contractors, shifting from hired labor to contract labor; (5) authoritarian management is yielding to a networking, people-style of management; (6) entrepreneurship within the corporations—intrapreneurship— is creating new products and markets and revitalizing companies inside out; (7) quality will be paramount; (8) intuition and creativity are challenging the "it's all in the numbers" business-school philosophy; (9) large corporations are emulating the positive and productive qualities of small business; and (10) the dawn of the information economy has fostered a massive shift from infrastructure to quality of life (pp. 45–46).

3. The changes that Naisbitt had forecast were observed by Shoshana Zuboff, in her book *In the Age of the Smart Machine: The Future of Work and Power* (New York: Basic Books, 1988). She describes the new workplace as one where "organizational leaders recognize the new forms of skill and knowledge needed to truly exploit the potential of an intelligent technology. They direct their resources toward creating a workforce that can exercise critical judgment as it manages the surrounding machine systems. Work becomes more abstract as it depends upon understanding and manipulating information" (p. 6). Zuboff observed that the workplace is in transition and that the new workplace would differ greatly from the old. "This technological transformation engenders a new approach to organizational behavior, in which relationships are more intricate, collaborative, and bound by the mutual responsibilities of colleagues. As the new technology integrates information across time and space, managers and workers each overcome their narrow functional perspectives and create new roles that are better suited to enhancing value-adding activities in a data-rich environment. As the quality of skills at each organizational level becomes similar, hierarchical distinctions begin to blur. Authority comes to depend more upon an appropriate fit between knowl-

edge and responsibility than upon the ranking rules of the traditional organizational pyramid" (p. 6). In this new environment, information technology shifts from being a servant to the automation of human work to being a producer of conceptual ideas that are much like patterns of human thinking. "Information technology is characterized by a fundamental duality that has not yet been fully appreciated. On the one hand, the technology can be applied to automating operations according to a logic that hardly differs from that of the nineteenth-century machine system—replace the human body with a technology that enables the same processes to be performed with more continuity and control. On the other hand, the same technology simultaneously generates information about the underlying productive and administrative processes through which an organization accomplishes its work. It provides a deeper level of transparency to activities that had been either partially or completely opaque. In this way information technology supersedes the traditional logic of automation" (pp. 9–11). This newly informated workplace requires a new set of measures. "Economists may continue to measure labor productivity as if the entire world of work could be represented adequately by the assembly line, but their measures will be systematically indifferent to what is most valuable in the informated organization. A new division of learning requires another vocabulary—one of colleagues and co-learners, of exploration, experimentation, and innovation. Jobs are comprehensive, tasks are abstractions that depend on insights and synthesis, and power is a roving force that comes to rest as dictated by function and need. . . . The informated organization is a learning institution, and one of its principal purposes is the expansion of knowledge—not knowledge for its own sake (as in academic pursuit), but knowledge that comes to reside at the core of what it means to be productive. Learning is no longer a separate activity that occurs either before one enters the workplace or in remote classroom settings. Nor is it an activity preserved for a managerial group. The behaviors that define learning and the behaviors that define being productive are one and the same. Learning is not something that requires time out from being engaged in productive activity; learning is the heart of productive activity. To put it simply, learning is the new form of labor" (p. 395).

4. Margaret Wheatley's previously cited book, *Leadership and the New Science*, has touched on the "fallibility" of holding a constant interpretation of scientific investigations. William Miller's book *Quantum Quality* (White Plains, NY: Quality Resources, 1993) bridges from a similar theme to emphasizing the need for breakthrough performance. He calls for quantum quality—rather than just continuously improving, changing the paradigm of the quality focus to making a leap in one of three ways: a leap in performance results of work processes, a leap in stakeholder benefits, or a leap in personal and team commitment to quality as a way of life (pp. 8–11).

5. John Naisbitt, *Re-inventing the Corporation*, p. 11.

6. Mark M. Klein, senior vice president of Gateway Management Consulting in New York City, has observed that most companies are outdated in their technology. "Most companies have legacy systems in place that reflect business practices of 20 to 30 years ago." Information systems organizations maintain this system and, as a result, they are viewed as inflexible and as unresponsive as the system that

they support. A Gateway survey noted that the priority setting between chief information officers and their chief executive officers did not align: The CIOs rated the following items as top priorities for their organization: cost cutting (71 percent), benchmarking (47 percent), Business Process Reengineering (2 percent), and organizational restructuring (0 percent). Their CEOs rated these same activities: cost cutting (24 percent), benchmarking (73 percent), Business Process Reengineering (88 percent), and organizational restructuring (77 percent). This data was in an article by Alice La Plante, "Does CIO Title Translate into Career Is Over," *Infoworld*, August 9, 1993, p. 56. She observes that the average term of a CIO is about five years and that about one third leave in an "unwilling" manner.

7. As described by Jon Prescot in his article, "Reengineering in a Global Economy," *Reliability Review*, September 1993, p. 24.

8. It is reasoning along these lines that has encouraged Xerox to proclaim itself "The Document Company" and to seek innovative solutions to document processing needs rather than just the information processing needs that serve a much smaller segment of an organization's knowledge base.

9. The initial and most complete book on this topic is by Charles Wiseman, who coined the term, *Strategic Information Systems* (Homewood, IL: Irwin, 1988). Stuart E. Madnick edited *The Strategic Use of Information Technology* (New York: Oxford University Press, 1987), and Claudio Ciborra and Tawfik Jelassi added to this subject's literature with their recent anthology *Strategic Information Systems: A European Perspective* (New York: John Wiley & Sons, 1994).

10. Such re-creating to maintain exciting quality and competitive advantage comes from a planned approach to product or service design that continues to deliver features that truly excite the customer—ones that anticipate unrecognized needs and increase the customer's value perception of the product (usually at no incremental cost to the prior generation product or service). This strategy is built upon the Kano model of customer satisfaction and excellence in design execution. The Kano model was developed by Dr. Noriaki Kano, a senior member of the Union of Japanese Scientists and Engineers (known by the translation of their acronym, JUSE). A more detailed explanation and illustration of this interpretation of the Kano model is found in *Strategic Benchmarking* (pp. 10–13).

11. The information management community has entered into the strategic planning dialog through two routes. First, they join the other staff functions by calling for a special iteration of the business plan that features their function as a special focus of the whole business. For example, the human resources community encourages the development of an annual human resource strategy; the quality community wants to have a strategic quality plan; and, of course, the finance community demands that prudent managers have an annual operating budget. The request of the information systems managers has been for an information systems strategy that ties together the requirements of the users with the capital investment strategy for hardware and the identification and prioritization of software development projects. Of course, none of these plans should be an independent document. Most businesses with mature planning systems have integrated these staff planning

documents into their annual business planning process. The second way that the information manager has entered into the corporate dialog for strategic planning is through the development of critical success factors for the business. Critical success factors (CSFs) are those things that must go well for an enterprise to ensure success. These factors identify what management must continuously pay special attention to. The concept of CSFs was initially developed by R. D. Daniel ("Management Information Crisis," *Harvard Business Review*, September–October 1961, p. 111). This concept was popularized by John F. Rockart in his *Harvard Business Review* article "Chief Executives Define Their Own Data Needs" (March–April 1970, pp. 81–93). Rockart suggested that a series of interviews between a systems analyst and members of the senior management team could identify the business's critical success factors and then derive the measures of performance that represent them. Rockart and C. V. Bullen then suggested that CSFs be used as a planning tool for management information systems ("A Primer on Critical Success Factors," CISR Working Paper #69, Sloan School of Management, MIT, June 1981). This use of CSFs involves interviewing managers throughout the organizational hierarchy and would result in a set of measures that were used throughout the organization. Information resources would then be targeted at enabling the organization to use this collective set of CSFs. A study of the applications of CSFs by M. C. Munro ("An Opinion . . . Comment on Critical Success Factors Work," *MIS Quarterly*, September 1983, pp. 67–68) indicates that reliable results may be obtained by using this approach. G. B. Davis ("Comments on the Critical Success Factors Method for Obtaining Management Information Requirements," *MIS Quarterly*, September 1979, pp. 57–58) raised some concerns regarding the CSF methodology. He suggested that the method may provide an information model that is simple and thought provoking; however, it would not necessarily be representative of the actual business environment. The problem with CSFs is that they do not provide a set of causally or even logically linked performance measures, as does the approach that I suggest using: the measurement map from the organizational goal level down to a stratification study of the operating performance measures. Certainly the development of the measurement map could use the same approach indicated for CSFs; however, it must be backed up with a logical check to determine if all key factors are really identified. The CSF method, by involving the senior managers and their reports in the definition of the model, does result in their acceptance of the result. The other strength of the CSF method is that it supports a top-down organizational analysis and planning process.

12. This is the theme of Soshana Zuboff's work, which she has so wonderfully illustrated in the opening chapters of her book: *In the Age of the Smart Machine*.

13. Thomas H. Davenport suggests some other implementation issues. He recommends that detailed process modeling should follow the completion of the systems model or else the focus on the desired business change will be lost. He also warns that because the process analysis and redesign can be completed within a few months, that the process owners may become impatient that the systems change is not equally fast—indicating the need for rapid prototyping of the new developments. He cautions against the use of packaged software that supports broad

business processes—it may need to be customized to meet the business need of your own organization. Davenport also cautions that the expense of implementation may lead the prudent manager to implement the changes over a period of time. I agree with Davenport's comments. ("Need Radical Innovation and Continuous Improvement? Integrate Process Reengineering and TQM," *Planning Review*, May–June 1993, p. 11).

14. Just as Xerox developed the WIMP or "windows–icon–mouse–pointing" computer environment, the personal computer, and object-oriented programming, the Xerox engineers also developed Ether-net as a means for connecting individual workstations together.

15. David Kirkpatrik, "Groupware Goes Boom," *Fortune*, December 27, 1993, pp. 99–106.

16. Maryann Alavi and Peter G. W. Keen, "Business Teams in an Information Age," *The Information Society*, Volume 6, 1989, pp. 179–195. This article provides some unique insights into the way that business teams will adapt to the coming groupware-generated working environment.

17. Erran Carmel and Joey George, "Joint Application Development (JAD) and Electronic Meeting Systems (EMS): Opportunities for the Future," University of Arizona, Center for the Management of Information, Working Paper, CMI WPS 91–06, 1991. This working paper describes how to facilitate software-user focus groups called Joint Application Development (JAD) meeting sessions to increase product innovation and compress the development time of new products.

18. The groupware application of electronic meeting management systems is the subject of two articles that feature the IBM Electronic Meeting System (EMS). These articles provide a more detailed look into the benefits and applications of groupware. Ron Grohowski, Chris McGoff, Doug Vogel, Ben Martz, and Jay Nunamaker, "Implementing Electronic Meeting System at IBM: Lessons Learned and Success Factors," *MIS Quarterly*, December 1990, pp. 368–383. A subset of this first group of authors developed an article on the type of facility that would be required to support such electronic meeting software: William Benjamin Martz, Jr., David A. Chappell, Edward E. Roberts, and J. F. Nunamaker, Jr., "Designing Integrated Information Facilities to Support Electronic Meetings," *Transactions of the IEEE*, November 29, 1991, pp. 394–402.

19. John Naisbitt foretells the future direction of technological change in *Global Paradox* (New York: William Morrow and Company, 1994—particularly Chapter 2 pp. 53–102).

20. William A. Sandres, "AMPEX: A Just-in-Time Approach from Procurement Through Production," *Target*, March–April 1993, pp. 37–41. In this case study, Sandres illustrates the performance improvements that come from streamlining information technology systems, rather than just adding technology systems. AMPEX, between 1989 and 1992, reduced the number of mainframe computers by 50 percent, cut the information systems staff by 60 percent, reduced the number of computer transactions for purchasing by 80 percent, cut the purchasing staff from 34 to 9 and the number of suppliers from about 2,000 to 135. Now, 80 percent of their part numbers come from just 6 suppliers, and 80 percent of

the purchased part volume comes from only 14 suppliers. They have redesigned their purchasing system by streamlining the data management requirements of the information system, not by just adding more capability to the current system.

21. John Naisbitt, *Global Paradox*, p. 89.

22. Zuboff, op. cit., p. 6.

23. GTE was shocked when it discovered its administrative bureaucracy was cutting its productivity in half. It worked on reengineering projects that consolidated nine regional data centers into four and cut $149 million in labor (25 percent of their workers) and overhead (85 thousand square feet of data center floorspace) from its 1992 budget. (See the articles by David P. Allen and Robert Natius, "Dreaming and Doing: Reengineering GTE Telephone Operations," *Planning Review*, March–April 1993, pp. 28–31, and Joseph Maglitta, "GTE to Save $149 Million," *Computerworld*, April 8, 1992, pp. 71–73.) GTE has recognized the first level of white-collar productivity improvement that is available from the consolidation of operations because of innovations in technology that enable streamlining of operations.

24. The net effect of a fully informed workplace will be to make the distinct technical skills of the knowledge workers less uncommon. The "technology" will be embedded in artificial intelligence; however, the judgment and application—the innovating skills—will still be in the heads of the workers. Teams of workers will use their (human) process skills to direct the flow of both the automated workplace and the informated workplace. As Shoshana Zuboff observed, while the new workplace will displace the current skills of workers (known as deskilling), the "informating power of the technology simultaneously creates pressure for a profound reskilling" (op. cit., 57).

25. John Naisbitt, *Megatrends*, p. 32.

26. I do not mean to imply that I believe such a staff consolidation would be either easy to accomplish or rapidly achievable. This transition would need to be planned carefully to achieve the full benefits from such staff synergy. Each of the staff communities wants a larger role in the management team's agenda. For example, one article encouraged information systems managers to reposition the information systems function from "a limited 'automated back office' to a more ubiquitous function involved in all aspects of the business" (John F. Rockart, "The Changing Role of the Information Systems Executive: A Critical Success Factors Perspective," Stuart E. Madnick, editor, *The Strategic Use of Information*, New York: Oxford University Press, 1987, p. 77). The consolidation of staff functions should not elevate one function over the others; it should recognize their common process foundation and also their unique technical contributions to creating a successful business.

27. Thomas H. Davenport has also suggested that "the highest level of integration is to combine process change groups, information systems, and the human resource function." "When they all report to the same executive, the chances of their collaboration are greatly increased" (op. cit., p. 12—see note 13 for more on Davenport's thinking).

Chapter 8

1. Peter M. Senge, *The Fifth Discipline: The Art and Practice of the Learning Organization* (New York: Doubleday Currency, 1990), p. 235.

2. Ibid., p. 234.

3. This brief description does not really do these four processes justice, so I felt that a little more detail would be appropriate. The following list describes elements that typically are part of each of the four processes. *Diagnosing Progress:* (1) Diagnosis of the performance of key business process performance; (2) use of data analysis methods and the principles of management by fact to evaluate significant overachievement or underachievement of the plan to the level of their root cause; (3) assessment of the planning process to determine what improvements should be made in the next planning cycle; (4) assessment of the organization-wide deployment of process management and quality tools using the organization's role model for excellence in process management—usually a customized version of the Baldrige Award criteria that is supplemented by ISO 9000 and the organization's cultural determinants of success; (5) the summarized findings of the diagnosis presented to management as input for setting direction. *Setting Direction:* (1) A reaffirmation of the cultural values that shape the organization's fundamental approach to relationships with customers, employees, and society; (2) the review, refocusing, or development of the enterprise vision—the challenging, achievable, and vivid picture of strategic intent for the organization's direction at a ten-year planning horizon; (3) the development of the organization's strategic direction—the statement of mission (driving purpose or reason for the existence of the enterprise), goals (a measurable end state that is desired to be achieved by a certain time frame), strategies (the means that are agreed upon as the route to achieve the goals), and objectives (the specific actions or projects that operationally define the implementation of the strategies into the workplace). *Deploying Direction:* (1) The cascade of objectives that is associated with management by objectives is modified to include a push-back or negotiation process. The direction set by senior management (values, vision, mission, goals, strategies, and objectives from the prior process) meets the results from a process analysis that is the product of the daily management system (yes, this is the same process analysis that is the subject of Chapter 5—interesting how these things relate in a system) and a catchball process is initiated. (2) Catchball is the process for engaging in productive dialog with both the vertical and horizontal organizational partners for the purpose of setting ends (targets) for performance, establishing means (work objectives for standing processes or chartering project teams to tackle new developments) to accomplish specific enterprise objectives, and securing consensus and commitment on the organization's operating plan. The catchball process is simply a structured dialog that is grounded in management by fact with the objective of achieving an agreed-upon implementation plan. (3) Translation of the enterprise objectives into actionable personal or team objectives marks the completion of the catchball process and the objectives cascade. At the individual contributor level, the set of annual objectives includes both daily management objectives and participation on teams that will deliver enterprise-wide strategic

objectives. *Managing Direction*: (1) Each strategy that is deployed to a process owner for execution should be addressed by an implementation plan (Gantt chart or equivalent) that describes the specific tasks, schedules, and process measures and targets that define successful completion. (2) It is the responsibility of process owners to conduct regular reviews of the progress that is achieved on this implementation plan. This allows a communication opportunity for performance review and resource management that may result in a reallocation of resources according to developing needs and the actual, rather than forecast, resource requirements of the improvement projects. (3) Concurrently, the daily management systems are monitored and managed using the PDCA methods discussed in Chapter 5—especially the problem-solving process and use of statistical tools to maintain control or continuously improve the work processes. (4) An escalation process is also part of managing direction. This process elevates those issues to management that are not capable of being managed within the boundary constraints that define the limit of empowerment for work processes within the daily management system. (5) Recognize and reinforce positive leadership behaviors that are observed in both individual and team successes.

4. Sarv Singh Soin, *Total Quality Control Essentials: Key Elements, Methodologies, and Managing for Success* (New York: McGraw-Hill, 1992). Soin describes the Hewlett-Packard approach to policy deployment. HP initiated its program in the mid-1980s and has been the benchmark for most other programs. Bruce M. Sheridan, *Policy Deployment: The TQM Approach to Long-Range Planning* (Milwaukee, WI: ASQC Quality Press, 1993). Sheridan describes the Florida Power & Light approach to policy deployment. FP&L received the Deming Prize in 1989 in recognition of the achievements of its quality system.

5. Brendan Collins and Ernest Huge, *Management by Policy: How Companies Focus Their Total Quality Efforts to Achieve Competitive Advantage* (Milwaukee, WI: ASQC Quality Press, 1993). Collins and Huge provide a readable definition of the methods of policy deployment that is usable by a wide audience. Yoji Akao, editor, *Hoshin Kanri: Policy Deployment for Successful TQM* (Cambridge, MA: Productivity Press, 1991). For purists, see Akao's book that describes all of the analytic detail of the implementation of policy deployment in leading Japanese companies. I was honored to prepare the overview chapter for this book. More detail of a tutorial nature is provided by some of the documents from GOAL/QPC, which are the result of their research committee's study of policy deployment and daily management. The report of the committee's summary is found in two research papers: *Hoshin Planning: A Planning System for Implementing Total Quality Management (TQM)* (Methuen, MA: GOAL/QPC Press, 1990) and *Hoshin Planning: The Foundation of Total Quality Management* (Methuen, MA: GOAL/QPC Press, 1989). GOAL/QPC's Bob King has published a paper illustrating the use of analytical tools (also called "the seven new management tools") to the planning process: Robert E. King, *Hoshin Planning: The Developmental Approach* (Methuen, MA: GOAL/QPC Press, 1989). In addition, two books have been prepared by a team of GOAL/QPC consultants to describe daily management practices: The first book focuses on "what is daily management," while the second book focuses on "how to set up a daily management system."

Casey Collett and Jack Moran were on both teams that produced these books: *Daily Management: A System for Individual and Organizational Optimization* (Methuen, MA: GOAL/QPC, 1991) and *Making Daily Management Work: A Perspective for Leaders and Managers* (Methuen, MA: GOAL/QPC, 1992).

6. A global benchmarking study of 15 companies that had implemented policy deployment was conducted to arrive at this generic model and the lessons learned. Questions asked fell into five categories: process description (15 questions), deployment approach (4 questions), support systems (8 questions), communication strategy (7 questions), and performance assessment (5 questions). The results of this study were used to develop a two-day course on policy deployment and are summarized in this chapter.

7. Americans visited Japan in the early 1980s after being stimulated by the NBC White Paper documentary "If Japan Can, Why Can't We?" They took with them their Western powers of observation and missed some of the subtleties of the Japanese management system. Specifically, they did not understand how the actions of teams and individuals were coordinated. *Hoshin* is not a visible practice. It is invisible in the sense that the posters and targets that illustrate the performance of work processes are only a manifestation of the coordination and priority-setting processes that delivered the result to the work process. For an excellent history of the way that *hoshin* developed from Peter Drucker's Japanese lectures on *The Practice of Management*, see the second appendix in *Hoshin Kanri* (citation in note 5). Just as it was difficult to observe *hoshin* in action in the Japanese culture, it is difficult to see it working in the Western culture. I am not sure of the true extent of its deployment, but I do know of over 40 firms that are using it including: Hewlett-Packard, Procter & Gamble, Intel, Xerox, and 3M, to name a few of the more "admirable" companies on my list.

8. Peter Drucker, "The New Society of Organizations," *The Learning Imperative: Managing People for Continuous Innovation* (Boston: Harvard Business Review Books, 1993), p. 13.

9. Jeffrey Pfeffer, *Competitive Advantage Through People: Unleashing the Power of the Work Force* (Boston: Harvard Business School Press, 1994), pp. 31–59.

10. SANNO Management Development Research Center, *Vision Management: Translating Strategy into Action* (Cambridge, MA: Productivity Press, 1991).

11. Following the elimination sequence that was introduced earlier (see Chapter 5), I recommend that organizations deal with the structure and processes of teamwork before they work on policy deployment. This is not a requirement, since many organizations have used a policy deployment approach to planning in traditional organizations as well. However, if your organization has decided to change its structure to team-based or empowered clusters, then you should seriously consider how to use policy deployment as an alignment and coordination method.

Chapter 9

1. Chrysler's new production system was introduced on the Chrysler LH, Jeep Grand Cherokee, as well as on the Dodge Viper. It was designed to move projects

from concept-to-car in less than three years, compared to 60 months under the old system. The system would allow no handoffs between design teams and production teams—a single team would be responsible for the entire project from design to production through after-sales and service. Ford had used a more limited team concept on the Ford Taurus and the Mercury Sable, and Honda has used teams to focus on project ownership for years; however, Chrysler has extended this concept further than either of these examples. Chrysler Executive Vice President Dennis Pawley explained: "We wanted to do this without Star Wars technology. We couldn't afford to launch a wholly new car with a project the size of GM's Saturn. With that kind of expense a [marketing] disaster would sink us." So, Chrysler focused on empowerment and team ownership of its project as the key ingredients for success. It appears to have worked. (From Stephen Kindel, "Styling and Design: Chrysler," *Financial World*, April 14, 1992, p. 42.)

2. Since the Viper is a high-profile vehicle—a drawing card to bring curious people into the showrooms—it represents a low-risk approach to test Chrysler's ability to push the envelope of project team synergy in the application of concurrent engineering. Concurrent engineering is also called simultaneous engineering. It focuses on the integration of the product development process from design through manufacturing. (The Chrysler approach is described in Eugene E. Sprow, "Chrysler's Concurrent Engineering Challenge," *Manufacturing Engineering*, April 1992, pp. 40–41.) Two books that provide broader survey information on this subject are John R. Hartley, *Concurrent Engineering: Shortening Lead Times, Raising Quality, and Reducing Costs* (Cambridge, MA: Productivity Press, 1992) and C. Wesley Allen, editor, *Simultaneous Engineering: Integrating Manufacturing and Design* (Dearborn, MI: Society of Manufacturing Engineers, 1990). The challenge of simultaneous product development and manufacturing process development is addressed by Preston G. Smith and Donald G. Reinertsen, *Developing Products in Half the Time* (New York: Van Nostrand Reinhold, 1991); Marvin L. Patterson, *Accelerating Innovation: Improving the Process of Product Development* (New York: Van Nostrand Reinhold, 1993); John Fox, *Quality Through Design: The Key to Successful Product Delivery* (New York: McGraw-Hill, 1993); Dan L. Shunk, *Integrated Product Design and Development* (Homewood, IL: BusinessOne Irwin, 1992); and V. Daniel Hunt, *Reengineering: Leveraging the Power of Integrated Product Design* (Essex Junction, VT: Oliver Wight, 1993).

3. Sprow, op. cit., p. 42.

4. James P. Womack, Daniel T. Jones, and Daniel Roos, *The Machine That Changed the World* (New York: Macmillan Publishing Company, 1990), p. 11.

5. See the entire summary in the MIT study: Michael L. Dertouzos, Richard K. Lester, and Robert M. Solow, *Made in America: Regaining the Productive Edge*, second edition (Cambridge, MA: Massachusetts Institute of Technology, 1989), pp. 18–20. The U.S. car marketing system assumed variety could not cost much, both labor and parts suppliers were an expendable asset of production, designs were to last for years, and quality didn't matter.

6. Henry Ford, *Today and Tomorrow* (Cambridge, MA: Productivity Press, reprint of Doubleday, Page and Company original, 1988), p. 103.

7. Frederick W. Taylor, *Scientific Management* (Westport, CT: Greenwood Press, 1972).

8. Ford, op. cit., p. 103.

9. Ibid., p. 118.

10. Ibid., p. 81.

11. Ibid., p. 124.

12. Womack, Jones, and Roos, op. cit., pp. 48–49. The historical development of the Toyota Production System and its growth to maturity is traced through five books. Shigeo Shingo, *A Study of the Toyota Production System*, revised edition (Cambridge, MA: Productivity Press, 1989); Taiichi Ohno, *Toyota Production System: Beyond Large-Scale Production* (Cambridge, MA: Productivity Press, 1988). These first two books are by the acknowledged architects of the Toyota Production System. David J. Lu, translator, *Kanban: Just-in-Time at Toyota*, revised edition (Cambridge, MA: Productivity Press, 1989); Isao Shinohara, *NPS New Production System* (Cambridge, MA: Productivity Press, 1988). This book describes the application of JIT concepts beyond the borders of the manufacturing business. Taiichi Ohno and Setsuo Mito, *Just-in-Time for Today and Tomorrow* (Cambridge, MA: Productivity Press, 1988), describe how JIT can be used together with information management systems as well as the manual card method of *kanban*. Ohno and Mito also express the relationship of their thinking to that of Henry Ford in his book *Today and Tomorrow*.

13. Taiichi Ohno, *Toyota Production System: Beyond Large-Scale Production*, p. x.

14. Yasuhiro Monden, "Toyota Production Systems," *Industrial Engineering*, January 1981, p. 106.

15. Ohno, *Toyota Production System: Beyond Large-Scale Production*, p. xiv.

16. Henry J. Johansson, Patrick McHugh, A. John Pendlebury, and William A. Wheeler III, *Business Process Reengineering: Breakpoint Strategies for Market Dominance* (New York: John Wiley & Sons, 1993), p. 2.

17. Ohno, *Toyota Production System: Beyond Large-Scale Production*, p. 25.

18. Ibid., p. xiii.

19. Gregory H. Watson, *Strategic Benchmarking*, p. 122. QFD is described further in Yoji Akao, editor, *Quality Function Deployment: Integrating Customer Requirements Into Product Design* (Cambridge, MA: Productivity Press, 1990) and Bob King, *Better Designs in Half the Time*, third edition (Methuen, MA: GOAL/QPC, 1989).

20. Ohno, *Toyota Production System: Beyond Large-Scale Production*, p. xiv.

21. Monden, op. cit., p. 106.

22. Ohno, op. cit., p. 23.

23. Donald E. Petersen ran Ford from 1980 to 1990—the first five years as CEO and the second five years as chairman of the board. Petersen, like most automotive executives, did not support the Japanese automotive industry's way of doing business. As he came into office, Ford was faced with billion dollar losses. Learning

from the Japanese was a hard thing for Petersen to accept. Consider the following quotation from his book *A Better Idea: Redefining the Way Americans Work* (Boston: Houghton Miffin, 1991): "Japan's view of the world was captured remarkably well by the popular historian Barbara Tuchman in a 1936 article in *Foreign Affairs* magazine: 'Unlike an individual, a nation cannot admit itself in error; so Japan's only answer has been to tell herself that her judges are wrong and she is right. To strengthen this contention she has built up the belief that she acts from the purest motives, which her fellow nations willfully misunderstand. The more they disapprove, the more adamant grows Japan's conviction that she is right. . . . So completely divorced is that Japanese mental process from the Occidental, so devoid of what Westerners call logic, that the Japanese are able to make statements, knowing they present a false picture, yet sincerely believing them.' That seems as true now as it was over fifty years ago. Even today, it would be futile for us to try to persuade the Japanese that their approach to trade and economic matters is wrong and that they should follow American practices. They believe in their approach, whether or not it is objectively wrong or right. The Japanese way of handling these issues is grounded in their tradition, and they hold on to that way because it is beneficial to their country" (pp. 209–210). Their way also seems to work. The Japanese concept of their trade practices is not judged in absolute terms as "right or wrong, " but in terms of "best and worst"—striving for *dantotsu*—being the best of the best—and the Japanese do not perceive the American way to be the best way. Certainly, the consumer market proves the Japanese to be correct, and the customer is the final arbitrator of quality.

24. Dertouzos, Lester, and Solow, op. cit., p. 117.

25. Michael Ward, Peter Cheese, Betty Thayer, Ichiro Sakuda, Daniel Jones, Rick Delbridge, James Lowe, and Nick Oliver, *The Lean Enterprise Benchmarking Project* (London: Andersen Consulting, 1993). This compared nine Japanese automobile manufacturers with nine of their British counterparts. The study indicates that the British manufacturers had a significant gap in their performance against the Japanese. The study showed that *all* of the world-class companies were Japanese (5 out of 18 participants), where world-class was indicated by having the combination of high quality and high productivity. These world-class plants had twice the level of productivity as the non-world-class plants and their quality was better by a hundredfold. In addition, the world-class plants were more highly automated and had higher production volumes, but this only accounted for 20 percent of the performance gap. The world-class plants have more active structures for shop floor problem-solving and involvement in improvement projects. In addition, the suppliers for world-class plants ship fewer defective parts than do the suppliers to the other plants—by a fifty-to-one ratio. This study indicates that European car manufacturers are also trying to close the two-to-one performance gap that was identified to the industry's best competitors, cited by James P. Womack, Daniel T. Jones, and Daniel Roos in their book *The Machine That Changed the World* (New York: Rawson Associates, 1990). This 1987 MIT study showed that the Japanese manufacturers had a two-to-one advantage in such productivity measures as assembly hours per car, assembly defects per hundred cars, and assembly space per car (p. 81). Interestingly, the New United Motors Manufactur-

ing Inc. (NUMMI) plant, a joint partnership of General Motors and Toyota located in Freemont, California, matched the world-class plants in Japan for quality and was only 20 percent off in productivity (p. 83).

26. Paul S. Adler and Robert E. Cole, "Designed for Learning: A Tale of Two Auto Plants," *Sloan Management Review*, Spring 1993, p. 86.

27. Gary S. Vasilash, "NUMMI: Proving That Cars Can Be Built in California," *Production*, February 1992, p. 40.

28. A detailed overview of the NUMMI production system is found in an appendix to David J. Lu, op. cit., pp. 177–184.

29. D. Michael Dodge, "Blueprint for World Class Quality," *Proceedings of the 20th International Conference on Quality*, April 13–14, 1992 (Cambridge, MA: Productivity Press, 1992), p. 122.

30. James Healey, "Firm Taps Rivals' Gains in Big Gamble," *USA Today*, October 21, 1992.

31. Marco Iansiti encouraged product development teams to take a systems focus toward their new product efforts in his article "Real-World R&D: Jumping the Product Generation Gap" (*Harvard Business Review*, May–June 1993, pp. 138–147). He defines a systems focus as the mutual adaptation of new technology, product design, manufacturing process, and user needs.

32. Kindel, op. cit., p. 42.

33. Jean Krawczyk, "Saturn: A Different Kind of Car Company," *The Quality Observor*, March 1994, pp. 21–22.

34. George Stalk, Jr., and Thomas M. Hout, *Competing Against Time* (New York: The Free Press, 1990), pp. 58–59, 139–140. This account of the rivalry between Honda and Yamaha is both a fascinating insight into the strategic operations of Honda and a warning against those who would take on the Honda machine—this is the kind of response that can be expected. At the end of the Honda-Yamaha wars, the president of Yamaha publicly apologized and announced that instead of challenging Honda, that Yamaha would work to secure the number two position behind it.

35. George Stalk, Jr., Philip Evans, and Lawrence E. Shulman, "Competing on Capabilities: The New Rules of Corporate Strategy," *Harvard Business Review*, March–April 1992, p. 65.

36. Karen Lowry Miller, Larry Armstrong, and David Woodruff, "A Car Is Born," *Business Week*, September 13, 1993, p. 67.

37. Stalk and Hout, op. cit., p. 59.

38. Miller, Armstrong, and Woodruff, op. cit., p. 72.

39. Womack, Jones, and Roos, op. cit., p. 13.

40. Dertouzos, Lester, and Solow, op. cit., p. 18. Four-wheel steering, four-wheel drive, turbocharging, and antilock braking systems were all introduced on foreign-made cars. In 1985 the three leading Japanese automobile manufacturers had filed more than twice as many patent applications as the U.S. Big Three manufacturers (p. 19).

41. Ibid., p. 20.

42. William J. Cook ("The End of the Plain Plane," *U.S. News & World Report*, April 11, 1994, pp. 43–46) reports a similar redefinition process in the aircraft industry. Boeing is changing the way that it makes aircraft and conducts business—it has asked its suppliers and customers to participate in the design of a "clean sheet" aircraft, the Boeing 777-200, for the first time in its history. It seems that the lessons of lean production are transferable across industry borders.

43. Womack, Jones, and Roos, op. cit., p. 19.

44. Taiichi Ohno, *The Toyota Production System*, p. ix.

45. All of the Japanese competitors are moving toward this time line efficiency that Ohno describes. Consider a news item in the September 1991 edition of *Business Japan* (p. 22) that talked about a new delivery capability that Nissan Motor Company had introduced. This system is called ANSWER (All Nissan Says Welcome to Every customeR)—an information system that informs customers of the delivery date of their car at the time of the order within two hours of the the order placement, and also tracks individual cars from order to delivery through the production and shipment processes. The ANSWER system is directly linked into Nissan's production scheduling system.

46. Robert W. Hall has identified the 12 challenges that face automobile manufacturers as they seek to develop agile manufacturing in his article, "The Challenges of the Three-Day Car," (*Target*, March–April, 1993, pp. 21–29). Hall defines agile manufacturing as delivering "what the customer wants, including design changes, when wanted, where wanted, at reasonable cost, with no quality glitches and no environmental degradation" (p. 21). To achieve this end, there are 12 challenges that Hall believes must be met by the automobile industry: (1) Break the dependence on economy of scale in production. (2) Create a system to produce vehicles in low volumes at reasonable cost. (3) Deliver a car with custom features very quickly—within three days after ordering. (4) Further downsize the scale of production operations. (5) Allow the same components to be configured in many different ways. (6) Create work stimulating to the people doing it. (7) Cultivate the automobile customer to participate in his or her own vehicle's service or order fulfillment. (8) Create an ordering system that will instantly check the combination of requests by the customer for engineering safety and feasibility. (9) Manage large masses of data and control their flow. (10) Recognize that the basic mission of an automobile company is to provide transportation service to its customers. (11) Learn how to remanufacture automobiles. (12) Redirect our competencies and our human institutions.

Chapter 10

1. Thomas J. Murray, "How Motorola Builds in Speed and Quality," *Business Month*, July 1989, p. 36.

2. Milliken & Company, a 1989 winner of the Malcolm Baldrige National Quality Award, has also integrated benchmarking with its strategic planning approach called POE for "Pursuit of Excellence" because of the influence of Tom Peters.

Peters had challenged Roger Milliken, owner and CEO of Milliken & Company: "It's not how good you think you are, it's how good your customers perceive you to be" (as quoted by Melanie Williams, "Wall to Wall Commitment," *Total Quality Management*, November/December 1992, p. 300). Milliken uses "Pursuit of Excellence" to describe its whole business strategy. Everything that the company does is part of their "Pursuit." The pursuit begins with a commitment to customer satisfaction that extends into every aspect of Milliken's business. Other aspects include: flattening the organization and moving management closer to the workers, using teamwork to address business challenges, developing supplier partnerships to improve the company's capabilities, and benchmarking both competitors and leading business practitioners to learn more about how to improve its own company. Milliken benchmarks the products and services of about 400 competitors, based upon concrete measures, to determine where to focus its own improvement efforts and product development investments (see *Business America*, November 20, 1989, p. 9). Benchmarking is the aspect of the "Pursuit of Excellence" that yields new ideas for improving business performance. As Newt Hardie, former vice president of quality at Milliken and now the deputy vice president of financial planning, has said: "Steal shamelessly or borrow honorably—you can't be world-class if you stay at home" (see Megan O'Leary, "The Fabric of Quality," *Chief Information Officer*, August, 1991, p. 40). But, to conduct a benchmarking study requires intensive prework. Milliken learned how to implement quality from Japanese companies. However, before going on the Japanese study mission, Milliken managers had to prepare by reading six books and participating in two intensive, three-day educational workshops. Although Milliken does not allow other companies to benchmark its own processes, it has persuaded many other companies to allow it access to their best business practices: Du Pont (supplier evaluation, safety, and security), Mobay (accounts payable), IBM (customer satisfaction, strategic planning, and employee education), 3M (innovation), Xerox (benchmarking), Goodyear (self-managed teams), Procter & Gamble (self-managed teams), Lenscrafters (time-based competition), Motorola (quality, stretch goal setting, statistics, and employee education), Frito-Lay (strategic planning), AT&T (strategic planning and customer satisfaction), and Sara Lee (flowcharting). This list indicates both the comprehensiveness and intensity of the Milliken benchmarking effort that is focused on improving business processes and practices, rather than the product side of competitive benchmarking, which was described earlier.

3. Benchmarking is an essential ingredient to making successful business transformations. Just consider the case of Allen-Bradley Company, founded in 1903 by Lynde Bradley with Dr. Stanton Allen providing the financing and becoming the first president. In 1985, it was sold to Rockwell International for $1.65 billion. The Allen-Bradley product line includes motor starters, bar code scanners, potentiometers, programmable controllers, industrial robots, ceramic and ferrite magnets, and industrial control software. Allen-Bradley is one of the three companies that Hewlett-Packard used in 1989 as a benchmark for advanced JIT/CIM manufacturing processes. How did it get to that position? Well, it all happened because the company saw the need for a transformation. In 1979, the Allen-Bradley board of directors had to consider their unlikely position. They had just finished a record

year with their highest sales, orders, revenue, and profits ever. According to Tracy O'Rourke, manager of Milwaukee CIM factory, "We had the most money in the bank in the history of the company." So, what was the crisis? Allen-Bradley manufactured electromechanical products and needed to transition to solid-state. According to O'Rourke: "Nothing that we were doing was suitable for that transition. That included the way we went to market, the way we competed, the way we manufactured, and the way we delivered quality. And to keep the profits and cash flow coming, we had to run a parallel effort of keeping what we had in electromechanical while moving over to solid-state" (as quoted by John Teresko in "Making CIM Work with People," *Industry Week*, November 2, 1987, pp. 50–51). In 1979, Allen-Bradley defined six major goals: (1) Convert to solid state; (2) expand the company's industry and customer base; (3) develop and make world-class products; (4) acquire a global market base; (5) implement a formal management training program; and (6) produce quality products at world-class manufacturing costs. Throughout the early 1980s, Allen-Bradley committed substantial resources to developing data acquisition and transfer technologies and, with these intelligent sensors, was on the leading edge of the factory automation business. In 1983, Allen-Bradley purchased Identronix, acquiring the RF technology that it had lacked to complete its technology suite. From that point in time, Allen-Bradley has become recognized as a leader in developing flexible manufacturing products such as integrated manufacturing cells. (See the article by James A. Dix, "Flexible Manufacturing Accommodates High-Tech Products at Allen-Bradley" in *Industrial Engineering*, September 1989, pp. 18–21.) Allen-Bradley itself has benchmarked to develop its product line manufacturing capability for the solid-state electronic controllers used in factory automation projects. "From a Hewlett-Packard plant in Colorado that made test equipment they learned how to integrate a number of suppliers into the smooth flow of the assembly line. Digital Equipment facilities in the Northeast taught them how to use a computer to eliminate waste when cutting printed circuit boards. In Japan, they visited a Sony tape recorder plant and watched in awe as it turned out enormous quantities of consumer items" (Jagannath Dubashsi, "Mastering Customized Manufacturing," *Financial World*, September 29, 1992, p. 42). The result of this learning was the development of a world-class factory. The CIM plant can produce up to 999 product variations in a lot size of one at a rate of 600 per hour. The product orders are received electronically, and the product is manufactured, tested, packaged, and shipped in under 24 hours. In the CIM plant, 60 percent of the machinery was built by Allen-Bradley, with the remaining equipment built to its own specification. As O'Rourke, now president of the company, says as he summarizes the CIM efforts of Allen-Bradley: "We've put our money where our mouth is" (as quoted in an internal Allen-Bradley magazine *Horizons*, July 1988, p. 10).

4. Thomas J. Murray, "Rethinking the Factory," *Business Month*, July 1989, p. 37. Murray quotes John Young of Hewlett-Packard: "You don't have to go to Japan, like you did ten years ago, to look for role models. You could make a tour of leading American companies and come away with all the ideas you need to win in the marketplace" (p. 34). Interestingly enough, in 1989, Hewlett-Packard's

manufacturing managers did just that by visiting Motorola, Ford, and Allen-Bradley.

5. Ibid.

6. Ibid.

7. As quoted in *Business Week,* June 6, 1988, p. 81.

8. For more information on flexible manufacturing and cycle time reduction at Motorola, see the following articles by Brian Dumaine ("Speed to Market," *Fortune,* February 13, 1989) and Lois Therrein ("The Rival Japan Respects," *Business Week,* November 13, 1989).

9. What is meant by Just-in-Time manufacturing and time-based competition? Time-based competition follows a simple formula: "Providing the most value for the lowest cost *in the least amount of time* is the new pattern for corporate success," according to George Stalk, Jr., and Thomas M. Hout (authors of *Competing Against Time: How Time-Based Competition Is Reshaping Global Markets* (New York: The Free Press, 1990), p. 31). Time-based competitors follow a set of methods to focus their organizations on flexibility and responsiveness: (1) Time consumption becomes the primary management measure. (2) Responsiveness is used to stay close to customers and increase their dependence upon the organization. (3) Value delivery systems are targeted to the most attractive customer segments. (4) Become the pacesetter for innovation within one's industry. (5) Grow faster with higher profits than competitors. (6) Confuse the competition through fast-paced strategy implementation. Time-based competitors deliver value two to three times faster than their competitors and form their strategy to result in delighting their customers as a result of their capability advantages from their time-responsive systems (see Stalk and Hout, op. cit., pp. 35–36). JIT is a complementary approach for time-based competitors. It focuses on increasing the clock-speed of the manufacturing process by eliminating delays and feedback loops for rework. JIT methods improve quality in parts supplied, increase the delivery reliability performance of the supply chain that delivers parts, and reduces the processing time for assembly of parts and test of the final product. The primary benefit of JIT is not the reduction in inventory levels that occurs, but the increase in the organization's responsiveness to customers. (See Joseph D. Blackburn, editor, *Time-Based Competition: The Next Battle Ground in American Manufacturing,* New York: BusinessOne Irwin, 1991, pp. 25–66 for a detailed description of the evolution of JIT.) Richard J. Schonberger's first book on JIT was *Japanese Manufacturing Techniques: Nine Hidden Lessons in Simplicity* (New York: Free Press, 1982). His nine lessons form the thesis that many companies pursued in the implementation of JIT—the forerunner of business reengineering methods. His nine lessons are: (1) Management technology is a highly transportable technology. (2) Just-in-Time production exposes problems otherwise hidden by excess inventories and staff. (3) Quality begins with production, and requires a company-wide "habit of improvement." (4) Culture is no obstacle; techniques can change behavior. (5) Simplify, and all goods will flow like water. (6) Flexibility opens doors. (7) Travel light and make numerous trips—like the water beetle. (8) More self-improvement, fewer programs, less specialist intervention.

(9) Simplicity is the natural state. The Hewlett-Packard Company is one of the pioneers in cycle time reduction through JIT. In his second book, *World Class Manufacturing: The Lessons of Simplicity Applied* (New York: The Free Press, 1986), Schonberger cited seven HP divisions as examples of organizations that have rejuvenated their processes through JIT. However, Schonberger missed at least five others that had implemented JIT in the early 1980s and made major improvements including: Lake Stevens Division, San Diego Division, Roseville Networks Division, Loveland Instruments Division, and Disc Memory Division. In Richard J. Schonberger's accompanying case study book *World Class Manufacturing Casebook: Implementing JIT and TQC* (New York: The Free Press, 1987), he provides more detailed descriptions of the implementation of JIT at four HP manufacturing sites: Fort Collins Division, Personal Office Computer Division, Computer Systems Division, and Greeley Division.

10. Distribution of products can provide a differentiating competitive advantage. Coca-Cola discovered that its distribution services actually formed an envelope around its product that was a large part of what its customers experienced about the product. Coke discovered that it must manage the logistical pipeline to the customer, just as carefully as it targets advertising at specific audiences in particular publications—that Coke needed to be responsive to a distinct set of customers whose business could be characterized by their required frequency of delivery (see the article by Joseph B. Fuller, James O'Connor, and Richard Rawlinson, "Tailored Logistics: The Next Advantage," *Harvard Business Review*, May–June, 1993, pp. 87–98).

11. Concentrating on the streamlining of distribution systems is a common theme in the redesign of manufacturing systems. In 1993, McKesson Drug Company received the third annual productivity achievement award for product distribution from *Modern Materials Handling* magazine. In the February 1993 magazine, McKesson was cited for implementing a portable distribution system at its Spokane, Washington, center. This system reduced handling item time 10 percent, while reducing mispicks by 72 percent—a $9,000 savings in the first month at a single center.

12. Product distribution can become a competitive advantage or a competitive albatross. Just consider the lesson learned by Compaq Computer. Compaq suffered a great loss of market share from a 1992 attack by Michael Dell and his Austin, Texas, based Dell Computer. The Compaq weakness was its reliance on a dealer channel distribution strategy. Dell had observed the fixed Compaq distribution strategy that created an opportunity for Dell to move in and gain share with a direct sales approach to the purchasers using deeply discounted products. As the market price for personal computers dropped sharply in early 1992, the dealer channels consolidated, leaving the resulting dealers with excess inventory almost equal to a month's revenue for Compaq. Without any alternative distribution channels, Compaq was forced to lose this revenue and watch Dell capitalize on the confusion in the market. Compaq ended the year with its first-ever loss and almost flat sales from the prior year—Dell finished with the highest revenue ever, closing the year with almost $2 billion in sales revenues (see Julie Pitta's article

"Why Dell Is a Survivor," *Forbes*, October 12, 1992, pp. 82–91). It was an expensive lesson.

13. Linkage of order processing directly to the factory through computer systems is another technology that finds its way into many business systems engineering efforts. In a reprinted internal Texas Instruments Executive Summary report, Larry Skinner, director of business engineering and information services, described the TI results from implementing Business Process Reengineering. Through the use of electronic data interchange (EDI), TI improved its order cycle time by more than 50 percent and reduced staffing by more than 30 percent—a $30 million annual saving (see Larry Skinner, "Business Process Engineering Executive Summary," in *Business Process Reengineering: Current Issues and Applications*, Norcross, GA: Industrial Engineering and Management Press, 1993, p. 153). External evidence of the TI commitment to excellence in CIM and reengineering is found in some of the recognition that has been given to its defense division. Texas Instruments' Defense Systems & Electronics facility in Sherman, Texas, was recognized with a LEAD CIM Award jointly presented by the Computer & Automated Systems Association and the Society of Manufacturing Engineers (*Industry Week*, November 2, 1987, p. 57). (Note: The LEAD award acronym stands for Leadership Excellence in the Application and Development of CIM.) This is the same division that received the Malcolm Baldrige National Quality Award in 1992.

14. Rita R. Schreiber, "The CIM Caper," *Manufacturing Engineering*, April 1989, p. 85.

15. These lessons in JIT implementation had most strongly influenced the management at Hewlett-Packard San Diego Division. In 1983 to 1985, the San Diego Division was faced with a need to make a major transformation in its product line and work processes. HP was clearly the world leader in graphical pen plotter sales. However, as thermal inkjet technology matured, it saw the need to maintain its leadership position in plotters while concurrently developing a capability to deliver new color inkjet products. Terry Siden, the manufacturing engineering manager, devised a strategy to build a single automated production cell that could assemble printed circuit boards for both the old style pen plotters and the new thermal inkjet printers on the same line. This project team divided its emphasis into the near-simultaneous development of the Colorpro and Paintjet products. Colorpro was under the manufacturing engineering management of Bob Procelli, who reported to Myron Bezenek. Myron coordinated the integration of the product designs and the development of the automated loading cell. The Joey cell project was most effectively managed by John Powell. It consisted of Panasonic chip inserters, Panasonic axial and radial lead component inserters, Seiko robots for odd-form components, and a lot of Hewlett-Packard cell controllers, logic analyzers, testing systems, and computers. The Joey cell was designed to produce products in lots of one based on a production schedule determined by input from the daily shipment requirements from sales. Joyce Douglas took both the final assembly and automated cell and merged them into a smooth production process. I had the privilege of working with the Joey project team during 1984 to 1985 and was present during the Motorola Bandit team's benchmarking visit to HP's

San Diego Division. This benchmarking visit sparked Motorola to purchase much of the software and subsystems that Hewlett-Packard had used for automated assembly of printed circuit boards and cell controllers. The use of these automated systems drove the need for high-quality parts for the robotic assembly and also enabled much of the reduction in time to market and manufacturing process cycle time. As John Young, Hewlett-Packard's former CEO, has said so many times: "Doing it fast forces you to do it right the first time."

16. Cycle time is an important focus in many business systems improvement efforts, and many companies follow similar processes to implement cycle time reduction efforts. For instance, OSRAM Sylvania, the nation's second largest manufacturer of incandescent, fluorescent, and high-intensity discharge lighting products, has extended its engineering from the manufacturing arena to include materials, purchasing, and distribution. (OSRAM GmbH is the subsidiary of Siemens A.G. that purchased Sylvania's lighting products group from GTE in January 1993.) The teams at OSRAM Sylvania used a six-step approach to improvement: (1) Research and map the business process. (2) Analyze the results. (3) Identify problems and prioritize solutions. (4) Develop and implement an improvement plan using employee involvement. (5) Measure the results of the new process. (6) Standardize the new, improved process (see Brad Bambarger, "OSRAM Sylvania's Time-Based Continuous Improvement Approach to BPR," *Industrial Engineering*, December 1993, pp. 14–18).

17. The emphasis on cycle time reduction and quality improvement is transferable to almost any type of activity. Consider the Naval Aviation Depot at Cherry Point in North Carolina, a winner of the President's Award for quality in government—it made a significant shift in its ability to perform its work processes. It decided that it had to improve its turnaround time, reduce work in progress, and reduce costs of repair drastically. It applied the principles of JIT and TQM, and in a 60-day period had reduced the turnaround time for aircraft repairs by 29 percent, engine repairs by 37 percent, and component repairs by 27 percent. It also reduced the cost of aircraft repairs by $9.4 million (see John S. Fargner, "Managing Process Improvement at the Cherry Point Naval Aviation Depot," *National Productivity Review*, Autumn 1992, pp. 533–547).

18. Many companies seeking to improve their operations management have merged the use of shop floor automation systems with computerized information systems. For instance, in 1990, *Management Today* magazine selected NCR Corporation's Dundee, Scotland, facility as one of Great Britain's five best factories. NCR Dundee, maker of automated teller machines, pursued a JIT strategy applying low-cost automation systems and management information and planning systems. The results of its efforts were to achieve a 99 percent on-time delivery rate, increase productivity 3.7 times, reduce head count by a factor of 1.5, reduce cycle time from 15 days to 2 days, reduce the supplier base from 480 to 165, and increase the local content in its product by purchasing 80 percent of their parts from British suppliers (see Steve Young and Brett Greerway, "Britain's Best Factories," *Management Today*, November 1990, p. 76–89.).

19. Rita R. Schreiber, op. cit., p. 85.

20. Ibid., p. 86.

21. Thomas J. Murray, "How Motorola Builds in Speed and Quality," op. cit., p. 37.

22. Teamwork and empowerment are common themes echoed in other leading automated plants. Consider GE Fanuc Automation North America, Inc., of Charlottesville, Virginia, a joint venture between General Electric and Fanuc of Japan that manufactures programmable logic controllers and computerized numerical controllers for the factory automation equipment market. GE Fanuc was honored by *Electronic Business* and *Electronic Packaging & Production* magazines with the 1991 electronics factory automation award. In 1992, GE Fanuc was named by *Industry Week* magazine as one of the best manufacturing plants in the United States. Using the General Electric "work-out" management technique for problem solving and sharing best practices, GE Fanuc CEO Bob Collins has shifted the culture from an authoritarian style to a coaching style. The plant's emphasis on continuous improvement through empowered teams has yielded a 52 percent reduction in organizational layers and a 74 percent reduction in the time to develop new products (see John Teresko, "American's Best Plants: GE Fanuc," *Industry Week*, October 19, 1992, pp. 50–52).

23. Many work process redesign efforts are not clean-sheet projects, but a reworking of a current production line populated with production workers. As a line is automated and people are removed, a company is faced with a dilemma—should they release the workers and claim a savings, or should they hold the workers and retrain them for another task? Corning CEO James R. Houghton has forged a commitment to labor based on the implementation of TQM. The Corning approach to labor relations is stated in its 1989 agreement that is titled, "A Partnership in the Workplace." The American Flint Glass Workers Union (AFGWU) workers have participated strongly in responding to this job security. When Corning opened its "factory of the future" in Blacksburg, Virginia, it chose to staff it with AFGWU workers even though it had the opportunity to have a nonunion shop (Ronald Fink, "Best Practice Company Labor Relations: Corning," *Financial Week*, September 29, 1992, p. 46). Corning's secret to its strong relationship with the AFGWU workers at the Blacksburg automotive filter plant is its active EI, or employee involvement, program. The six elements in the Corning EI process are: (1) Create a clear, compelling vision with participation from all areas of the workforce. (2) Share information about customers, costs, markets, and performance with the workers. (3) Ask the people to design their own work processes. (4) Use self-managed work groups throughout the organization. (5) Make continuous improvement a normal part of work. (6) Involve the entire organization. Larry Bankowski, president of the AFGWU, believes that: "Partnership allows more decision making by employees and requires the company to be interested in the whole worker—brains as well as hands. The result is more wealth for the company and the employee" (quoted in "Employee Involvement: How Corning Creates an Environment for People to Implement Quality," *The Productivity Newsletter*, October 1992, p. 5). Rob Henderson, plant manager for Erwin, New York, sister plant to the specialty ceramics operation in Blacksburg, Virginia, is convinced that American workers are going to make the difference: "Once people get a taste of the decision making process, it is irreversible. There

are a lot of talented people out there, capable of making intelligent decisions if they are given the complete set of information. . . . This is good stuff. It will really have an impact. And it can't be stopped" (quoted by John H. Sheridan in his article "A Philosophy for Commitment," *Industry Week*, February 4, 1991, p. 13).

24. Rita R. Schreiber, op. cit., p. 86.

25. Ibid., p. 88.

26. Forging strong supplier partnerships is not a Motorola secret; Coleman Outdoor Products has also had success with this strategy. First implemented in 1988, supplier partnerships have used JIT techniques to reduce inventory by more than one third at the end of 1992. In return for their commitment to rapid delivery of high-quality parts, Coleman shares its production forecast with suppliers and guarantees them 100 percent of the business for their particular commodity (see Susan Avery, "Using Suppliers to Drive Change," *Purchasing*, March 18, 1993, pp. 54–57).

27. Rita R. Schreiber, op. cit., p. 89.

Chapter 11

1. Danny Miller calls this the Icarus paradox. Like the mythical Icarus, successful companies can become so locked into the formula that gave them their initial success that they don't read the signals for change. Thus, TI's technology-research and cost-cutting strategy did not carry it into the 1980s and required its own restructuring. The story of this phenomena is very interesting and is told well in Miller's book *The Icarus Paradox: How Successful Companies Bring About Their Own Downfall* (New York: Harper Business, 1990, pp. 19–20).

2. Glenn Rifkin, "The 1980s: A Retrospective," *Computerworld*, December 18, 1989, p. 55.

3. After joining Compaq as the director of corporate quality, I became amazed at the insight of the senior management team that established a history of quality from the very beginning. In the first year of its operation, Compaq sent all of its exempt employees to attend the Crosby Quality College. Its first annual report (1984) stated its quality commitment: "One of the primary goals at Compaq is to set the standard for quality in the computer industry. Although an ambitious goal, it is one to which the Company's management is solidly committed. Not only are we striving to produce products without defects, but we also plan to be known for quality in every activity of the company." To my knowledge, Compaq was the first company that was founded on the principles of Total Quality Management. These principles pervade its way of working and are evident throughout its actions in this case study.

4. An indicator of the lack of confidence in computer companies was the fact that the initial stock offering for Compaq stock sold at $11 per share, instead of the targeted $18. This was despite the backing of successful venture capitalist Ben Rosen. Stephen T. McClellan, *The Coming Computer Industry Shakeout: Winners, Losers, and Survivors* (New York: John Wiley & Sons, 1984), p. 211.

5. Even the company's name change in 1983 signaled the organization's dedication to its core product, the portable computer: The "Compaq" name is a contraction of *communication* and *portable*. When asked where the "q" came from, Rod Canion reminisced that the marketing company thought that it gave a "techie" sound to the company's name, but to the senior management team it indicated the open commitment to quality.

6. Mark Ivey, Barbara Buell, Jonathan B. Levine, and Neil Gross, "Doing Unto Compaq As It Did Unto IBM?" *Business Week*, November 19, 1990, p. 122.

7. Compaq maintains the most extensive software compatibility testing system in the industry. They test every new system to ensure that it will run the most popular software in the industry. In fact, internal Compaq mythology has it that one question asked by its competitor's service departments when they are faced with a software compatibility problem is: "But will it run on a Compaq?" This question is asked as the definitive method to determine whether the problem is software or hardware induced. If it runs on a Compaq, then it should be able to run on any personal computer from a software design viewpoint—therefore the problem must be with the competitor's hardware.

8. Ivey, Buell, Levine, and Gross, op. cit., p. 130.

9. For a good description of the change mechanisms that trigger corporate restructuring, see the third chapter in Gordon Donaldson's book *Corporate Restructuring: Managing the Change Process from Within* (Boston: Harvard Business School Press, 1994).

10. Interestingly enough, the Harvard Graduate School Case Study on Compaq illustrates the very vulnerability that was pointed out by Dell's market actions. In making the transition, Compaq survived a very vulnerable period in its history. To quote Richard Swingle, director of product marketing at Compaq, commenting on the introduction of the new low-cost lines: "There will be some substantial cannibalization. Either you eat your own children or someone else does" (*The Wall Street Journal*, June 15, 1992). Compaq had grown up into a new epoch in the history of its growth.

11. Many of the internal product design features that Compaq engineers put in place for either the sake of reliability or serviceability resulted in too much cost when compared against the products of its competitors through a product tear-down analysis. Two obvious differences were that competitors used tin connectors on their circuit boards, while Compaq used gold for its greater reliability in high-humidity environments, and some competitors used plastic instead of metal for the support frame inside the computer case. Compaq had to track best design practices of its competitors on two dimensions: not just for technical advances and reliability, but also for the degree of the design's cost-competitiveness.

Chapter 12

1. Thomas Tel, "Service Comes First: An Interview with USAA's Robert F. McDermott," *Harvard Business Review*, September-October 1991, p. 117.

2. Even the mission of USAA reinforces its tradition of service to its owner-members. The mission of USAA, its subsidiaries and affiliates is to provide products and services of the highest quality at competitive prices to satisfy the financial security, asset management, and quality of life needs of USAA members and their families. USAA's independent lines of business will function, to the extent permitted by law, as a single integrated business organization whose culture and reputation for integrity foster an association built upon trust and confidence. This mission is reinforced by its creed, dedicating each member to: "serving each other on a personal basis with integrity and dependability; sharing each other's insurance risks equitably and economically; and sharing opportunities, through selected products and services, to fulfill our mutual lifetime needs for security, financial success, and better quality of life."

   As a member of USAA since 1971, I [Watson] can honestly say that this company has been dedicated to its principles as long as I have been a member. I wonder how many of us are proud to have insurance from our insurance company? I don't know the answer, but I do know that I am proud to be a part of such an excellent organization.

3. Thomas Tel, op. cit., p. 119.

4. When McDermott took over, he found things that he didn't like. "The systems were archaic. In auto insurance, every application and letter that came in went through 55 steps" (Thomas Tel, op. cit., p. 125). However, McDermott didn't look at technology as a panacea that would correct all ills. The first project he initiated was an automated policy-writing system that was based on punch cards, and then he gradually moved the company to on-line systems. Now USAA is toying with multimedia and expert systems as add-ons to its state-of-the-art image processing capability. "Information technology has to be a strategic weapon—not just a cost center" (p. 125). Now, a five-minute phone call takes the place of the 55 steps—a one-stop, on-line capability that redesigned the process to take advantage of the technology.

5. When "the General" took command at USAA in 1969, he had a four-pronged attack to employ against the evils of poor productivity. First, he attacked using a weapon of automation to redefine the approach to policy writing. Second, he wanted to eliminate employees—through a natural attrition process, rather than a drastic reduction in force. Third, he wanted to educate and upgrade employees—perhaps he carried forth this emphasis from his days as Commandant of the Air Force Academy. Fourth, he decentralized and pushed decision-making authority to the front line where the members were engaged. Thomas Tel, "Service Comes First: An Interview with USAA's Robert F. McDermott," *Harvard Business Review*, September–October 1991, p. 119.

6. General McDermott has been the visionary driving USAA toward a "paperless environment" through the use of technology. A former fighter pilot, he blends the military metaphor with the strategic planning lessons of a Harvard MBA to call for an extended, planned campaign using technology to create business success. McDermott's direction for USAA was stated: "Systems and communications technologies are strategic weapons and it is imperative that we take full advantage of the opportunities that new and emerging information processing technology

will offer to us over the next few years. Our success, and even survival, will be closely tied to how well we will be able to compete in the marketplace on technological grounds." Harvard Business School Case study on United Services Automobile Association (revised January 1989), p. 1.

7. Thomas Tel, op. cit., p. 119.

8. How does USAA exploit its need to change? USAA conducts detailed business process assessments. It explicitly analyzes each job and operation in the company to determine answers to some tough questions: Does this job need to exist? Does this department need to exist? Is this work being performed in the best possible way? Is this support system or organization infrastructure necessary?

9. In recognition of his contribution in leading USAA in its application of advanced technology, and citing specifically the image processing and storage system, the Conference Board presented its Excellence in Technology Award to McDermott in 1989.

10. USAA uses a process similar to the measurement map described in Chapter 5. It calls its tool a family of measures (abbreviated as FOM) and uses FOM to track the quality of individual and unit performance. The question addressed by the FOM is whether an individual or unit is showing improvement in its process. If there is no improvement indicated by the process measure, then the solution is to look at what areas need training or process improvement. Without the use of the FOM as a tool, an organization would not be able to judge where to focus its efforts on process improvement. The basic measures included in the USAA FOM are: quality of work completed, quantity of work completed, timeliness in delivering the service, resource capacity (time spent working to perform the output), and customer satisfaction with the output.

11. The American Modern Home Insurance, The Principal Financial Group, and other insurance companies did not learn some of the same lessons that USAA had put into place until the early 1990s. Robert Janson, "Thanks to Its Employees, This Re-engineering Effort Worked," *Journal for Quality and Participation*, December 1993, pp. 78–80. Charles E. Rohm, "The Principal Insures a Better Future by Reengineering Its Individual Insurance Department," *National Productivity Review*, Winter 1992/1993, pp. 55–64.

12. Thomas Tel, op. cit., pp. 126–127.

Chapter 13

1. Darell Rigby, "The Secret History of Process Reengineering," *Planning Review*, March–April 1993, pp. 24–27.

2. Thomas H. Davenport, "Need Radical Innovation and Continuous Improvement? Integrate Process Reengineering and TQM," *Planning Review*, May–June 1993, pp. 6–12.

3. Richard Chang, "Improve Processes, Reengineer Them, or Both?" *Training & Development*, March 1994, pp. 54–58.

4. Jon R. Katzenbach and Douglas K. Smith, "The Rules for Managing Cross-Functional Teams," *Planning Review*, March–April 1993, pp. 12–13.

5. David A. Garvin, "Building a Learning Organization," *Harvard Business Review*, July–August 1993, pp. 78–91.

6. Thomas J. Housel, Chris J. Morris, and Christopher Westland, "Business Process Reengineering at Pacific Bell," *Planning Review*, May–June 1993, pp. 28–33.

7. Gene Hall, Jim Rosenthal, and Judy Wade, "How to Make Reengineering *Really* Work," *Harvard Business Review*, November–December 1993, pp. 119–131.

8. Richard C. Palermo, Sr., and Gregory H. Watson, editors, *A World of Quality: The Timeless Passport* (Milwaukee, WI: ASQC Quality Press, 1993), p. 41.

9. "Re-engineering Europe," *The Economist*, February 26, 1994, pp. 67–68.

10. Kurt Singer, *Mirror, Sword and Jewel: The Geometry of Japanese Life* (Tokyo: Kodansha International, 1973), p. 118.

11. F. Timothy Fuller, "Eliminating Complexity from Work," *National Productivity Review*, Autumn 1985, pp. 327–344.

12. Katzenbach and Smith, op. cit., pp. 12–13.

Chapter 14

1. Michael Hammer and James Champy, *Reengineering the Corporation: A Manifesto for Business Revolution*, p. 200.

2. Donald L. Kirkpatrick, *How to Manage Change Effectively* (San Francisco: Jossey-Bass, 1985), p. 35.

3. Rosabeth Moss Kanter, *The Change Masters*, p. 248.

4. The primary source for these principles of redesign is Michael Hammer's article in the July–August 1990 issue of *Harvard Business Review*: "Reengineering Work: Don't Automate, Obliterate." Other contributions came from: B. Ray Helton, "Twelve Universal Re-engineering Solutions," *Quality Observer*, March 1994; Theodore B. Kinni, "A Reengineering Primer," *Quality Digest*, January 1994; John A. Byrne, "The Horizontal Corporation: It's About Managing Across, Not Up and Down," *Business Week*, December 20, 1993.

5. Robert B. Kaplan and Laura Murdock, "Rethinking the Corporation: Core Process Redesign," *McKinsey Quarterly*, Number 2, 1991. Kaplan and Murdock outline a five-phase approach to core process redesign: Phase 1: Identifying the process; Phase 2: Defining performance requirements; Phase 3: Pinpointing the problems; Phase 4: Developing a vision; and Phase 5: Making it happen (pp. 35–43).

6. Timothy R. Furey, "A Six-step Guide to Process Reengineering," *Planning Review*, March–April 1993. Tim was a copresenter at a November 1993 Xerox workshop on reengineering. At that time, we shared our approaches and noted their similarities. Tim's six-step model follows: (1) Identify the process's customer-driven objectives; (2) map and measure the existing process; (3) analyze and modify the existing process; (4) benchmark for innovative, proven alternatives; (5) reengineer the process; and (6) roll out the new process (p. 20).

7. Thomas H. Davenport and James E. Short, "The New Industrial Engineering: Information Technology and Business Process Redesign," *Sloan Management Review*, Summer 1990. Tom Davenport has influenced many of the Xerox reengineering projects in England and the United States. His model for business process redesign: (1) Develop business vision and process objectives then prioritize objectives and set stretch targets; (2) identify processes to be redesigned—identify critical or bottleneck processes; (3) understand and measure existing processes—identify the current problems and set the baseline performance; (4) identify information technology levers—brainstorm new process approaches; and (5) design and build a prototype of the process (p. 14).

8. John Farrell, "A Practical Guide for Implementing Reengineering," *Planning Review*, March–April 1994. Farrell presents a five-phased Ernst & Young approach to the new "art" of Business Process Reengineering: (1) Assessment; (2) reengineering; (3) design; (4) construction; and (5) implementation (pp. 41–42).

9. Rosabeth Moss Kanter, op. cit., p. 250.

Reengineering
Bibliography

One trait that causes me to treasure certain books is that they help me to proceed beyond them. This annotated bibliography and the extensive use of footnotes are part of my attempt to do that for each reader. The following list of books provides a beginning point for further research on this topic. Of course, I placed it at the end of my own book so that you would finish reading my book before I recommended that you take a journey through another author's text. Under each citation below, I have made comments and opinions about these authors and their work. These thoughts are mine and do not reflect the editorial opinions of my publisher or anyone on his staff. That makes me the one who is responsible for these judgments—either bad or good, depending upon your perspective. In any case, I wish each dedicated reader who has gotten this far the good sense to know when to give up the pursuit of knowledge and start changing your business for the better. Now that I am finished with this book, I think that it is time to tend to the redesign of my own business practice.

Andrews, Dorine C. and Susan K. Stalick, *Business Reengineering: The Survival Guide* (Englewood Cliffs: Prentice-Hall, 1994).

Andrews and Stalick have joined the bandwagon with another information-centric book on business process reengineering. Does not extend the knowledge base on reengineering, but it is a very readable book.

Arnold, Robert S., editor, *Software Reengineering* (Los Alamitos, CA: Institute of Electrical and Electronics Engineers (IEEE) Computer Society Press, 1994).

Arnold has pulled together a set of articles and papers that provide an opportunity to get acquainted with software reengineering. These selected articles represent a software-centric approach that does not cover all aspects of business process improvement.

Currid, Cheryl, et. al., *The Reengineering Toolkit: Fifteen Tools and Technologies for Reengineering Your Organization* (Rocklin, CA: Prima Publishing, 1994).

While Currid has also provided an information-centric approach to reengineering, she has done a great service by clearly explaining how the "leading" technologies operate and how they can be used for business process improvement. This makes it a valuable extension of the literature on reengineering.

Davenport, Thomas H., *Process Innovation: Reengineering Work Through Information Technology* (Boston: Harvard Business School Press, 1993).

Davenport's book on business process redesign focuses on information technology as the enabler of process innovation that leads to dramatic business improvement. He recognizes the need for a more holistic approach and seeks to integrate benchmarking and Total Quality Management into support roles for the redesign effort. Davenport also recognizes the importance of organizational development of human resources during implementation. Process innovation must be guided by the strategic business context and a vision of the future process state. Discussions of business process redesign projects are included for IBM, Xerox, Digital Equipment, Continental Bank, Federal Mogul, and Westinghouse. Davenport is with Ernst & Young and teaches at Boston University's School of Management.

Donaldson, Gordon, *Corporate Restructuring: Managing the Change Process from Within* (Boston: Harvard Business School Press, 1994).

Donaldson's book is written from the perspective of a financial advisor. He shows how firms, based on their own self-assessment of performance, can restructure their financial and governance structures. For a board of directors to execute its capacity for intervention and fundamentally restructure its corporation should be approached with care and caution. Essential ingredients for voluntary restructuring are convincing proof of the need for change, opportunities for near-term improvement, consensus among the board members and top management, and a visible mandate for change. The two most common mandates are the retirement of the CEO, and a sudden and significant deterioration in performance. Projects and case studies are included for Armco, Safeway, Household International, General Mills, Burlington Northern, and CPC International. Donaldson is on the faculty of Harvard Graduate School of Business.

Green, Mark and John F. Berry, *The Challenge of Hidden Profits: Reducing Corporate Bureaucracy and Waste* (New York: William Morrow and Company, 1985).

Bureaucratic strangulation of corporations results in wasteful practices. Some of these practices include: the failure to motivate employees; managers who are more interested in self-promotion than in leadership; a concentration on acquisition rather than innovation; compensation pegged to position rather than performance; excessive corporate legal expenses; indifference to quality and the ultimate cost of goods; waste from government-business alliances that often protect the corporation from competition. Green and Berry are reporters.

Hammer, Michael and James Champy, *Reengineering the Corporation: A Manifesto for Business Revolution* (New York: McGraw-Hill, 1993).

This is the one that created all of the fuss. This best-selling book by Hammer and Champy tells management to seek quantum leaps in performance—tenfold improvement—rather than just settling for incremental improvements of 10 percent to 20 percent annually. They present a set of seven principles for reengineering that guide the successful transition of companies to saving hundreds of millions of dollars a year. Case studies include Bell Atlantic, Taco Bell, and Hallmark Cards. Hammer has his own company that specializes in reengineering while Champy is with CSC Index, Inc.

Hunt, V. Daniel, *Reengineering: Leveraging the Power of Integrated Product Development* (Essex Junction, VT: Oliver Wight, 1993).

Hunt's book focuses on the reengineering of the product development process. He observes that there are three different opportunities for reengineering: new products (23 percent of process redesign opportunities), functional processes (65 percent), and corporate-wide business processes (12 percent). Hunt focuses his book on the product development opportunities and encourages development of an integrated product development process: a systems approach to reengineering products and their related processes (business processes, design processes, manufacturing processes, and support systems). The approach entails a complete restructure of the product life cycle. Hunt describes practices that have been put into effect at Hewlett-Packard, AT&T, and Boeing. Hunt is with Technology Research Corporation.

Institute of Industrial Engineers, *Business Process Reengineering: Current Issues and Applications* (Norcross, GA: Industrial Engineering and Management Press, 1993).

This book is a collection of articles on Business Process Reengineering from 1990 until the middle of 1993. IIE is a professional society of industrial engineers.

Johansson, Henry J., Patrick McHugh, A. John Pendlebury, and William A. Wheeler III, *Business Process Reengineering: Breakpoint Strategies for Market Dominance* (New York: John Wiley & Sons, 1993).

The authors describe the Coopers & Lybrand approach to redesign of core business processes—those processes that cut across boundaries, functions, and departments and deliver market differentiable advantage. The authors urge management to concentrate on breakpoints—the achievement of excellence in one or more value metrics where the marketplace clearly recognizes the advantage and where the ensuing result is a disproportionate and sustained increase in market share. They integrate Just-in-Time manufacturing and Total Quality Management with reengineering in a very pragmatic way.

Lowenthal, Jeffrey N., *Reengineering the Organization: A Step-by-Step Approach to Corporate Revitalization* (Milwaukee, WI: ASQC Quality Press, 1994).

Lowenthal considers reengineering to be the fundamental rethinking and redesign of operating processes and organizational structure, focused on the organization's core competencies, to achieve dramatic improvements in organizational performance. He presents a thirteen-step, four-phase process for reengineering with lots of practical tools. Missing are the case studies that will convince readers that this approach is workable. Lowenthal is with Performance Solutions International, Ltd.

Mills, D. Quinn, *Rebirth of the Corporation* (New York: John Wiley & Sons, 1991).

Mills describes the transition from hierarchical organizations to organizations that are built around clusters. A cluster is a group of people who are drawn together from different disciplines to work together on a semipermanent basis. Six different types of clusters may be formed: core team, business units, staff units, project teams, alliance teams, and change teams. Examples from Du Pont, GE Canada, and British Petroleum illustrate the application of these ideas. Mills is on the faculty of the Harvard Graduate School of Business.

Morris, Daniel and Joel Brandon, *Reengineering Your Business* (New York: McGraw-Hill, 1993).

Morris and Brandon present a worthwhile, readable book on reengineering. They offer a nine-step process: (1) Identify possible projects; (2) conduct initial impact analysis; (3) select the effort and define the scope; (4) analyze business and work process baseline information; (5) define new process alternatives: simulate new work flows; (6) evaluate the potential costs and benefits of each alternative; (7) select the best alternative; (8) implement the alternative selected; (9) update the positioning models and information.

Naisbitt, John and Patricia Aburdene, *Re-inventing the Corporation: Transforming Your Job and Your Company for the New Information Society* (New York: Warner Books, 1985).

Naisbitt and Aburdene describe how to merge two essential elements of corporate transformation—new values and economic necessity—and through their synthesis create a company that is better prepared to move ahead in the information age. This book is on a journalistic journey into the need for business improvement because of the forthcoming labor shortage. To compete for the best people, organizations will focus on factors that increase individual productivity.

Petrozzo, Daniel P. and John C. Stepper, *Successful Reengineering* (New York: Van Nostrand Reinhold, 1994).

Petrozzo and Stepper integrates its approach to reengineering across three components of the business: business processes, organizational support systems, and information systems. They present a four-phased approach to reengineering: (1) Discover; (2) hunt and gather; (3) innovate and build; and (4) reorganize, retrain, and retool. A good book, but it has a simplistic perspective of TQM.

Roberts, Lon, *Process Reengineering: The Key to Achieving Breakthrough Success* (Milwaukee, WI: ASQC Quality Press, 1994).

Roberts presents a potpourri of tools that can help during Business Process Reengineering. While there is a basic methodology for reengineering, it is not clear that the tools are usable as Roberts has suggested. No practical examples are reported. Case studies include Ford Motor Company, Bell Atlantic, Johnson Filtration Systems, Xerox, and Westinghouse Electric. These case studies appear to be synopses of open literature.

Schneider, William E., *The Reengineering Alternative: A Plan for Making Your Current Culture Work* (Burr Ridge, IL: Irwin, 1994).

Schneider offers a more humanistic approach to business process improvement by reverting back to an emphasis on corporate culture. Particularly valuable is the questionnaire for cultural self-assessment of your organization. Schneider's work adds to the literature by contributing to the non-machine side of quality improvement: emphasizing human efforts and shared values.

Shores, A. Richard, *Reengineering the Factory: A Primer for World-Class Manufacturing* (Milwaukee, WI: ASQC Quality Press, 1994).

Shores has brought together a disjoint collection of manufacturing-related tools without showing how they work together. Reengineering appears to be a thematic afterthought that is only discussed in about four paragraphs. If you want to know about some manufacturing processes, this book is acceptable. If you want to know about reengineering manufacturing, then read about Motorola in my book. This book lacks detailed case studies to demonstrate the methods.

Shunk, Dan L., *Integrated Process Design and Development* (Homewood, IL: Irwin, 1992).

Shunk's book does not claim to be about reengineering, but it has as much to say about redesign as some that do claim to be in the "mainstream." Shunk cites four keys to the new integration of process design and development: (1) A systems approach; (2) modular manufacturing; (3) a new approach to accounting in manufacturing; and (4) statistical quality control. Shunk's book shows how to make every area in the company work together by describing the fundamental building blocks of an integrated process. Case studies include Nippondenzo, Allied Signal's Garrett Engine Division, and an anonymous manufacturing company. Shunk is on the faculty of Arizona State University.

Index

281

About the Author

GREGORY H. WATSON is a business advisor to senior management teams of leading companies in Europe, Latin American, and the United States. Previously he was vice president of product development for Xerox Quality Solutions—the corporation's quality consulting group—and vice president of quality for the Xerox copier business. Greg was vice president of benchmarking services at the American Productivity & Quality Center, where he was instrumental in establishing the International Benchmarking Clearinghouse. He has also held senior executive and quality management positions with both Compaq Computer Corporation and the Hewlett-Packard Company. Prior to his business experience, Greg served for 11 years in the United States Navy in a variety of operational, staff, management, and research positions, attaining the rank of lieutenant commander.

Greg is a certified quality engineer and a senior member of the American Society for Quality Control (ASQC) and the Institute of Industrial Engineers. He currently serves on the board of directors for ASQC as a director-at-large. Greg was a member of the GOAL/QPC Research Committee (1989–1991) and the board of examiners for the Malcolm Baldrige National Quality Award (1991–1992). He is presently a senior examiner for the New York State Excelsior Award (1993–1994), a judge for the American Productivity & Quality Center Benchmarking Award (1993–1994), and a judge for the Texas Quality Award (1994). Greg is also a member of the advisory boards for the American Productivity & Quality Center (1991–1994), the Rochester Institute of Technology's Center for Quality and Applied Statistics (1993–1994), and the *International Journal of Benchmarking for Quality and Technology Management.*

Greg is the author of *Strategic Benchmarking* (New York: John Wiley & Sons, 1993) and *The Benchmarking Workbook* (Cambridge, MA: Productivity Press, 1992), as well as editor of *The Benchmarking Management Guide* (Cambridge, MA: Productivity Press, 1993), and *A World of Quality: The Timeless Passport* (Milwaukee WI: ASQC Press, 1993). In addition, he has contributed many articles to quality journals and magazines and has made numerous speeches and public presentations on management topics.

Greg and his family live in the rolling glacial drumlins outside of Victor, New York.